DISCARDED

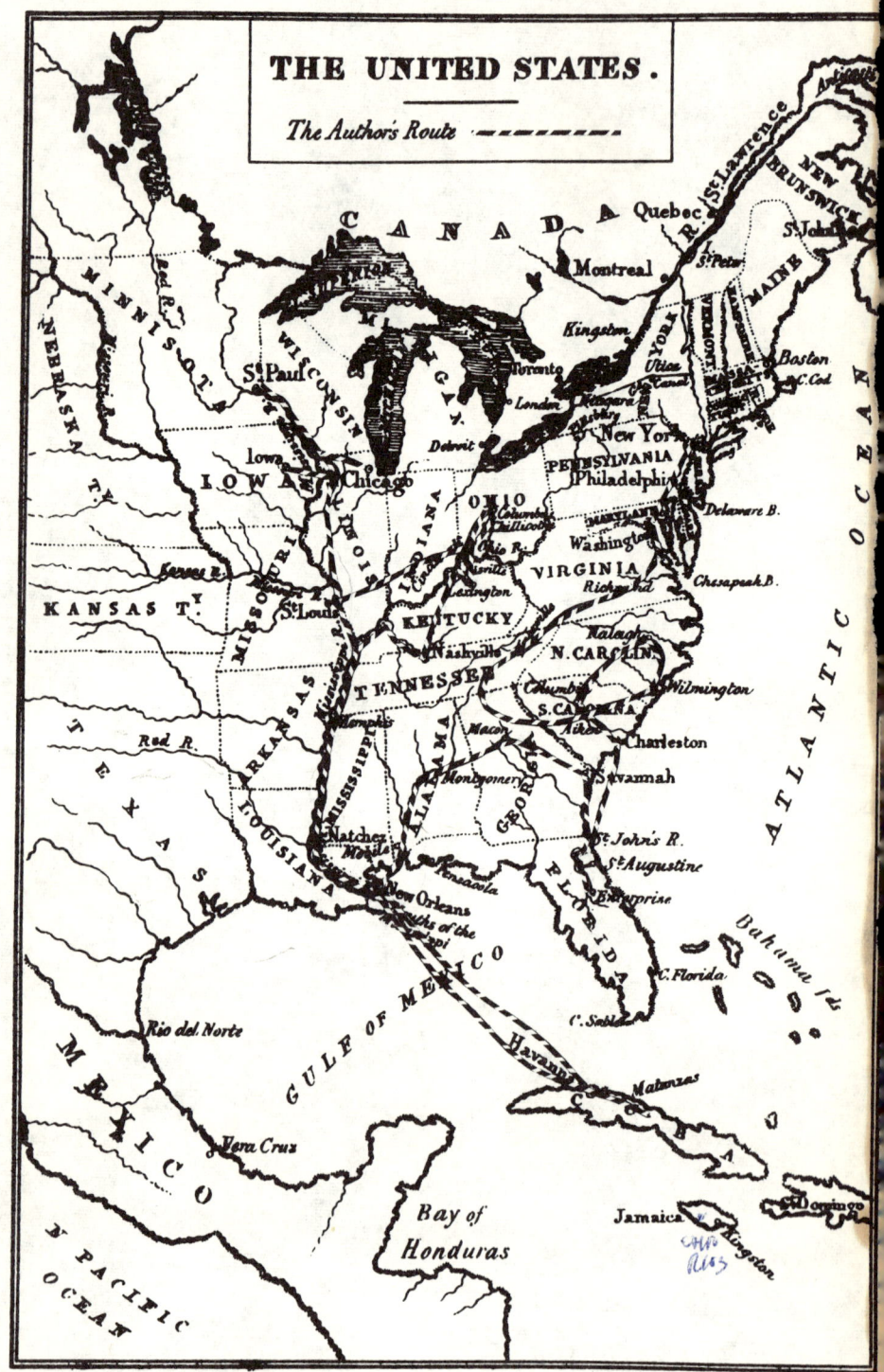

LETTERS

FROM THE

SLAVE STATES.

BY

JAMES STIRLING.

NEGRO UNIVERSITIES PRESS
NEW YORK

Originally published in 1857
by John W. Parker and Son, London

Reprinted 1969 by
Negro Universities Press
A DIVISION OF GREENWOOD PUBLISHING CORP.
NEW YORK

SBN 8371-1379-2

PRINTED IN UNITED STATES OF AMERICA

CONTENTS.

	PAGE
INTRODUCTION	vii

LETTER I.
Chicago—St. Paul—A Local Legislature 1

LETTER II.
The Prairie—Prairie Railways—Prairie Difficulties . . 10

LETTER III.
Emigration to the West—Long Winters 17

LETTER IV.
Henry Ward Beecher—Lecture on Patriotism—Spurious Democracy—Sovereignty of the People—False Equality—True Democracy 23

LETTER V.
Future Dangers—American Industry—Kentucky—Stagnation—Social Contrasts 36

LETTER VI.
Slavery—Slave Physiognomy—Slave Agitation—Free Negroes—Difficulties of the Free Negroes—The Slave's love of England 46

LETTER VII.
State of the South—The North is Democratic—The South is Aristocratic—The Line of Division—State Rights—Cause of Whig Failure—The Slavery Dispute—Aggression of the South—Spirit of Disunion—Spirit of the North—Southern Fanatics 58

iv   CONTENTS.

                                                                                       PAGE

LETTER VIII.

Presidential Election — The Republican Party — The Democratic Party—The Fillmore Party—Virtual Defeat of the South—Democratic Differences . .   80

LETTER IX.

Union or Disunion—Desire for Territory—The Secret of Power—Moral Disunion—Love of Social Distinctions—Social Progress   94

LETTER X.

Cuba—Slavery in Cuba—What Cuba may be—Socialism and Slavery—Serfdom and Freedom—Bledsoe's Defence of Slavery—Slavery Sophisms—West India Emancipation—Doubts of the Slaveholder . . .   106

LETTER XI.

Louisiana—Longing for Cuba—Universal Suffrage—Mob-government — English Ambassadors — What our Ambassadors should be—Duty of the English Press   124

LETTER XII.

Thuggism in New Orleans—Lynch-law—The London Policeman—Police in America—Hotel Life: its Causes; its Effects—American Domestic Affection —Extravagance in Dress—Southern Friends—Texas   139

LETTER XIII.

Mob-taxation—Pauper Suffrage—General Walker—Cotton—Essential to the South—Cotton produced by Free Labour   163

LETTER XIV.

Backwardness of the South—Sparseness of Population—Chances of Sugar Planting   177

LETTER XV.

English Thoroughness—American Superficiality—Want of a Leisure Class—Loss and Gain—Protectionist Fallacies—Evils of Protection in America—Economical Ignorance in America—The Example of England 184

LETTER XVI.

A Slave's View of Slavery—Illinois and Georgia—Stagnation in the South—Nat. Lewis—The American Alliance—American Newspapers 200

LETTER XVII.

Florida—The Seminole War—A Yankee in the South—White Trash—Progressiveness of Free Society—Florida Squatters—Florida and Minnesota. . . 213

LETTER XVIII.

Street Obstructions—Free and Slave Labour—Slaves unfit for High Farming—Slavery ruinous to the South 228

LETTER XIX.

Liberia a Failure—Difficulties of Emancipation—Elevation of the Slave—Self-Emancipation—Antipathy to the Free Negro—Gain of Emancipation—Decline of South Carolina—Charleston 237

LETTER XX.

Orphan Hospital—Military Academy—A Southern Lecturer—A Slave Sale—A Converted Abolitionist . . 252

LETTER XXI.

Sandhillers—Duelling—Affrays—Habit of Carrying Arms 261

LETTER XXII.

American Capitals—The Post Office—Abuses and Mismanagement—Private Enterprise the Remedy—Lynch-law 274

LETTER XXIII.

Condition of the Slaves—House Servants—Field Hands—Farm Servants—Slave Trade—Slave Disaffection—Causes of Disaffection—Insurrectionary Movements—The Remedy 284

LETTER XXIV.

Prospects of Slavery—Economical Influences—Demand for Labour—The South divided—The Frontier Slave States—Loss and Gain of Slave Breeding—Arkansas and Texas—Lowlands and Uplands—Abolitionism in the South 302

LETTER XXV.

West Virginia—Abolition Sentiments—The Scotch in West Virginia—Revivals—Climate of West Virginia—East Virginia 323

LETTER XXVI.

North and South—The Slave Power—Slavery doomed—Appeal for the South—Improbability of Disunion—Strength of National Feeling—Disunion a Bugbear 337

LETTER XXVII.

Future of America—England and America—New York Press—Dollar-worship 353

LETTER XXVIII.

Scarcity of Food—Paper Money—Manifest Destiny—American Physiognomy 362

LETTER XXIX.

The Success of America—Its Causes and Limits . . . 370

INTRODUCTION.

It may be proper to give some explanation of the form in which the following pages appear, as well as of the abrupt commencement of the 'Letters' at a distant point in the interior of America.

On the 20th August, 1856, the Author landed at New York, with the intention of making a somewhat extended tour in the United States. During the autumn months he visited the principal points of interest in New England, the State of New York, and Upper and Lower Canada, returning to New York by Lake Champlain and the Hudson. Passing then by Philadelphia, he crossed the Alleghanies to Pittsburg and Cleveland, arriving about the middle of October at Chicago, the Key of the Far West. From this point his course was to the North-West, and subsequently to the South, as indicated in the 'Letters.'

During his journey, the Author was in the habit of writing to a friend at home remarks on the people and country he was visiting. This was particularly the case in the South, where the social and political circumstances of the country forced on his attention topics of great importance. It was afterwards suggested that some portions of these communications might be interesting to the public; and in accordance with that suggestion these 'Letters' are now published.

In preparing a private correspondence for the press, much matter of merely personal and temporary interest has of course been suppressed. All that part also which referred to the North-East portion of the States has been excluded, as relating to subjects made familiar to English readers by many recent publications. Accordingly the first letter inserted in this volume is one that speaks of Chicago and the Far West.

It has been thought desirable, however, to retain as nearly as possible the original form in which the letters were written, and it is hoped that the greater freshness of an actual correspondence will more than compensate the fragmentary nature of the treatment.

The title, 'Letters from the Slave States,' has been adopted, both because the great bulk of the letters were written from the South, and because the most important topics treated of relate more immediately to the interests and institutions of the Slave States.

LETTER I.

St. Paul, Minnesota, 25th October, 1856.

Ever since I came into the States, I have been hearing of Chicago, as the great feature of the new Western world, and was therefore prepared for a wonderful city. But the reality exceeded my expectations. It is a city, not in growth, but in revolution; growth is much too slow a word for the transformation of a hamlet of log-huts into a western New York, in the space of a few years. Ten years ago Chicago had 4000 or 5000 inhabitants; now it has 100,000 : some say 120,000. Property has risen in proportion, and fabulous fortunes have been made. You hear of a man being forced to take a few acres for a bad debt, and finding himself in a year or two a millionaire; another selling by the lineal foot what he bought the other day by the acre. The proprietor of the Tremont House, where I lodged, was a poor tailor, who, when travelling westward a few years ago, stopped at Chicago. Presently he built a log-tavern, and called it the 'Tremont:' this was burned down, and he built another on the opposite side of the street. This, too, was burned down; and he then built the present 'Tremont House' on its site. It is an immense pile, and people thought him mad at the time; but Snip had an eye for futurity. He let his hotel unfurnished for 12,000 dollars, and now gets 24,000 dollars, and when the lease is out he will probably rebuild it, and have the finest hotel in the States.

There were about a dozen new churches building when we were at Chicago and some streets formed quite an avenue of spires. Let us hope that the exhortations of the kirks will be of sufficient weight to counterbalance the corruptions of the stores. I fear, however, that here, as in old Scotland, the church or meeting-house is too often but a place where the sharp trader throws off, as he thinks, the week's accumulation of sin, and starts afresh on Monday morning for six days more worldliness.

The situation of Chicago was originally so low that there could be no proper drainage. They are, therefore, now raising the whole town some three feet. This gives the town at present a most peculiar look. When you walk along even the principal streets, you pass perhaps a block of fine stone-built stores, with splendid plate-glass windows (finer than any in New York), with a good granite pavement in front: a few steps on you descend by three or four wooden steps to the old level of the street, and find a wooden pavement in front of low, shabby-looking wooden houses. The opposite side of the street presents probably the reverse. In some places the wooden causeway of the street may be raised, while the foot-pavement is low; or the granite pavement may be raised to the new level while the middle of the street is still the old plank-road, two or three feet below. At the Tremont House both are on the old low level, and only the high granite curb-stone, over which you have to clamber, reminds you of the reform yet to come. On every side magnificent blocks, stores, hotels, and churches are rising, many of them built of a beautiful white stone, that is very hard, and seems to me a kind of limestone. Along the shore of the Lake there is a terrace of private dwellings of this white stone, that in size and architectural effect will bear comparison with the newest and best houses in Belgravia.

From Chicago we crossed over to Dunleith (opposite Dabucque), by the Chicago and Galena' Railway. From Dunleith we came up to St. Paul by steamer. The Upper Mississippi is very picturesque; the bluffs are bold, and their craggy summits have often castellated forms. The foliage of the trees at the time of our passage was chiefly a rich brown, varied by a bright yellow, which harmonize well together; the ground is also covered with a reddish herbage, something like our heather; and as the woods are not close, but admit of the ground being seen through the trees, the bluffs altogether had a most beautiful russet hue, at once rich and harmonious. The river runs much in narrow channels formed by islands, and we were frequently sailing close by these islands, finely timbered, and with here and there a woodcutter's cabin. The river, as a stream, has not in this part the magnificent steady roll of the St. Lawrence, but this, to my mind, is amply compensated by the greater variety and beauty of its marginal bluffs.

St. Paul is one of the five great cities *to be*, of the Mississippi—New Orleans, Memphis, Cairo, St. Louis, and St. Paul. I believe in the two Saints, one heading the lower, and the other the upper navigation of the Mississippi, and both backed by large districts of fertile land; but the three other greatnesses I must take leave to doubt. By a recent enumeration St. Paul counts 9975 inhabitants; and at this day probably exceeds 10,000. The situation of the town is beautiful. It stands on a plateau, rising some eighty feet above the river, and behind rises an amphitheatre of heights, which will afford a magnificent site for the coming city. On the opposite side of the river are still more beautifully wooded heights, where the eye of the land speculator, in 'fine frenzy rolling,' already discerns the splendid villas of the 'merchant-princes of St. Paul.' Meanwhile St. Paul is a city of mud; and when you attempt to traverse it you are at once brought down from the gorgeous Future to a very splashy Present.

As an instance of the rise in the value of real estate in these countries, I may give you the experiences of a canny Yorkshire watchmaker whose acquaintance I made at St. Paul. He landed here four years ago (when, he says, there were more Indians than white men), and bought a town lot for 250 dollars. For the neighbouring lot 7,500 dollars have been offered and refused; and as my friend's principal lot stands on the street leading from the steam-boat wharf to the hotel, (showing the sagacity of his original choice,) he may well look for a further advance. To the thinking man, who has witnessed this sudden rise in values, and this immense rush of emigrants and speculators, the question naturally occurs, is all this progress sound? or is it built on a sandy foundation? Speaking of Minnesota alone, I should say that her success, to the whole extent predicted by sanguine men, is somewhat problematical. The four great elements of success in such new countries seem to me to be,—1st, an energetic population; 2nd, a fertile soil; 3rd, a favourable climate; 4th, easy means of communication. The first element Minnesota possesses in perfection; the second she also possesses in an eminent degree. Her soil in great part is, I believe, superior to that of Canada West, though not, perhaps, equal to the western portions of Illinois. Still the soil is quite capable of bearing good crops of wheat, the grand criterion of success, under favourable circumstances.

This brings us to the question of climate; and that, I believe, from all I have heard, is as yet a moot point. To grow good winter wheat, with such regularity as will make it an average paying crop, you must either have such a degree of warmth in winter as will dispense with the necessity of a covering of snow, as in central Illinois, or you must have a sufficient coating of snow to protect the plant during the winter, as in Western Canada, without having such a depth as prevents the admission of air, and so 'chokes' the young plant, as to a certain extent occurs in Lower Canada. Such I believe to be the theory of the thing. But the facts are difficult to ascertain, partly because there has not yet been sufficient experience of the climate to pronounce definitely on its average nature, and partly because one cannot rely on the interested statements which are made to you.

My own impression is, that there will not be sufficient snow, as the climate is decidedly drier than that of Canada West, and there is less rain. If so, the wind sweeping over the prairies, which in general are lightly timbered, would destroy the covering necessary to protect the wheat. In answer to this, you are told that there are no such winds in winter; but this I doubt. Time must show. At all events, however, they may grow good spring wheat and other grains. The climate, in point of health, is said to be admirable, and many invalids come hither to be restored, even such as are suffering from pulmonary complaints. The dryness of the climate is very favourable to them; and I have even heard of hæmorrhage of the lungs being stopped by a residence here. But to return.—The fourth element of success, or easy communication, is, I fear, wanting to Minnesota. The only natural means of external communication, of any value, is the Mississippi, and that is closed some five months in the year. So soon, therefore, as the settlers can supply themselves, and the internal or local demand ceases, and they have to cast about for an external market, I fear that Minnesota will be somewhat in the predicament of Robinson Crusoe's boat. The ready answer to this objection is, that they will by that time have railways.

But railways to this country will take a long time to make. The country is not so favourable as in the Southern prairies, where an 'air-line' costs little more than the price of iron. They count much on the projected line to Superior City; but the road is to make—the country is to settle—and the city is to build.

Such are some of the doubts which occur to a cautious Scotch intellect; but such scruples are here passed by with a shrug or a pshaw. The folks here have no time to doubt; and they have a faith which can remove mountains, and build cities and railways in their place. Only such hopeful, undoubting men, can pioneer civilization. We must follow quietly in the rear, lending them a little money, and giving them a little advice. The former they will readily take—the latter not quite so readily. This territory will probably apply this winter for admission as a State. They have sufficient numbers, perhaps 130,000 or 140,000. They are rather divided between two feelings, a wish to enjoy the honour of being a State, and a reluctance to incur the burden of paying their own government. Ambition will probably triumph over economy; and I presume there will be no objection made to their admission. The territorial Legislature meets at St. Paul this winter, when the matter will probably be settled

A LOCAL LEGISLATURE.

Some of the members of this body must be curious specimens. The present representative from one of the Northern districts is an Indian half-breed, and journeys to St. Paul on a sledge drawn by dogs, camping out o' night, and living on pemmican. So nearly does American civilization border on savagery.

LETTER II.

COLUMBUS, OHIO, 4th November, 1856.

I HAVE now travelled about 1000 miles over prairie, and begin to have some idea of the nature of the country and the course of its development. For practical purposes, you may divide the Northern States into three divisions—that east of the Alleghanies; that between the Alleghanies and the Wabash; and that west of the Wabash. The middle division consists mainly of the northern portion of Ohio and Indiana. Now the first and second divisions were originally all under forest. The first division has been in great part subjected to culture, and only stumps remind you of its ancient state. In the highly-cultivated parts, such as the neighbourhood of Boston, New York, and Philadelphia, stumps are rare; but in New York State they are yet abundant, and in many parts of New England. The northern part of Ohio and most of Indiana are yet in great part under forest. The cultivated portions

THE PRAIRIE.

are spaces cleared and reclaimed by the labour of the backwoodsman. Finally, the prairies are open land, cleared by nature, if ever they were forest, and all ready for the plough of the husbandman. Here the pioneer is not the backwoodsman with his axe, but the 'prairie-breaker' with his team and plough. You turn up the soil, and at once you are a producer of corn and wheat.

But there is compensation in everything; and these teeming wildernesses, especially those east of the Mississippi, had one great want, they had no natural means of communication. Illinois, in particular, the most fertile of all, had few rivers, and those of small account. While the lands to the east of her had, besides the Lakes, the Hudson, the Ohio, the St. Lawrence, the Delaware, &c., with all their magnificent tributaries, the prairie lands were for hundreds of miles inaccessible by internal navigation. Communication, the great means of exchange, and so of civilization, was wanting. Man could produce, but he could not trade; he had no market, and so could only live an isolated, and, therefore, unprogressive life. But civilization gave what nature denied; thus providing for her own advance. The railway supplied a cheap and easy means of communication; it gave the producer a market, and so gave value to his labour. The railway is the soul of

Western civilization. The result is seen in the astonishing tide of emigration that of late years has set westward, and in the rapid settlement which is taking place all over this region.

There seems a natural, pre-ordained fitness between the railway and the prairie; for the prairie is as eminently suited to the formation of railways, as railways are essential to the development of prairies. For hundreds of miles you have only to raise the turf, and lay your sleepers; for hundreds of miles you need neither grading nor bridging; no engineering; hardly any surveying. In one long, unwavering line your iron road passes over the level plain. And that plain, remember, costs nothing; or at most a dollar and a quarter per acre. The artificial hindrances are still fewer than the natural ones. There are no cities to be circumvented, or bridged over, at enormous cost; no gentlemen's seats whose 'amenity' is to be preserved at the cost of the plundered proprietors; no pig-headed opponents or greedy rivals to ruin you with parliamentary expenses. Absolutely, the rails and labour are your sole expense. And, in passing, let me express my astonishment, and, I may say, disgust, that, under such circumstances, a people, boasting itself first among civilized peoples, should ignorantly and suicidally cramp their enterprise by an antediluvian protective duty. Such a duty is a tax on progress. Is it not lamentable, nay, provoking to see a young nation, while putting on its 'shoes of swiftness,' thus recklessly clog itself with the cast-off absurdities of the Old World? It is a blunder which, I believe, can only be explained by supposing a want of thorough education in the American people. The very notion of this folly stings me like a mosquito every time it crosses my mind.

But, again: the prairies absolutely make their own railways without cost to any one. The development of the country by means of a railway is such, that what was yesterday waste land is to-day a valuable district. There is thus action and reaction: the railway improves the land; the improvement pays for the railway. Latterly grants of land have been made to railway companies for the purpose of forming new lines, the Government reserving alternate sections with the railway. In this way the Government loses nothing: for the price of the land it gives away is more than made up by the enhanced price of what they retain. The Illinois Central expects to have the line clear, and some million acres to boot. That is their story; I do not endorse it; but still the principle remains as I have stated. Lands have been granted in Iowa and Wisconsin for the same purpose. If you look at a railway map of

America, and calculate the immense extent of land which their roads, completed and projected, must bring into practical operation as food-producing countries, you can yourself estimate the amount of social and political development which is here in progress. De Tocqueville calculated the rate of Western progress at nineteen miles per annum. At this moment it must be reckoned by hundreds of miles. Nebraska will be settled immediately. Cities are already rising on the Missouri. I believe there is nothing in history to compare with this seven-league progress of civilization. For the first time in the world we see a highly-civilized people quietly spreading itself over a vast untenanted solitude, and at one wave of its wand converting the wilderness into a cultivated and fruitful region.

It is, indeed, the peculiarity and high privilege of the American people that it began its history with all the means and appliances of high civilization. It had not to grow out of barbarism; it had only to give new development to the civilization of the Old World. Hence one reason of its remarkable progress. This truth is brought home to you when you find in the Far West all the most recent adaptations of engineering and other sciences. Think, for one item, of 22,000 miles of railway and 40,000 miles of telegraph in America! It is to me a satisfaction to think that we Englishmen are aiding, by our capital, in this great work. We, too, are putting our hand to the 'prairie-plough,' whose furrow is the path of human progress. The day is gone by for narrow selfishness and national rivalries. The wise, at least, rejoice at progress wherever it exists, and sink national jealousies in a cosmopolitan unity of occupations, ideas, and aspirations.

The prairies, then, are becoming settled; but here, as elsewhere, man's lot is not without its trials and troubles. Two great necessaries, wood and water, are scarce. The former can be brought at a moderate expense by railway; but the want of water, and especially good water, is a more serious evil. All over the prairies, except in some favoured spots, they have to dig from twenty to forty feet for water; and when they get it, it is hard, and much impregnated with lime. It seems to me that, from this cause, Illinois, and such prairie land as is similarly situated, can never be densely populated, but must be used in large sections for agricultural, and, perhaps, pastoral purposes, while towns and cities of any magnitude must be situated on the rivers. Another evil is the unhealthiness of the prairie. Illinois has a particularly bad name in this respect. Some say that it arises greatly from the progress of cultivation; that the turning up of vast masses of decaying vegetable matter produces miasma; and they point to New York State, and Ohio, where formerly disease existed to a degree now unknown. There is probably truth in this, but I fear it will be long before Illinois will be really healthy. An intelligent physician, who has resided twenty years in the country, told me he perceived no improvement as yet.

LETTER III.

CINCINNATI, 10th November, 1856.

Chambers, if I remember well, recommends Canada West for British emigrants of the poorer classes. In this I cannot agree. The climate of Canada, though healthy, is very severe; but a stronger objection to me would be the unsatisfactory state of Canadian politics. A colony, at best, is but a provisional political organization; but in Canada there is, besides, the element of discord and perplexity arising from the division of the Provinces. This difficulty will not be easily surmounted. And there seems corruption in their government quite as great as in the States. Then, considering the matter economically, Canada is a forest land, which requires the labour and cost of clearing; and the poor man who sits down in such a wilderness generally finds that the most he can do is to have his land cleared and productive when he has spent a lifetime's labour on it, and is about to hide his bones in it.

On political and economical grounds, therefore, I should consider a prairie farm in the States a much more eligible venture. Here the emigrant has, at least, a settled government, and can at once proceed to put the plough into his land. Suppose he settles in Iowa State, some fifty miles west of Iowa city; he can have an improved farm, *i.e.*, with house, fences, &c., all ready for occupation, so that the settler can proceed at once to cultivate the soil, at from ten to fifteen dollars an acre. This is better, if he can afford it, than buying raw prairie at five to eight dollars. Here he finds a fruitful soil ready for the plough, a tolerably healthy climate, water for the digging, and, in some districts, running streams; while some of the coarser woods, such as black walnut and hickory, are at hand, and fir can be had at moderate cost from the Mississippi. The emigration itself furnishes him a local market, and by the time that fails, railways will secure him a more permanent, though perhaps less profitable, market. There is probably not snow enough to make winter wheat a sure crop, but spring wheat and Indian corn, or as they call it here simply 'corn,' will ensure him a fair return for his labour. At the start he hires a 'prairie-breaker,' to break up his land, which will cost him from two and a half to three dollars per acre; between the furrows made by the heavy prairie-plough he drops corn-seed, and will probably have nearly thirty-six bushels per acre, which, at twenty-five cents, gives him nine dollars, and this will pay all expenses of 'breaking,' reaping, &c., and leave him something handsome over. The corn is sometimes sold 'on foot,' at five and six dollars per acre; so that the settler need have no trouble about want of labour, &c. In this way, you see, an emigrant would very soon have his land clear; whereas, in Canada, he must be years before he can call the land his own, or have any practical use of it.

In Indiana, I am told, it is common, after felling the timber, to let it lie for three years to rot, before commencing to clear the ground. By that time the prairie settler would be in full swing on a free farm, with a railway at his elbow. A man would need to land in New York with 200*l*. in his pocket; with that he might, with sobriety and industry, soon realize a fair competence. At this moment the rush of emigration is towards Minnesota; but this, I believe, is greatly because the government land offices in Wisconsin and Iowa are shut till the railway companies claim the lands which have been granted to them. On the whole, a poor man would probably do best in Iowa. The lands are cheap, the country tolerably healthy, and the climate less severe than in Minnesota; indeed, some people consider Iowa to be the garden of the West. In the western portions I understand there are streams swarming with trout; and it is remarked that men and trout flourish in the same regions. Probably the clear water, and the undulation of surface necessary for running brooks, may be the ground of this fact, if fact it be.

If a man has a little more money in his pocket, and is willing to stake his health for some additional profit, then let him go to Illinois. The land is dearer, but still cheap, and it is fertile. There he has markets on every side: railways carry him to the Mississippi on the West, or to the Lakes on the North-east. He has all the advantages of the great markets of St. Louis on the one side, and of Chicago on the other. If he can afford it, and wishes to have the advantages of civilized society, then let him buy an improved farm in Ohio; there he will find good land, good society, and an agreeable climate. There is land to be had in Texas for thirty-six cents an acre; and I am told the climate is delightful, or rather, you can have any climate you choose, according to elevation. For grazing purposes, I fancy the more hilly parts of Texas are superior to anything in the States; but then you have the objection of slavery. This, however, is not an insuperable objection, for there is a large German population in Texas who do not use slaves, and are cultivating cotton successfully with free white labour. Missouri, too, but for its slavery, presents great attractions of fertility, climate, and cheapness of land. And perhaps nowhere would you do better than in Old Virginia, were it not for the blight of slavery.

One great drawback at present to the cultivation of the prairie is the long time, four or five months, during which they have to feed their cattle in winter. The first frost destroys the grass. But agricultural science is here in its infancy. Nature has done so much, that man has not roused himself to action. I have no doubt that science will overcome these natural difficulties. Better grasses will probably stand the winter better; and, at all events, other food may be easily raised. I have heard of surprising crops of beet and turnips; and, with a little wooden housing, I doubt not cattle-breeding may become a most lucrative business. In the meantime, it has been neglected for grain-growing, which paid better, and cost less trouble. This may soon be reversed.

As I mentioned before, we have travelled 1000 miles over prairie, but the space seems shorter to the recollection than you would suppose. The truth is, that we measure space, like time, by sensations; and when there are few objects in space, or few events in time, we have little idea of extension. In other words, monotony makes both the road and life seem short. The Americans amuse themselves laughing at the smallness of England; and certainly, estimated in square miles, she is small enough. But, if we consider what she contains, her bulk swells to vastness. The extent of their territory is a favourite consideration with Americans: to such enthusiasts I would propose as a salutary corrective a day's railway travel on a prairie 'air line.' It would be a fervid imagination, indeed, that could resist its soporific tendency.

The pork-trade of Cincinnati interested me deeply; much more so than her picturesque mistake of wine-growing, which could only exist under prohibitory duties. The provision-trade of Ohio, on the contrary, is a branch of that grand division of labour by which nature sets one nation to produce the food, another the clothing, and a third the luxuries of the world, and so unites all in the fellowship of a common industry. Pork-curing is nauseous in its details, but it is blessed in its effects. The sewers of Cincinnati run blood; yet pork is a bond of nations, and the peace of the world is cemented by lard.

LETTER IV.

CINCINNATI, 19th Nov., 1856.

ON Sunday last I had an opportunity of hearing Henry Ward Beecher preach, and on Monday evening I heard him lecture. I was glad of this opportunity, not only because I wished to hear the man, but because a popular teacher is in some sort a gauge of the intellectual standing of the people that delights in him. On the whole, I have been disappointed with Beecher. He is a man of genius, but his power is pathological rather than intellectual. There is vigour and novelty in his mode of expression, but the thing expressed is old and commonplace. The warp and woof of his discourse is poor and antiquated, but is concealed from the vulgar view by a rich covering of fancy, pathos, and humour. No wonder, then, that he is a popular orator, for it is the very essence of popularity to present old ideas in a new garb, thus flattering the vulgar mind that it is adopting new notions, when in truth it is only receiving back its old threadbare prejudices in a new and becoming dress. That such oratory should pass current as sterling thought among the American people, confirms me in an opinion which has been growing on me, that education here, though diffused, is shallow.

Beecher's text was: 'Cast thy care on the Lord, for He will care for thee.' He dwelt greatly on the evil of 'care,' in the sense of anxiety, as opposed to joyfulness, which he said was the natural temperament of the true believer. He attributed the 'care' of the modern world to its faithlessness; that is, to its want of true Christianity. In a remarkable passage he told his hearers when they went forth next day, and the next, and the next, to the public streets, to mark the countenances of those they met, and take note how many of them wore the appearance of joy. 'You will find *all*,' he said, 'marked with lines of "care."' 'I am accustomed to address large audiences,' he continued, 'and nowhere do I see any expression but that of anxiety and care. Joy has departed out of the world because there is no real Christianity in it.' This was to me a notable testimony to the universality of that anxious physiognomy among Americans, which has struck me ever since my landing. But Beecher is wrong in extending the remark to all nations. There is care enough in the faces of certain individuals, and even classes, among us; but as a rule, the English physiognomy is *not* care-worn; on the contrary, it is joyous and contented; and even the corpulency of John Bull is a testimony to the truth of the rule, 'Laugh and grow fat.

There was nothing thrilling in Beecher's discourse. There was much fine word-painting, some pathos, and once or twice expressions so nearly approaching the ludicrous as to cause a titter through the church; but the essence of his sermon was just such commonplace orthodox theology as you might hear in any Calvinistic conventicle in a second-rate Scotch town. To me it was mortifying to hear such antiquated teaching in so new a place. It seemed to me here thoroughly incongruous. Surely the master-mind of Young America might bring forth some doctrine more fresh and invigorating than that which puzzles the brain and corrupts the will of Calvinistic Europe! Beecher is a consummate actor: he thoroughly understands effect; not that I think him insincere; I should think him a decidedly earnest man; but he does not disdain the aid of external means to rouse and attract his audience. To me he seems much less impressive than Caird was in his best days. Beecher is a better actor, but Caird was a more fervid preacher, therefore a more powerful one.

Though there was an immense crowd, and hundreds had to leave the church door, yet there were a great many children present. This was, doubtless, owing to that spirit of indulgence which prompts American parents to refuse nothing to their children, not even what is unreasonable. What had children to do there? They could not enjoy the discourse, they were only playing the dog in the manger, taking up the room of those who would have enjoyed it. But they liked the fun and excitement, and so their parents let them go. In the pew before us were three girls of ten or twelve years of age, who thoroughly disturbed the congregation. When told to be quiet, they stared boldly in our faces, as asking 'What is your business?' This indulgence of children in America is no trifling matter: it is sapping the virtue and self-control of the whole nation, and threatens to undermine all lawful authority.

On Monday evening Beecher lectured on 'Patriotism.' Here, again, I remarked the same richness of imagery, and the same baldness of thought. The intellectual thread of his discourse might have been borrowed from a school-girl's theme, but his illustrations were powerful, striking, and varied. The main ideas developed were intensely popular, in fact, the mere ordinary notions of the democratic mind at this hour, not without a strong dash of American prejudice. He deprecated the influence of great men, as opposed to the intellectual equality of a true democracy. He thanked God, he said, for having removed Clay, Webster, and Calhoun from amidst them, for it destroyed the temptation towards hero-worship which had beset the people; 'and since their death,' he added with a sneer, and lowering his voice almost to an 'aside,' 'He has not led us into further temptation.' This last trait may give you some idea of Beecher's humour, which is mainly sarcastic, and depends much for its effect on the artistic management of his voice. You will agree with me, I think, that to desire a low monotony of intellect among the people, lest any one should overtop his neighbours, is as unphilosophical as Carlyle's wish, that mankind should look up from a low level of degradation to the one Great Man. The true ideal surely is, that all men should raise themselves, each according to his own gifts and powers, and that the gifted ones among us are instruments in the hands of God for advancing the general progress; the teachers and ensamples of humanity. Great men are not to be worshipped, neither can they be dispensed with.

Beecher dwelt complacently, and to the great satisfaction of his audience, on the 'new ideas' of America in reference to politics, and the 'self-government' of the New World, as opposed to the monarchical rule 'from above,' in the Old World. This self-adulation in regard to their political superiority is too common, and seems to me unwarranted. The Americans have as yet promulgated, so far as I know, no 'new ideas' in regard to the nature of government. On the contrary, I would say of the political ideas current in the Union (as has been often said of other things) that what is new is bad, and what is good is not new. Americans flatter themselves that they have a mission to enlighten the world as to the possibility and advantage of what they call 'self-government;' but it seems to me that, in many respects, they do but dish up the stale maxims of European theorists, and these not the wisest. True self-government is the noblest gift of man. But by self-government I mean the power and habit of every individual man to think and act for himself, irrespective of any prying, would-be-Providential Bureaucracy. This gift the Americans have, and I honour them for it; but they have it in common with ourselves. But that spurious 'self-government,' which here resolves itself into the supreme rule of Irish Rowdyism, is not a Government to be proud of. If we must have class-legislation, as well be ruled by the upper as the lower class. We shall, at least, have fewer tyrants; and a despotism 'from below' seems to me no whit better than a despotism 'from above.' It is small gain to a nation that ' Five Points' should oppress ' Fifth Avenue' instead of ' Fifth Avenue' misruling ' Five Points.'

Democrats on both sides of the Atlantic have a confused notion of the fundamental principles of liberty and equality, which, properly understood, may be resolved into one. They see in liberty only the freedom to exercise the unrestrained will of the individual; in equality, a gross similitude of material circumstances. Whereas, true liberty is that subordination of all wills to an universal law of justice, which secures to each its own unrestricted sphere of action; and equality in the highest sense is the equality of men as free-intelligences, which such a subordination effects. Well understood, therefore, liberty is not opposed to law: rather law is the essential condition of liberty. But the vulgar in all times have confounded the spiritual, unseen law of justice and the material government which is its necessary embodiment. Justice must be administered by some organized power ; and for as much as the holders of that power have often turned it to their own uses, shallow and impatient men have jumped to the conclusion that all law, all government, all authority is despotism. Hence, monarchy means with them tyranny, because many kings have played the tyrant; and democracy means liberty, because every man gets his own way. But all this is sheer confusion of thought. Where the universal law of justice prevails, no matter in what form, or under what name, there we have liberty; but where that law is disregarded or dishonoured, we have despotism or anarchy, according as the law is abused by its appointed representative, on the one hand, or disregarded, from want of any efficient embodiment, on the other.

The founders of the American Union understood this distinction, and sought to give power to the Government, while forming checks to despotism; but the people of America have gone astray from the 'wisdom of their ancestors,' and have weakened more and more the authority of the law, till now it is all but powerless for good. The old Federalist party does not exist even in name; so unpopular is the idea of a strong Government. And the fear and hatred of authority has penetrated even into the school and the household, and teachers and parents are ashamed and afraid to exercise the rightful authority of their station, so inveterate is the popular prejudice in regard to law, and so complete the confusion of the American mind as to despotism and authority.

Equally indistinct and unphilosophical are the

SOVEREIGNTY OF THE PEOPLE. 31

popular democratic ideas with regard to the sovereignty of the people. If, as is usual in democratic communities, we confound 'the people' with the numerical majority of the nation, and set up their will, be it holy or unholy, as the supreme arbiter of affairs, we confound the brute force of numbers with the divine authority of right and justice, and thereby lay the foundation for a whole system of political blundering. This confusion of ideas lies at the root of all the Democratic legislation which has been deteriorating the constitution of the United States for these last fifty years, impairing the power, and dimming the purity of the Government. It is this popular fallacy which has proved the stronghold of the Democratic party, and enabled it to induce the unthinking masses to sap the authority of the Government, until it can protect neither life nor liberty. By acting on this vulgar prejudice that party has subjected every important office, even the sacred one of judge, to the fitful fancies of a vulgar crowd. In a word, by means of this popular fallacy, the Democratic party has very nearly reduced the Republic of the United States to an Irish mobocracy. Government is a means, not an end. The end in view is the predominance of justice. If that end be attained, it matters little by what machinery it is worked out. If it be not attained, then the most specious constitution is a blunder and a failure.

In England, I think the just will of the people is, on the whole, fairly represented by the Government, though I believe it is more in spite of our 'constituted authorities' than by means of them. Intelligent public opinion—with occasional interregna of stupid John-Bullism—is the real ruler of England. In so far we are, therefore, essentially a self-governing people. Are the Americans, in this sense, a self-governing people, or are they ruled by that numerical majority of the people, which is neither the wisest nor the justest? I hesitate to answer. Intelligent Americans have themselves hesitated to answer this question to me. Some events, such as the late election, would lead one to fear that the unwise and unworthy multitude predominates; and yet I cannot overlook that latent force of virtue and wisdom which makes itself as yet too little felt in public affairs, but which assuredly is there, and which will come forth, I am convinced, when the hour of trial comes, to save the country.

The popular notion of Equality is no less superficial than that of Liberty. The Democrat prizes an outward, material equality; not the essential, inward equality that is rooted in man's humanity, and that exists in spite of all outward differences.

Hence he is not satisfied with essential equality: he must have an outward monotony of condition. The people must all ride in the same car, and sit at the same table, and vote at the same polling-place. It is considered a degradation for one to serve another; and the very name of servant is abominated. In all this there is a want of true wisdom and true dignity. It is right to assert the dignity and worth of manhood, but it is a weakness and a folly to rebel against those civil and domestic distinctions which originate in the nature of things, and which therefore carry no real dishonour with them. Why should not a poor man consent to ride in a less luxurious car, paying a proportionate fare, as well as live in a less luxurious house, paying a proportionate rent? So with service. There is nothing essentially degrading in one man performing certain menial offices for another. The degradation arises only when the office is performed in a menial spirit In itself, all labour, even the most menial, is honourable, when performed in the true spirit of duty. The Americans will cease to disparage domestic service when they learn to take a higher view of human equality. The false views of equality now rife lead to contradictions and compromises that are sometimes almost ludicrous; for the force of things is always in contest with false ideas.

A distinction of class is pretty generally maintained among the travelling and hotel-living public by virtue of the national chivalry for the 'ladies.' On some lines there is a 'ladies' car;' in the hotels there are 'ladies' parlours,' 'ladies' ordinaries,' a 'ladies' saloon,' and so on; in all of which I could easily see that part of the object, if not the whole, was to get quietly and decently over the theoretical equality among the 'sovereign people.' It is rather curious to hear their mode of address: a labourer is always 'this gentleman;' whereas a gentleman in dress and appearance is 'this man.' In the one case, the poor man must be raised to a level with the gentry; in the other, the gentleman must be levelled to an equality with the people. To be called a 'man,' therefore, is an acknowledgment of your gentility: to be called 'gentleman,' infers your want of position. A master-tailor said to me to-day, pointing to a coatless, cross-legged snip—'This gentleman will fix your button.' Had he told the man to sew on my button, he would have said, ' Sam, fix this man's button.' But with all this confusion of ideas and with all these practical absurdities, I still am pleased even with this external and very imperfect assertion of man's dignity and equality. With all its blunders and absurdities, it is better than the stolid subservience of the lower classes, such as is preached and taught by our English parsons to their degraded chaw-bacons. Men cannot all at once learn the true nature of such divine notions : the first step is to grasp some rude adumbration of the ethereal thing. In time they will pass from the husk to the kernel. Our own Scotch working-class is in the same stage of development : they have learned to despise subserviency, but they mistake rudeness and coarseness for independence. When the poor feel more assured of their essential equality with the rich, they will put off their present harsh and morose manners. So when the Americans understand better true equality, they will tolerate the necessary distinctions of society.

LETTER V.

LOUISVILLE, KENTUCKY, 23rd Nov., 1856.

THE late election gave scope for serious reflection in regard to the future of America. Hitherto the States have had almost entirely a rural population: they were peopled by a yeomanry: hence their equality, and power of self-government—hence, too, the rationality and peaceableness of their Government, on the whole. But how will it be when, with the development of commerce, and still more of manufactures, a large urban population comes into existence and into power? Will the American constitution stand the wear and tear of an 'Age of Great Cities,' with their Alsatias, and all the vice, and ignorance, and lawlessness that that word infers? Will the 'Model Republic' be proof against a 'dangerous class?' Will the ballot-box, and universal suffrage, and elective chief magistrates, protect the commonwealth against the evils of Socialism, Red Republicanism, and all the other crudities of Proletarian ignorance and licence? Hitherto the prairie has been the safety-valve of the American Constitution. But how will it be when the thickly-peopled West shall no longer afford a vent for discontent? The density of population in the United States is now 7.90 to the square mile; in England it is 332 to the square mile. Will the American Constitution bear a pressure of 332 inhabitants to the square mile? The American nation may, and, I doubt not, will wrestle victoriously with these social and political hydras; but it will be in virtue of its strong Anglo-Saxon common sense, and not by any help derived from its ultra-democratic institutions, but the contrary. They will be a clog and a hindrance in the hour of trial; and if the country be saved, she will be saved in spite of them. And remember, this is not the flippant dictum of me, a passing stranger in the land, it is the grave opinion of the best and wisest of her own sons. Even from the grave, the patriots of the Revolution and their worthiest successors call on the country to pause in their levelling and law-destroying career.

In reference to this view of the peculiar dangers to which American Republicanism is exposed, I have been struck from the hour of my arrival with the fearful impolicy of Protectionism in the States. Protectionism here is a political, no less than an economical blunder. The natural tendency of American development, by the settling and cultivation of vast tracts of rich land by a population of educated but not wealthy emigrants, is precisely the condition of things best adapted to unfold the excellences of the American constitution, and repress its evil tendencies. By letting things take their natural course, American statesmen would have secured the rapid formation of so large a class of intelligent freemen as would have thoroughly neutralized the brutal mobs of a few large towns, and at the same time would have ensured the most rapid and perfect development of the material resources of the country. But, by following the stupid old system of Protection, they have not only diverted industry from its true and most profitable course, but have prevented the creation of a large class of yeomen, who would otherwise have been called into existence, and in their stead have created the mobs of New York, Philadelphia, and all the other manufacturing districts, which now make every reasoning American tremble for the future of his country. That ignorant men should fall into such a blunder would not surprise me; but what does surprise and annoy me is, that among all the most enlightened intellects of America, so very few should see these truths in all their scope and fearful significance.

On the whole, I am convinced the industry of America is not in advance of ours; on the contrary, in thoroughness it is far inferior. It is only in a certain originality of conception and boldness of enterprise that she may excel us; and this advantage is compensated by the evil of overhaste and presumption. With more daring innovations, America has also more sorry failures. This may be applied to her industrial, as well as to her political system. The imagination of the Americans is more vivid than ours; they are a younger people; their rapid increase gives a larger proportion of young minds; the whole tendency of their development is to excite and fire the imagination. Hence there is more tendency to invention, which depends on vivacity of the imagination; but, on the other hand, there is less of that cautious weighing of difficulties, which depends on a due subordination of the fancy to the understanding; there is less doubt, and consequently more blundering. Thus we see that the Americans took the lead in ship-building, and jogged us out of our 'dogmatic sleep;' but even here she went too fast, and stumbled in her haste; and now I am told by naval men they are coming back from their extreme clipper build, which would not carry cargo, and displeased both shippers and underwriters, and are returning to comparatively bluff bows.

We should also distinguish between different branches of industry, in speaking of American progress. It is here as elsewhere: where the human intellect has been stimulated by necessity, it has done wonders; where nature has worked for man he has been slothful and stationary. The great want of labour has forced the American to seek for substitutes; hence the reaping and mowing machines, and other ingenious implements which have half-delighted, half-alarmed the English public; but on the other hand, the fertility of the soil has led to a rude agriculture, which would shock our most backward farmers. On this point I can quote the authority of Mr. Alexander, of Kentucky, a most judicious and impartial witness, who writes thus to a Louisville paper:—'The present may be truly called the age of progress, and as our people are fond of experiment, it is not surprising that America should deserve and receive credit for making rapid advances in useful discoveries. These experiments and discoveries seem, however, to be mostly confined to mechanics and the arts, and the farmer, here as elsewhere, seems the last to leave the beaten track in search of improvement and profit.' As a citizen of the world, as well as a consumer of the products of labour, I should rejoice if the Americans were still more inventive than they are; as it is, I suspect their merit in that direction is somewhat over-estimated.

The face of the country in Kentucky is 'rolling' —*i.e.*, it is almost universally undulating. You do not see a ridge of hills and then a plain, now a valley and now a table-land, as in England, and even in Scotland; but there seems an almost constant succession of undulating country, seldom rising into hills, and seldom stretching out in level plains. Except where the land has been cleared, it is covered with timber, sometimes in a beautiful park-like manner. In America there seems a tendency in Nature to do everything by wholesale. There are regions of plain, then regions of hill; instead of the less imposing, though more beautiful, 'hill and dale' of the little 'Old Country.' Then they have whole regions of fresh water, and rivers running from end to end of the land, instead of our little lakes and brooks and burns. Things here are on a grand scale —'that's a fact.'

The original settlement of Kentucky partook much more of a military occupation than a purely agricultural emigration. All the inhabitants lived under the protection of a military fort, and at night were 'forted in' with their cattle. Before I came to Kentucky I had often heard that it was inhabited by a taller, larger race of men than any others in America, and from the moment I put my foot in the State I found this corroborated by my own observation. The men are not only of a larger size, but have a franker, jollier, freer Old-English look, than most Americans. I inquired from various Kentuckians what could possibly be the cause of so marked a phenomenon; but though all admitted the fact, none could suggest a reason. They generally turned it off with a joke as to good food and the like. To me it seems pretty evident that the history of the State accounts for the physiognomy of its inhabitants. It was won by the rifle. For years it was the rallying-point of all the adventurous bold spirits who loved danger for its own sake, and who had the physical endurance and nerve fit to cope with the toils and dangers of a hunter's and warrior's life. Here, only men of vigorous constitution and hardy frame could find a continuing city; the weak, if by chance they come, must soon be cut off; a powerful winnowing would leave only the strong. And it is the descendants of these strong, bold men whom we now find in the fields of Kentucky, six feet and upwards, with broad athletic frames, and full, broad, open faces; as different as can well be from the sharp, lean, furrowed physiognomy of the Eastern States. I confess it was a great relief to my mind when I found at least a plausible solution of an enigma that had thoroughly puzzled me since my first entrance into the State.

The social state of Kentucky seems very back-

STAGNATION. 43

ward. The moment you cross the Ohio you are painfully struck with the contrast, and as you advance into the interior things get worse and worse. You miss entirely that progress which is the charm of the East and the wonder of the West. Here things seem all at a stand-still ; there is no go-aheadness ; you never come across a new 'city' rising in the wilderness. Nowhere do you hear that extraordinary combination of hammering, planing, and sawing, which on every turn of the Upper Mississippi announces a new and bustling settlement. Here everything is old-fashioned : you would think the country had been settled before the flood. The farm-houses, with their tumble-down barns and pig-houses, speak of poverty and ill-requited labour. The people themselves are mostly clad in homespun garments of antediluvian cut and colour. They travel much, men and women, on horseback, with perhaps a child on a pillion, or a saddle-bag, if the man is on a long journey. The roads, as such an equipage indicates, are of the worst, and a road is always a fair criterion of civilization. Sometimes you find a 'pike' or turnpike road gravelled, or even Macadamized ; but more frequently you have to trust to ' mud roads'— a phrase which explains itself. Yesterday a traveller, who had just arrived by land from Memphis, begged me not to attempt that route, unless I was prepared to drag the stage myself, for that the stage had stuck up to the axles, and all the passengers had to help to drag it out of the mire. There are some odds-and-ends of railroads in Kentucky and Tennessee, but no important line has been finished. Even of the main line between Louisville and Nashville, only 30 miles are completed, and that in an imperfect manner; the rest, 160 miles, are promised in some three years, but I would not ensure the completion of the whole line in five.

As if things were not sufficiently backward, the Legislature of Kentucky has passed a Usury Law, making six per cent. the legal interest. As you may suppose, capitalists who may get ten per cent. legal interest by sending their capital to Chicago, or elsewhere in Illinois, or who may invest their funds anywhere advantageously in land in the West, do not leave it in Kentucky. The folly is so transparent, that I asked the friend who gave me the information, how men could be so besotted? His explanation was, that the hireling politicians, who here form the State Legislatures, mostly briefless lawyers and the like, must please their constituents; and that as the bulk of these think a Usury Law a protection to the poor, a Usury Law is passed, without much reference to the ideas of Smith or Bentham. Does all this smack of superior intelligence? Still this brave American does not despair of the future of the country. 'We have been too prosperous,' he says, 'and must have our trials to sober and instruct us. We have waxed fat, and kicked, and now we must learn by hard experience.' This, I think, is the truth of the matter. I cannot conceive that Providence would ever suffer a nation to prosper so conspicuously as America has done, and then suddenly to collapse; on the other hand, I doubt not that her prosperity will receive some severe checks, and that ere long. The mission of this people, in spreading Anglo-Saxon civilization over the Western world, will assuredly be accomplished; but the new birth will as surely be accompanied by throes and travail. Even now, methinks, I hear the moanings of coming sorrow.

Even in passing through the country, here in the South, I think one notices marks of a greater inequality of social condition than exists in the North. There is not the same appearance of equably disseminated comfort. There are handsome dwellings here and there, and there are poor, mean-looking homesteads; but one misses the neat farm-houses that dot the landscape of New England, and speak of comfort, equality, and intelligence. In the North there is a population of comfortable yeomen; in the South you have rich planters and poverty-stricken peasants.

LETTER VI.

Nashville, Tennessee, 1st December, 1856.

Now what shall I say of slavery? I have as yet said nothing; but you will not do me the injustice to think me indifferent to that matter. On the contrary, that, of all others, is the subject nearest my thoughts; and I may say, ever since I entered into the Slave States, it has pressed like nightmare on my breast. Oh, it is an accursed thing; and the nearer one comes to it, the more hideous it is. It seems to me almost as if I were travelling in an enchanted land, with giants, and gnomes, and bad genii, and slaves. There is something in slavery so utterly incongruous with all a civilized man's ideas, and habits, and sympathies, that I never can get rid of a certain feeling of unreality about the whole thing. Even when the bare, disgusting fact is pressed unmistakeably on my notice, my mind relieves itself from the dilemma by unconsciously conceiving it as a mere passing shadow that for the

SLAVERY.   47

moment darkens the earth. And this, moreover, is
the result, no less, of my soberest reflections. This
system cannot last; assuredly it is doomed. It must
and will disappear, and that speedily. If there be a
God in heaven, it must away. I am not fanatical,
I hope. I recognise the practical difficulties with
which the question of American slavery is environed.
I have no cut-and-dry remedy to propose; and I
sincerely pity the white men who labour under this
affliction, and to whom this plague has been handed
down by their and our forefathers. But I ask, at
least, for a due appreciation of the evil, and some
approximation to a better state of things, some
progress towards the right, some mitigation of
wrong.

I do not, will not judge of slavery by its
physical effects. Even if all planters' stories were
true, and the slave were really as 'happy' as they
would have us believe, it would alter my hatred
of slavery not a jot; on the contrary, such a
consummation were to me the supremest evidence
of its accursedness. If slavery could really so
brutalize men's minds as to make them hug their
chains, and glory in degradation, it would be, in my
eyes, doubly cursed. But it is not so; the slaves are
not 'happy,' and I thank God for it. There is manhood
enough left in them to make them at least unhappy

Therefore there is hope for them. What would the worm be that could not even turn? I hold that man is 'an end unto himself,' and that to use him as a 'brute means' to the ends of other men, is to outrage the laws of God. This is to me the 'Law and the Prophets' in the matter of human liberty; and I disdain to enter into any huckstering, pettifogging calculations of 'happiness.' I take my stand far above the atmosphere of happiness or unhappiness when I argue the question as a matter of right and wrong.

But even as to this same 'happiness' of the slave much might be said, and that not favourably. It is true that, on the whole, and taking in the slave population of all the States, statistics prove incontestably that the treatment of the slaves must be reasonably good. A beneficent law of Providence has ordained that man does not multiply fast under excessive misery; and the slaves multiply fast. The slave population of America, even without allowing for manumissions, has increased since 1790 at the rate of six per cent. per annum, as I calculate. Therefore, it has not been supremely miserable. This is to me a much more cogent statement in favour of good treatment than any tale of 'patriarchal' sway; for patriarchs, even in the best of times, were far from being saints, and in modern times the breed has probably not much improved. But granting so much, I still deny the positive 'happiness' of the slaves. By universal consent, the slaves of the Northern States are the best treated; and yet, even here, in Kentucky and Tennessee, I maintain they are not happy. You need only look in their faces to see they are not happy. The slave physiognomy, even in Kentucky, struck me as depressed, and in some places gloomy. There is, indeed, but too much cause for gloom, even among the best treated. Their present may be comfortable, but their future is always insecure. Let their master be ever so benevolent, yet he may die, or he may fail, or he may run in debt; in either case the 'happy' slave may be sold, handcuffed, and sent to the South. This happens every day.

At a roadside inn where we slept we found the slaves, especially the females, were very ill-treated, being frequently 'whipped.' I could have sworn it from their hang-dog look. The landlord was an ill-conditioned fellow, and his wife still worse. The day we left the house, a beautiful, calm, sunshiny Sunday morning, I learnt, after we had started, that one tall, melancholy-looking mulatto girl was to be flogged as soon as we went off, because our breakfast had been somewhat late. I declare it made me sick to think that we were brought so close into contact with this atrocious system, and I regretted heartily that I had shaken hands with our host, who, so soon as our backs were turned, would tie up this poor woman, and flog her with a whip, knowing that we 'Old Country people' would then be out of reach of her screams.

I find, too, that even in these Northern Slave States cases of gross cruelty occur. I overheard a conversation in a stage between two Southern people, in which, after sporting the usual commonplaces about the comfort of the negroes, one added that no doubt there were exceptions; that he knew one man in Kentucky who used his slaves 'barbarously,' and that such things ought to be prevented by law. From another source I heard of a drunken scoundrel who possesses some forty slaves, and systematically flogs them; and of a second, who, though a married man, has four negro slaves with whom he regularly cohabits, and procreates slave children. In short, it is atrocious, even at the best: what then must it be at the worst, in those Southern dens of infamy where no traveller can penetrate? Here, the *fear* of the South makes the poor wretches tremble: what must be the fate of those who have to meet the dread reality? The system, too, is getting worse; the chains of the slave are getting tighter and more galling. Fear and suspicion, the

SLAVE AGITATION. 51

natural results of the agitation of this question, induce the slave-owner to keep a tighter hand over his people : this irritates ; more force again is required, and so things go in a vicious circle.

The slaves of the more Northern States have somehow become more intelligent than they were. I have been quite struck with the intelligence and frankness of some of those with whom I have conversed. They know very well the state of matters between the North and the South, and they are evidently biding their time ; they know also the feelings of Englishmen, and speak very openly to them. Their owners are aware of this intelligence, and it makes them more suspicious and more severe. They cannot abide free negroes. Indeed, it is now unlawful in Kentucky to manumit a slave. Suspicion is the Fury that whips, in retribution, the slave-master.

At this moment there is evidently a great agitation in the minds of the slave population. All over the country there have been insurrectionary outbreaks. Now, where is all this to end ? Insurrection causes severity; but can you compress human emotion ? When it comes to nailing down the safety-valve, it is a bad look-out for all concerned. The slave-owner may turn round and ask me what, then, is my solution of the problem. I for one have no solution to offer; but this I say, a solution must be found, or a worse thing will happen. If the South cannot find a solution of this slave problem, God will find one for them, and that, trust me, will be a violent one. Southern writers tell us that, if the negroes are to be freed, one or other of the two races must be destroyed. They cannot exist together, say they, and the result of freedom must be the 'utter extermination' of one race. It is not difficult to guess which race they propose to exterminate; but the extermination of four millions of people is no such simple matter, though passionate editors talk so glibly of it. The immediate future of slaves and slave-owners in the South is very dark. Hatred and revenge on the one hand; fear and suspicion on the other; these are sorry elements of a social system. And the slaves are becoming not only more intelligent, and therefore more powerful, but they are also rapidly becoming more numerous. They have increased from 697,897 in 1790, to 3,204,373 in 1850. Now they probably number 4,000,000. This rapid growth, it seems to me, must force on a 'solution' sooner or later. A caste may be held down, but how can a people be kept under? It is to be observed that while this increase of numbers makes some solution of the difficulty more inevitable, it also makes it more perplexing.

FREE NEGROES. 53

A whole people cannot be removed; the whites say they will not live in a land in common with the blacks, if free and equal. What then is to be done? This is the difficulty that staggered De Tocqueville, and made him all but hopeless. It is, doubtless, a great difficulty; but Providence has led men before out of greater difficulties.

Closely connected with this question is the position of the free negroes in the North; and accordingly that occupied some of my attention while there. On the whole, I was agreeably surprised with the intelligence and seeming prosperity of that class, as also with their improved relation to the whites. Some with whom I conversed were men of superior mind and some education. From them and other sources I learn that their situation has been much ameliorated within these last few years. They are treated much more as equals than formerly, and in some respects are comfortable. They are not now excluded from public conveyances in New England, and in some States are even allowed to exercise the franchise, as well as to possess it. In Boston, ever in the van of American civilization, one of the chief law practitioners is a coloured man. I saw lately, in a *London Illustrated News*, a story of a free negro being turned out of a railway car in Pennsylvania. This may be true, as the anti-nigger prejudice is always strongest in States adjoining the Slave States; but, on the other hand, I have myself travelled with coloured people in cars and steamers, and never saw them put out, or ignominiously treated. Indeed, they allow themselves that they are now much better treated in this respect; though one very intelligent man from Ohio told me he had never been allowed to enter what is called the 'ladies' car' (*i.e.*, as I have explained before, the principal or exclusive car), though he had tried, just to see what would happen. All this proves irresistibly that the old prejudice of colour is not unconquerable; on the contrary, that it is rapidly giving way to better and more rational feelings.

De Tocqueville argues that freedom would make the position of the blacks worse than ever, as the very feeling of social equality would intensify the prejudices and hatred of the whites. And so it would be at first; but De Tocqueville has not, I think, made sufficient allowance for the influence of time in softening prejudices, when once the original cause was removed. The experience of the last few years seems to me most hopeful in this respect. But perhaps the best refutation of De Tocqueville's notion is to be found in the statistics of the mulatto population. Increased mixture of blood is surely the best criterion of decreasing

DIFFICULTIES OF THE FREE NEGRO. 55

aversion. Now the census of 1850 tells us, that while mulattoes form only one-twelfth of the slave blacks, they form more than half the number of free blacks. Looking at all these circumstances, I cannot but think that if only freedom were once established there would be a gradual admixture of the races, and the negro, partly through an infusion of Anglo-Saxon blood, and partly through the civilizing influence of Anglo-Saxon industry, would gradually rise to be a very respectable, if not superior man.

In the meantime, the free negro of the North has some great difficulties in his way. Foremost of these is the difficulty of learning or profitably exercising any skilled trade. White men will not work in the same workshop with a coloured man. He is thus, in most cases, prevented from learning a trade. But even if he should overcome this difficulty, he would find himself shut out from employment. White people will not employ a coloured workman if they can help it. The consequence is, that although in the Slave States many artificers are slaves, in the Free States coloured men are generally obliged to adopt such menial or simply labouring occupations as require little skill and training. These free coloured men make capital servants; I, at least, prefer them to the Irish. A lady in Canada told us that she would rather give a dollar a day to a negro washerwoman than half a dollar to an Irish. Some hotels have the one class, some the other: they are seldom mixed; though in the West I have seen even Americans acting as stewards along with mulattoes. They are extremely observant; they notice your slightest look or gesture; and I am told they have an intuitive perception of the rank and station of persons, an invaluable quality, I should think, in a hotel servant. The free negroes and mulattoes of the North have nothing whatever of the nigger gibberish; and indeed even here, in Kentucky and Tennessee, I have heard little or none of it. On the contrary, the coloured men in America seem to me to speak better, or at least more agreeably to an English ear, than the whites. They have no twang, and no sing-song. There is something, too, soft in their voices, and this with a certain native courtesy and gentleness, gives quite a charm to their manner, so at least it appeared to us, though I must confess I have heard others express themselves differently. In such cases, however, I thought there was prejudice at bottom. It is but fair to add, that the negroes here, both free and slave, are quite aware of the views and sympathies of 'Old Country' people; and perhaps that may have secured for us more than usual respect and attention from these poor creatures. A free man, and a very intelligent one, a barber at St. Paul's, told me that the first thing the slaves teach their children is to love England. He further told me that many free men, himself among the rest, are preparing to cross over to Canada, where, though they cannot earn so much money, they enjoy the rights and status of equal citizenship. Poor creatures, may they prosper! It is a proud thing for an Englishman to be loved and honoured by the oppressed, as the best assertor of human freedom.

LETTER VII.

NEW ORLEANS, 16th December, 1856

WE made many pleasant acquaintances on board the Cumberland and Mississippi steamers. When well-educated Southerners know that you mean no harm to them or theirs, although you may differ from them in opinion, they are most kind, one introducing you to another, and so passing you along a whole chain of kindly hospitalities. On the other hand, the lower set of people are morose and suspicious. They dog your steps, and watch your every word. I had to endure more espionage on the Mississippi than in Austrian Italy. There you have to do only with paid professional spies: here your fellow-traveller is your spy. Yet, after all, this suspicion is a necessity of the slave-owner's position. He must be watchful, for all around him there is danger.

The South seems to me in that mood of mind which foreruns destruction: there is a curse upon the land. Materially, its progress is naught; were it not for its cotton, it would be as wretched, poverty-stricken a country as Mexico. There is no enterprise, no capital. Then, in a social point of view, it is a sheer, downright despotism, without liberty of thought or speech. Fear and suspicion have taken possession of their souls, and no wonder. The North is becoming daily more earnest in its just resistance. The infatuated South has herself abolished the Compromise which was her safeguard. The din of the conflict has reached the slaves, awakening dim hopes. Hence abortive attempts at insurrection, which will be put down by brute force; but the spirit of insurrection is a devil that will not be so easily laid, and sooner or later the fears of the South will be changed to a dread reality. Even at this moment the planter lays himself to bed with pistols under his pillow, never knowing when the wild whoop of insurrection may awaken him to a bloody fight. The whole South is like one of her own cotton-steamers—such as I have just left, filled from the hold to the topmost deck with the most inflammable matter; everything heated up to the burning point, a furious draught blowing from end to end, and a huge high-pressure boiler in her belly, pressed to bursting. Is it pleasant to live in such a country? I have slept for nights over the boiler, and can tell you it is very far from pleasant.

It is a gross blunder to speak simply of the American Democracy. The American Government is one half democratic, one half aristocratic There is a *bonâ-fide* Democracy in the North, founded on a material equality of condition; but the South is a downright Oligarchy. Most European errors in respect to American affairs, arise from not distinguishing sufficiently the varying phases of American society, both as regards time and space. Here is a marked instance. We speak of 'Democracy in America' without sufficiently adverting to the great and fundamental differences in the two great sections of the States, the North and South. This difference I call fundamental, because it is not founded on any temporary or partial circumstance, not even, I believe, on the division into Free and Slave States—which is rather a consequence than a cause—but which lies deep in the very essence of the national character. The North is essentially Puritan; the South, Cavalier. They are so historically, and they are so in all the characteristics of their development. In the New England States, and the Western and North-western States, which have been chiefly formed by them, we find, above all, that energy and love of freedom which drove their forefathers across the ocean, and enabled them to subdue a savage race, and a yet more inhospitable soil. In the natural course of modern progress their energy has taken an industrial form; and hence those marvels of industrial development which strike one with surprise, from New York to St. Paul, and which, ere long, will make the vast wildernesses of North America blossom like a garden.

Further, the original character of their material condition is yet strongly impressed on their political system. They were all men of moderate means, men of the middle class, who came out on terms of equality, without any aristocratic privileges, and without any marked differences of station, to suffer and labour together; their holdings were small, and they were very equal. The natural constitution for such a community was a Democracy; it was a Democracy by necessity of position as well as by the idiosyncrasy of the citizens. To such a people no form of government but one essentially Democratic was possible. Even under the King of England, New England was essentially Democratic. The head was, indeed, a monarch; but all the real internal business of the colonies was transacted by the self-governing community; the townships and their 'select men' were the real rulers. Hence, for New England, the Revolution was no revolution: the head became elective instead of hereditary; a President was substituted for a King; and the Revolution was complete. The internal mechanism of self-government existed already; the laws, for the most part, were retained; and the States were merely confederated colonies, *minus* a mother country. The citizens were all labourers, and labour was therefore honourable.

From these original elements, acting on a large extent of fertile territory, have proceeded the freedom, the equality, the prosperity, in a word, the progressive democracy, in the true and good sense of the word, of the North; for we need hardly take into account the countervailing influence of slavery in the Northern States. It is true it prevailed in all the thirteen original States but one at the date of the Revolution; but it was so clearly antagonistic to the character and position of the Northern States, that it speedily disappeared from them. Where man and labour are honoured, slavery cannot permanently exist: it can exist only as an exotic, feebly, and for a time; and so it was here. The North is free from slavery because it was essentially opposed to slavish ideas: the character of the people could not tolerate such a system. The present division, therefore, of the States, as Free and Slave States, does not rest fundamentally on the existence or non-existence of slavery; but rather that social distinction has its origin in the characteristic idiosyncrasy of the two sections of the American people. True, slavery is now the nominal and ostensible bone of contention; but a

THE SOUTH IS ARISTOCRATIC. 63

deeper, and, therefore, more dangerous cause of disunion, is that difference in the nature of the two peoples, which has caused this difference in their domestic institutions.

The North, then, was originally, and is yet, Puritan and Plebeian; the South, on the contrary, was Cavalier and Patrician; Virginia and the Carolinas were settled mainly by English gentry, with a sprinkling even of the nobility. They brought with them not only their aristocratic feelings, but even their aristocratic laws, entails, and the law of primogeniture. And though these laws, as such, have been repealed, the spirit and custom, which are stronger than all laws, and without which all written law is but waste parchment, exist more or less to this day; and in the older Southern States it is the custom for the eldest son to take the family estate, where it yet exists, and portion off the younger children. The South, then, is to all intents and purposes an Aristocracy, nay, an Oligarchy; for in addition to aristocratic feeling, there is also an anti-democratic inequality of fortune. This is best seen by the holdings of slaves, the chief form of Southern property. The whole slave-holders in the States, in 1850, amounted only to 347,525, and of this number only 92,257 own 10 slaves and upwards. Here, then, we have the essence of an Oligarchy; a fraction of the population monopolizing the principal property of the community.

The politics of the country are quite in keeping with this state of matters. The South is ruled by its leaders; the poor of the community, the 'white trash,' go with their lords. This aristocratic nature of Southern society, by dishonouring labour, has tended, even more than the climate of the South, to perpetuate slavery. What is there in the climate of Virginia, or of its offspring, Kentucky, in that of North Carolina, or *her* daughter Tennessee, to favour slavery? On the contrary, the climate is rather harsh for the African constitution, and the products of these States, especially the northern parts of them, are such as are not well suited for slave labour. No, it was not the climate, but the aristocratic tendencies of the people that preserved slavery in the South when it was abandoned in the North. But slavery, once established as a permanent institution, reacts on the minds of the dominant race. Labour, unhonoured by a patrician race, becomes dishonourable when identified with slave-labour. Thus industry is sapped at the very root, and all progress is paralysed.

In passing through the two sections of the States, the difference is apparent to the material eye: in one, nothing but progress and prosperity; in the other, comparative poverty and gloom.

The line which divides the North and South is not simply geographical, not merely Mason and Dixon's (the Arrowsmiths of America), it is political and it is social. On the one hand you have the industrial energy and political independence of a self-governing yeomanry; on the other, the stagnation of a people, where the rich are too proud to work, and the poor are too subservient to be free; while one-third of the whole population is practically reduced to the status of beasts of burden. Of what use is it to talk of Democracy here? Can true Democracy exist under such conditions? I think not. The truth is, the South is under the rule of an Oligarchy, and it is only confusing our ideas by a vain babble of words to speak of Democratic liberty or equality in the fifteen Southern States of the American Union.

We must remember, however, that here, as in all American affairs, a rapid change is taking place. The one class of the North is rapidly subdividing into three, a rich mercantile class (a *parvenu* Aristocracy of wealth), a middle class, and a mob. That is especially in the great cities. In rural districts the old yeomanry still prevails, and is the backbone of American society. The effect of a wealthy, powerful, and highly-educated class in the States has yet to be developed. No doubt, in another generation, it will be great. Similar changes, in consequence of industrial development, are also modifying society in the South; but these changes take place more slowly; and for all practical purposes we may still regard Southern society as consisting of aristocratic planters and 'white trash.'

The above considerations explain, I think, what otherwise seems strange, viz., the influence which the South has hitherto almost invariably exercised on the national councils. With a minority of States, with less than a third, thirty-two per cent., of the white population, how is it that the South has managed to appropriate to herself so large a share of official influence and executive power? The answer seems to me to be, that the aristocratic nature of Southern society is more fitted for political organization, and therefore the small but compact phalanx of Southern leaders has generally been able to out-manœuvre the more numerous but less manageable hosts of the North.

In the same manner we can explain what at first sight seems a contradiction, the tendency of the Southern aristocracy to hold by the Democratic party. I do not mean the present unholy alliance between Southern oligarchs and Northern mobs, for that is an affair of sheer political trading, the planters backing up the *canaille* of the cities for the sake of **nig-**

gerdom. But ever since the days of Jefferson the South has supported a policy seemingly at variance with aristocratic tendencies. The solution of the difficulty is to be found, I believe, in the twofold nature of the American constitution. The Southern was a Democrat in federal politics, precisely because he was an aristocrat in his own State. He had all the pride of power, and could not bear to think of his dignity as a Virginian or Carolinian being lost in an indiscriminate mass of plebeian Yankeedom. Hence the 'State-rights'' principle, which has been all along the essence of Southern Democracy, which lies at the root of all their opposition to federal power, and which is the favourite policy even of those Southern States, such as South Carolina, where the internal government of the State is most aristocratic. Had it not been for this peculiar personal feeling in the patricians of the South, Jefferson would have found fewer followers in his democratic schemes, and the course of American history might have been altogether different. As it is, the patricians of the South have combined with the populace of the North to pull down all the safeguards against mob-government which the wisest founders of the constitution had so laboriously built up. Unfortunately for themselves, their success has been complete, and now they can only attain their political ends by a base subserviency to the Rowdyism of the nation.

Thus the Democracy of the Southern States has ever been of a spurious nature. They did not wish to limit the power of Government from any love of popular ascendancy; on the contrary, they sought to curtail federal ascendancy, lest it should be detrimental to State independence, where they themselves were paramount. Their object, in all the phases of this long struggle was more private than public, founded on interests rather than ideas, on selfishness rather than considerations of the public weal. Their opposition to 'internal improvements,' and to a 'national bank,' and their 'Free-trade' movement, in itself an admirable policy, thus lost the dignity of disinterested and purely speculative measures, and partook more of sectional hostility and party spirit. And now, finally, the South has made its democracy subservient to its base pecuniary purposes; and the good of the commonwealth is sacrificed to a low, peddling traffic in slave-labour.

The alliance of Southern patricians and Northern plebeians has hitherto given almost unvaried success to the democratic party. During half a century democratic principles have been, more or less, in the ascendant; and the consequence has been a gradual deterioration of the constitution, deplored by all wise Americans. But I think the career of success would not have been so signal, or so continuous, had not the Whig party erred by taking up ground on principles wholly opposed to truth. The false is a fatal ground to do battle on ; protection and centralization are principles, in political affairs, which must tend to the ruin and disgrace of any party that takes its stand upon them. Had the Whig party abided by their fundamental principles of a Government strong enough to enforce the law, and independent enough to secure justice, it must, sooner or later, have carried with it an intelligent and law-loving people ; but when its greatest men lent themselves, ignorantly or jesuitically, I know not which, to bolster up an indefensible system of monopoly in trade and jobbery in government, we cannot wonder that the prestige of superior wisdom deserted their cause, and with it political success and power. The defeat of the Whigs was a just retribution, and one from which I trust they may yet learn wisdom, and gain renewed strength. By making itself the champion of protection, the North was put in a false and humiliating position; its politics had the look of mere selfish huckstering ; and when, notwithstanding, its organs assumed, on other questions, where their pecuniary interests were not affected, a high moral and religious tone, we can hardly wonder that the South should twit them with hypocrisy and cant. But now it is the turn of the South to suffer from adopting a principle of conduct irreconcilable with justice and right reason. Once for all, the South has taken its stand on the principle of domestic slavery, and nothing but ruin can befall a cause that builds on a foundation so utterly unsound.

You see, then, that, in my opinion, the present antagonism of North and South has really originated in their opposed social idiosyncrasies and habits. There is no doubt, however, that this fundamental opposition of North and South has *now* taken the form of a dispute as to slavery. Henceforth, and for all practical purposes, the sectional division of the American States rests on the question of free or slave labour; and no worse foundation could civil discord have, for, on the one side, it raises up all the basest and most malevolent passions of our nature; while, on the other, it excites hostility so determined as to make civil strife a virtue. When we look back a few years, we see that this question of slavery, which has now grown to such paramount importance, has acquired this pre-eminence partly by accidental circumstances, partly by the errors and misdeeds of American politicians. At the date of the Declaration of Independence, slavery, though common to all the

States but one, was unanimously doomed in the public estimation. It was felt to be an incongruity that must soon pass away; so much so, that any express declaration to that effect was considered unnecessary. The constitution carefully avoids the very name of slavery, its founders hoping, no doubt, that soon the thing itself would disappear, and therefore desiring that no verbal memorial of so vile a thing should stain the page of their Republican constitution. This hope seemed for some years in a fair way of being fulfilled. One State after another abandoned slavery; while the external slave trade was abolished by the act of the nation. Even in Virginia and Kentucky, measures for the abolition of slavery were lost by the merest fractional majorities. It seemed as if the end of slavery were at hand. But, strange to say, the same trade which has raised the condition of the white labourers of England has riveted the chains of the black labourers of America. 'The accident of cotton' has been ruinous to the negro. It has increased the money value of his labour, and opposed to every appeal of enlightened humanity the more cogent argument of nefarious gain. The Southern Slave States want slaves to pick their cotton; and the more Northern Slave States raise the supply to meet the atrocious demand. Both sections are interested in the continuance of this internal slave trade;

the one as producers, the other as consumers of niggers.

The other circumstance which has given prominence to the slave question as a source of civil discord, is the spirit of aggrandizement which has taken possession of the politicians, if not of the people of America. The addition of Louisiana and Florida to their territory, besides driving out the Indians from the country east of the Mississippi, has greatly extended the area of Southern production, and correspondingly increased the weight of the slave interest in the States. Then followed the occupation and ultimate annexation of Texas; out of which again grew the Mexican war, and the acquisition of California. The admission of the latter country as a free State was a new source of contest. The South fearing the preponderance of the Free States, tried to extend the Missouri Compromise line across the Rocky Mountains to California, the southern portion of which would then belong to the slave territory, an extension sanctioned perhaps by the letter of that law, but certainly not dreamed of by its framers. Ultimately the strife was laid for the moment by Clay's compromise measures of 1850: in other words, the Fugitive Slave Law was thrown as a sop to the South, and thereupon they admitted California. But the slave interest, now daily growing in power, as cotton and sugar increased in importance, and now fairly aroused to the political necessities of their position, passed from defensive measures to aggression; and in 1854 they flung down the barrier which the Missouri Compromise of 1820 had set up against the advance of slavery. They now claimed the right, as American citizens, to proceed unmolested with their *chattels*, to the unsettled portions of the national territory; and when they could not obtain their ends by fair means they resorted, as in Kansas, to brute violence. Thus the present crisis in American affairs seems to me to be the retributive plague with which Providence has visited the land, in punishment of its highhanded violence towards weak and peaceable neighbours. For a moment the national sin seemed rewarded by glory and prosperity; but the punishment was at hand, and now strife and dissension are consuming the vitals of the nation. So true is it, that nations, no more than individuals, can sin with impunity.

Southern slaveholders and Northern Doughfaces never weary of telling you that the whole strife has arisen through the agitation of the Abolitionists, and perhaps they honestly think so. But this is the usual mistake which men make in attributing every result to palpable material agencies, and overlooking the less visible but far more powerful spiritual causes. No doubt slavery and abolitionism act and react on each other. The spirit of contradiction turns Southern men from ameliorations which they might otherwise have attempted. They will not be dragooned into humanity. Nay, to avoid the influence of abolitionism, they even render the condition of their slaves harsher than it might otherwise have been. And this again intensifies the zeal of the abolitionist to sheer fanaticism. But in all this there is nothing fundamental and original. Abolitionism arose because slavery began to grow in strength, instead of gradually disappearing from the land. Abolitionism was a natural and necessary phenomenon in an age and country where high-minded men existed in the presence of an abominable institution. It is, therefore, sheer weakness and silliness in the Slave States to attribute to this cause the perpetuation of their accursed system. Love of gain and lust of conquest are the two passions which have perpetuated American slavery; not the remonstrances of the good, nor even the ravings of the fanatical.

Had slavery jogged on in the same quiet inoffensive way as in the beginning of the century, the Union might have been spared the present disastrous struggle. But the great increase in the number and value of slaves has excited disgust in the North, and fear and jealousy in the South. Hence crimination and recrimination, bad feeling and hostile measures. Men, with more love of peace than principle, have in vain tried to damp down the threatening fire by measures of compromise. As usual the compromises have pleased neither party; and now both sides agree that the time for compromise is gone by. A crisis is at hand. A spirit of disunion has taken possession of both parties; they regard each other with jealousy, if not dislike; and the language of the two geographical sections of the States savours more of the rancour of avowed enemies than the loving-kindness of brethren. I am satisfied that there is not in either section a settled purpose of a dismemberment of the confederation, but beyond all doubt a moral disunion already exists, which must be modified, or it will ultimately lead to actual separation. Already there is a conflict of opinion, sympathy, and interests which, if continued and exacerbated, must result in civil war or separation. Although slavery is the prominent and absorbing issue in the present sectional struggle between North and South, the old constitutional antagonism may still be seen, from time to time, underlying the more palpable politics of the day. In the South, we still find practical questions mixed up with speculations as to the principles of society, which smack strongly of the old aristocratic leaven; and though in public politics republican equality is grudgingly admitted, in private the Southron expresses unmeasured disdain for his Yankee brother.

The South now takes high ground; it no longer stands on the defensive. It not only vindicates slavery as a just and good institution, but it declares that it must be extended; it demands its introduction into the territories as a matter of right, and many scruple not to declare that they will not be satisfied till they have carried slavery up to the very doors of Boston. With an equal consistency of fanaticism, some demand the re-opening of the slave trade. 'If it is a right thing,' say they, 'to possess slaves, it is a right thing to acquire them.' This logic is incontrovertible: only it proves rather too much.

Such is the spirit of the South. The free North, on the contrary, is more than ever alive to the evil of slavery. It feels acutely that America stands convicted before enlightened humanity of a prodigious incongruity; and it feels, moreover, that the South is no longer satisfied with the *status quo*, but desires to push her institutions across the old lines. It fears that Southern aggression will wrest from the free North those rich territories where she hoped to find a profitable field for her labour and capital, and a useful safety-valve for political discontent.

With a view to the future development of the empire, no less than to social quiet, the possession of the fertile prairies of the West is of infinite importance to the North. Here, therefore, interest combines with principle to stimulate the thinking population of the free Northern States to resist by every lawful means all aggression on their hitherto free territory; and when that aggression took the shape of brutal violence in the case of Kansas, there was little wonder that a spirit of resistance was awakened, which dared every danger, even that of civil broil. The consequence of this state of feeling in the two great sections of the empire, was the late Presidential election, when North and South were arrayed against each other, and slavery was the subject of the contest. So overwhelming has this question become, that all less absorbing interests have been lost sight of, and all older party-organizations have been broken up. The result has been a nominal triumph, but, as I think, a real defeat of the South. The strong minority which the North was able to bring together in so short a time, and under all the disadvantages of broken party-ties, new organization, and old party prepossessions, not to mention the official power of their opponents, was a virtual victory. And this is the feeling of the South. They regard this Presidential victory only as a respite, not as a final and triumphant settlement of the question at issue; and hence their present object seems mainly to be, to prepare for the time when fortune may give the victory to their opponents. The Senate is the point to which American politicians mainly look. The Free States have already a majority of two. Minnesota, when admitted, will make their majority four, and the South fears that if Missouri were surrounded by Free States it might renounce slavery, which would raise the Free majority in the Senate to eight. There is no wonder, therefore, that they strove hard to make its neighbour Kansas a Slave State, and, when fair means failed, used foul.

The South is now anxious to turn to account the respite it has gained by Buchanan's election. Their object is to prepare for future defeat, which they deem, if not inevitable, at least probable. Hence the extreme fanatics of the South desire to make themselves so independent of the North as to be able to separate, or, if it comes to that, to fight. They wish to be able to emancipate themselves from the Union, as the colonies emancipated themselves from the British Empire. Hence their press, and their conventions, and their Governors' messages advocate all manner of Southern undertakings to supersede Northern enterprise. Why, they ask, should they patronize their Northern enemies, instead of encouraging Southern industry? They propose, therefore, to have

Southern lines of steamvessels to Europe; Southern manufactures of all needful articles now bought from their Northern neighbours; a Southern manufacture of cannon and other arms; a Southern Pacific railway, &c.; and then, to provide for spiritual as well as material wants, a Southern literature, Southern schools and colleges, and, what I would impress on our National School zealots, Southern *school-books*. Where the capital and the brains are to come from does not appear; such prosaic considerations seem beneath the notice of tropical politicians in their present state of frenzy. Now, what shall we say of people who can talk so sillily on matters of paramount importance? Observe, too, the total ignorance of rulers and writers, not to mention the vulgar, in this country, of everything pertaining to political economy. The simplest relations of capital and labour to industrial enterprise are overlooked, and men talk of national industry as if it were an affair of patronage and encouragement, a thing to be extemporized by the resolutions of a convention or the flourishes of a subservient press.

LETTER VIII.

New Orleans, December 25, 1856.

In my last I gave it as my opinion that the present antagonism of North and South does not originate in the slave question, but is founded on a deep-seated social difference in the two sections; that this social difference had given rise to the distinction of Free and Slave States, and that, finally, this social distinction, intensified by the current of industrial and political events, culminated in the Kansas troubles, and sought a solution in the late Presidential election. Let us now look for a moment to the nature and probable consequence of that election. Like most foreigners, I find it very difficult properly to appreciate the constitution of American parties. Their party-names are so numerous and so extravagant, that they tend rather to mislead than to inform; and, moreover, the objects in dispute are generally so different from those which occupy the attention of political parties on our side of the water, that we feel at first absolutely bewildered in the seeming chaos of opinion.

In the South, the Fremont party was, we may say, *nil:* the votes polled for him amounting to some 1200; though, doubtless, there were many secret Fremonters among the supporters of Fillmore in the South. In the North, Fremont was supported by the so-called Republican party, a new organization, with a well-chosen name (always of some importance in party conflicts), and, I would fain hope, a prosperous future in store for it. That a new party, extemporized for the occasion, with many difficulties to contend against, should have made so good a fight—polling about forty-five per cent. of the popular vote, and thirty-eight per cent. of the electoral vote, speaks well not only for the intelligence and worth of the North, but for the future welfare of such States as shall hereafter be under the guidance of that party.

It is usual here, and elsewhere, to say that the old Whig party is dead; but I cannot think such is the case. No doubt, the blunders of the Whig party have thrown a temporary slur on its principles, and made the old name a dishonoured one, but it is not in the nature of things that the wise, conservative, law-loving spirit of the old Whig party should utterly die out. Whiggery is not dead;

under new names, and in different developments, it must have its due influence on the United States of America, so long as worth and wisdom have there an abiding place. I cannot doubt that most of the best men of this party adhered, in the late struggle, to the Republican cause; though, no doubt, many of the more cautious ones voted for Mr. Fillmore. It may, indeed, be said of the Republican party, that it consisted of a fusion of all that was best in all other parties. It contained the most liberal Whigs, and the most conservative Democrats. It was a party, in short, of all those party men who were above mere party. That so many of the staunch old Democrats joined the Republican ranks is a circumstance highly creditable to the middle classes of the Northern Union. Only men capable of appreciating things as opposed to names would have had strength of mind to make this change. It is no easy matter to leave a party, and requires an amount both of moral courage and intellectual power not easily to be found in masses of men. But the yeomanry of the Northern States have proved themselves equal to the crisis; and by so doing have shown the world that they are worthy of the great work to which they have been called. These noble sons of noble sires are the true Democracy of the Western World, and will rescue popular government from the contempt and derision which the spurious, self-styled Democrats of the South would heap upon it. These 'small-fisted farmers' of the North *are* capable of self-government: they understand the true meaning of freedom, and they never will submit to have their free soil tainted with the accursed thing. With these sturdy yeomen of the fields were ranked the middle classes of the towns—for the most part the sons and kinsmen of the yeomen, who had left their paternal acres to cultivate trade, manufactures, commerce, or learned professions in the more crowded haunts of industry This, the most rising, and soon, perhaps, to be the most important class of Northern society, was another strong element of the Republican party. All honour to them, and thanks, for they were fighting the battle not of America only, but of the civilized world. Theirs was the cause not only of Republicanism but of Humanity and Progress.

In the South the Republican party may be said not to have existed, or, if it did exist to any extent, it appeared under a different name, and need not be here dwelt on. The Democratic party was all in all in this struggle: the Democratic candidate was a mere piece of lumber. The strength of the Democratic party was constituted by a coalition, which, like most other political coalitions, owed its existence to an abandonment of principle in favour of interest. Properly speaking, the Democratic party had really no Democratic principle in view. They did, indeed, make some vain show of the old party measures; but these were mere blinds, and the true and essential object of their policy was to secure the permanence, and if possible the extension, of slavery The Democratic party was, in truth, a Southern party, adopting the interests and views of the South. It consisted, first, of the Planter party. This was a mere matter of political convenience. The aristocrats of the South have been for sometime aware that it is only through the agency of the ignorant democracy of both sections of the empire that they can carry out their objects with regard to slavery. Hence they adhere steadfastly to this party, some of them conscientiously, in accordance with their State rights prepossessions, and others, I believe, simply from interested views with regard to slavery. It must be humbling, one should think, for the educated and refined patricians of the South to let themselves be dragged through the dirt of Democratic politics for a shabby pecuniary purpose; but what will not men do when they consider their interests to be at stake? Did we not see the haughty nobles and squires of England unite with Chartists and chaw-bacons, in opposition to the middle classes of their country, when the question concerned a few shillings in the quarter of wheat? Now slavery, in the estimation

THE DEMOCRATIC PARTY.   85

of a planter, is for him a question not only of wealth or poverty, but also of personal safety and danger. Abolition for him means ruin, murder, rape. No wonder, then, that he is somewhat fanatical, and will not listen to reason on the subject.

As I mentioned in my last letter, the small number and high station of the planter aristocracy is highly favourable to political organization, whereas the dispersed or isolated position of the Northern yeomanry is precisely the reverse. The farmers of the North and North-west are very numerous; they are scattered over an immense wilderness; they live almost all alone; how can they act in concert? In this contrast, I believe, lies great part of the success of the Democratic party, headed and led by the Southern aristocracy. It is no difficult matter to collect in one city, or even in one parlour at Charleston or Saratoga, the heads of this Southern organization; and thus give a unity and force to their purposes which can ill be met by the head-less, plan-less North. In such a case, the North can only trust to the force of truth, of principle, of right, as stirring simultaneously the bosom of each individual voter; it can only oppose moral union to political organization.

This, then, was the aristocratic element of the Buchanan party, and in unholy alliance with them was the mob of both North and South; the 'mean whites' of the Southern cities, river-banks, and plantations, and the *canaille* of the great towns of the North, principally Irish. The 'white trash' of the South, though not themselves holding slaves, have all the passions and prejudices of slave-holders in the most exaggerated form, and, moreover, have a personal dislike of the negroes which the planters do not at all share. On the contrary, all planters of any heart or principle feel a certain interest in the welfare of their 'people,' and, in many cases, even affection for them. But the white *canaille* of the South regard the slaves as interfering with their interests as free labourers; they detest them as rivals, and they look with no small envy on their care-free condition. The worst enemy of the slave, therefore, is the 'mean white;' it is by him that the poor negro is whipped and hung in times of excitement, and hunted down when he tries to end his misery by escape. They, too, are the 'border ruffians,' ever ready with revolver and bowie-knife. These, then, form, we may be sure, a formidable phalanx in the Democratic army of the South.

The Northern mobs were all Democratic, seduced principally by the party-name. Irish Repealers are the natural enemies of all governments; they will always be found, therefore, on that side which is said

THE DEMOCRATIC PARTY. 87

to be the most hostile to law and lawgivers; and such they account the Democratic party. These mobs we may set down as actuated by sheer ignorance and stupidity; they knew not what they did. If they could but see the truth, the labourers of the North had a very strong interest in keeping open to their labour the whole virgin territory of the States. Every new Slave State is a lessening of the area of their employment while they continue labourers, and a lessening of the extent of land available for their occupation when they shall become capitalists. But truths so simple and patent as these were too abstruse for the apprehension of New York and Philadelphian mobs. Without being able to give one plausible reason for their preference, they were fanatical for Buchanan; and they were unanimous in their fanaticism. I conversed with many Irishmen, and could find no one with a rational motive for supporting Buchanan: and in the public Democratic meetings which I attended there was an equally meagre amount of common sense argument in favour of their cause. If Interest determined the Southern Democracy, Ignorance led the Democracy of the North.

Besides these two great divisions of the Buchanan party, there were two minor ones. First, a considerable number of Northern middle-class men, chiefly moneyed men and traders, joined the ranks of the Democracy from fear of sectional disturbance, or even disunion. This was the Doughface party. A Doughface is one of those men who is averse to all high principle, and who stigmatizes all enthusiasm as fanaticism. He is ever crying 'Peace, peace,' when there is no peace; and by his short-sighted, soulless policy will, in all probability, precipitate that very crisis which he sacrifices all principle to avoid. Secondly, there was a sprinkling of Southern men in Northern States, whither they had emigrated, carrying with them their Southern passions, and who turned the scale in favour of a bastard Democracy in more than one State. It was thus that Illinois and Indiana were wrested from freedom, in spite of all the efforts of Northern intelligence and virtue.

The Fillmore party consisted, in the North, of cautious, perhaps timid, but conscientious Conservatives, who thought Fillmore would preserve a *juste milieu*, and maintain the rights and honour of the North, without sacrificing the just pretensions of the South. In the South it included Old Whigs, Know-nothings, and, I have no doubt, many out-and-out Free-soilers. There is, I have reason to know, a not inconsiderable class of men in the Southern States, especially in the more northern ones, and in all the commercial cities, who see clearly the evils of slavery, and would fain see it done away

THE FILLMORE PARTY. 89

with were a feasible mode suggested. These men, however, do not openly avow their sentiments. They dare not do so. Not only their trading profits and social comfort would be risked by so doing, but their very life would be endangered. There is a terrorism at work in the Southern States which effectually keeps down every open expression of dissent from the prevailing orthodox creed of slavery: and how few have the courage to beard this dominant rule, is seen by the paltry vote given for Fremont by six millions of white freemen in the Southern States of this Model Republic. It is remarkable that the cities of the South, in many instances, opposed the country just as in the North, but in an opposite sense; for while here the country was generally democratic, the cities were frequently in favour of Fillmore. This, I believe, proceeded greatly from the circumstance that the trading and middle classes of the South have sufficient intelligence to see the evils of Slavery, and would resist at least its extension; while the mobs of the cities, on account of the scarcity of white labourers, are not sufficiently numerous to control the city vote as in the cities of the North. The great number of individuals who in the popular vote supported Fillmore in the South is one of the few features of the late election that tend to inspire confidence in the future of these unhappy States. It discloses the fact of a strong, half-latent, conservative force; and the question of questions is, how far this force may be able to resist, or even control, the more vehement action of the violent party in its own States.

With such elements of contention as I have described, it is not astonishing that Buchanan was successful; the more especially as he was powerfully supported by the whole strength of official influence. How powerful that influence must be in the United States may be conceived from the fact of every office under Government, down to that of the paltriest tide-waiter or Far West postmaster, being dependent on the success of the Democratic candidate. This total want of independence on the part of the Government officials seems to me one of the worst features of the American constitution as at present existing, not only in a political, but a social point of view.

Whether the North has any reason to regret the issue of the late Presidential election may very much be doubted. My own opinion is, that the North has gained all the advantages of a victory without its inconveniences. In a crisis like that which hangs over American affairs, it is a questionable boon to be placed at the helm of the State. Had the Republican party carried their candidate, they would have had tremendous difficulties to encounter. In all probability the South, even if it did not go the whole length of secession, would have thrown every possible impediment in the way of the Government. It is probable that some of the Southern States, if not all, would have refused to send representatives to Congress, and thus have seriously embarrassed the administration of affairs. In such a crisis, a party newly organized, with an untried President of no official capacity, would have been sorely tried. If it blundered, or even if it were unfortunate, it would have lost its prestige, and disunion would have diminished its strength. The passions of the South, already sufficiently excited, would have been inflamed to the highest pitch; and no one can tell what folly and madness on the part of the slave-owners a Fremont Administration would have had to encounter. Nor is it to be omitted, that the slave population, in case of Fremont's success, would very probably have been excited even to the extent of insurrection; regarding, as they do, the Republican party as the champions of their cause. This would have still further infuriated the South, and increased the difficulties of the Administration. As it is, the onus and the difficulties are all on the side of the Democratic party. Their candidate is successful; but to me it seems they have gained a position rather of danger than of honour.

The organs of the successful faction confess already

that their opponents have gained a virtual victory: already they are casting about for means to prevent the ultimate defeat which they foresee. Had the Free soilers had but one candidate, and so saved many useless votes, or had they had a more worthy candidate, the result even of the last election might have been different. What, then, may not be the result of *next* election, when the Republican party shall have had time for thorough organization and consolidation, and when they shall have an opportunity of putting forward a candidate really worthy of the cause? Moreover, by that time the Free State of Minnesota will have been added to the Republican side; perhaps even Nebraska; so that even should Kansas be gained to the Slave States, the balance will be at least preserved. On the other hand, the pro-Slavery party will have to encounter all the difficulties which the Free-soil party has escaped. It will have the onus of Government; and the burden will be such as no previous administration had to sustain. It will have to rule an empire divided into two hostile factions: it will have to decide questions the most perplexing and irritating; and in all this its policy will be opposed, if it remain true to its avowed principles, by the best, wisest, and wealthiest citizens of the United States.

But by far the greatest difficulties of the Buchanan Administration will be found in the intestine feuds of the party. The Buchanan Democracy is no homogeneous organization, growing spontaneously out of a noble or even intelligible principle : it is a mosaic of interests ; a crude combination, with no principle of cohesion save the one miserable principle of hostility to better men than themselves. Now, the moment of success to such a party is also the moment of dissolution. Their object gained in the defeat of the common enemy, they will turn and worry one another. What real interests or sympathies has the Irish loafer of New York in common with the aristocratic slave-holder of South Carolina? Even during the canvass the two different shades of opinion could not be concealed, though in the heat of the conflict men had not leisure to dwell upon the fact. It is notorious that in the North 'Buchanan and Free Kansas' was the rallying cry, while in the South it was 'Buchanan and Slave Kansas.' Together, they made Buchanan President ; but being President, how is he to please both parties? Not even an American President can ' serve two masters ;' and Buchanan will find that both his masters are severe ones. That the upshot of their victory is very doubtful seems to be the secret conviction of the South. Only thus can we understand the present state of feeling among the violent politicians of that section. It is only in anticipation of disgrace and defeat that they would think it necessary to prepare beforehand for secession and independence.

LETTER IX.

HAVANA, 1st January, 1857.

THERE is, I find, a party in the South conscientiously, and almost fanatically, in favour of disunion; and the whole South might be very easily brought to coincide in the disunion movement by any imprudent or aggressive course of policy on the part of the North. There is a party called the 'Southern Party,' which is distinctly in favour of a separation. This party is striving at present to prepare for the separation which they expect and desire, by making the South what they call 'independent' of the North. It consists mainly of the aristocratic democracy of the South. Its head-quarters are, of course, to be found in South Carolina, that hot-bed of agitation and nullification. But this party would, I believe, carry along with it, even in its most insane policy, a great proportion of the low white population, all that part, namely, which I have already described as participating in the passions and prejudices of the planters, though not in their interests. Hatred of 'Abolitionism,' (which with them is identical with ' the North,') on the one hand, and jealousy of the nigger on the other, will ever make this miserable mob a ready tool in the hands of a fanatical party. Opposed to this extreme party is all the Conservative intelligence of the South. That this element is powerful, we know by the strong Fillmore minority of the late election. But whether it may be powerful enough to withstand and overrule the fanatical favourers of disunion is what I cannot undertake to say: and it appears to me that amid so many elements of uncertainty in the future, both from the excited state of men's minds in the States themselves, and the complication of surrounding circumstances, no wise man would venture to foretell the probable issue of American affairs during the next four years. Among the Americans themselves, the majority look on a separation as impossible; on the other hand, many consider it quite possible; and a few look on it as certain, at all events, within a generation. Men are probably swayed unconsciously by their hopes and fears, in coming to a conclusion. Those who regard disunion as synonymous with civil war, comfort themselves with the idea of its impossibility: they who take a less gloomy view of its effects, are probably less incredulous as to its advent.

Most Americans, I think, are of opinion that a peaceable separation is an impossibility, and that, if it comes to disunion, it must come to civil war. Some say that there would be so many irritating questions in regard to national property, the army, navy, archives, &c., that they could not be amicably adjusted. Others, again, think that the Northern Slave States, which, in case of separation, would be Border States, would be so exposed to harassing evils in the way of fugitive slaves, &c., that they would not peaceably submit to a separation. For my part, I think these fears exaggerated, as also the apprehensions of evils to result from a separation of the empire. In the first place there is quite sufficient territory, and to spare, to form two great empires. The Free States have an area of 612,597 square miles; the Slave States of 851,508, while France and Great Britain together only make up 329,057, or not much more than half of the Free States. Besides this, there are 1,472,061 square miles of territory to divide; so that each of the new empires would possess nearly a million and a half of square miles of land. Nothing but the most insatiable desire for land would complain of such an allowance of the earth's surface.

The value attached to the possession of an immense territory in America seems to me a weakness, attributable partly to their vivacious imagination, and partly to their ignorance of political economy. In private and in public affairs it is a very common, but very shallow error to look on land as the great source of power and wealth, whereas it is not the extent, but the productiveness of the land possessed that is the measure of individual and national wealth and power. It is true, as the Americans are fond of telling us, that all England might be drowned in one of their Lakes, but does that fact afford even an approximate measure of the comparative greatness of the two nations, in a material, not to say spiritual, point of view? Have not all great nations been, at first at least, small ones? Mere bulk is as little a test of strength in countries as in individual men. Nay, I am inclined to think that the extent of territory in the Northern States is a source of positive weakness rather than of strength. There is more soil than can well be cultivated for ages to come: agriculture is therefore perfunctory, and the whole industry of the country participates, in some degree, in this imperfect mode of conducting business. The development of the country is rapid, but it is decidedly superficial. There is a want of concentration in American civilization: the people is spread over a vast surface of land, and its efforts, though vigorous and sustained, are necessarily imperfect. Population, notwithstanding its vast increase from within and from without, does not keep pace with the growth of territory. In 1840 the density of population was greater than in 1850. At the former period there were 9.55 inhabitants to the square mile; in 1850 they had diminished to 7.90 In England there are 332.00 inhabitants to the square mile; in Belgium 388.00. Surely for some centuries to come the Northern States would have full scope for their energy in cultivating their present area up to the pitch of England or Belgium, without scattering their people, and wasting their resources in an exhausting struggle with the deserts of the Far West. Concentration, not extension, is what America wants. The New England States contain only 65,038 square miles of the worst soil on the Continent, and yet how large a proportion is theirs of the industrial, financial, political, and intellectual greatness of the people of the United States? Let the Americans look to New England as well as to Old England, and learn there the real source of national greatness.

In passing, I may remark that this exaggerated idea of the value of mere *territory*, as a source of national power and greatness, is at the bottom of the American admiration of Russia. Confounding area and power, they attribute to Russia the 'mission' of conquering the whole of Western Europe. This is to me a most extraordinary hallucination, only to be explained as above. One would think the late war might teach all nations that power, now more than ever, is an affair of capital and credit. Why did Russia and France both long for peace, but that their resources were exhausted? England, on the other hand, though she had suffered nothing but disaster and disgrace, relieved only by the glory of her mere fighting soldier and sailor, was ready, nay, anxious to prolong the contest. It seems ridiculous to talk of the universal dominion of a Power that cannot raise fifty millions to make a railway. The truth is, the power of nations may be pretty accurately measured by the prices of their public stocks. English Three Per Cents. at ninety-five, French at seventy, and others in their due proportions, afford a fair criterion of national power. Nowhere does the prevailing ignorance as to the real sources of national greatness lead to more erroneous conclusions than with regard to the progress of England. The increase of our power depends mainly on accumulations of productive capital, the extent and value of which the vulgar intellect has no means of calculating. Hence the progress of British power is generally under-estimated by foreign nations, who, with the usual confusion as to territory and power, for the most part measure the growth of England by the swelling of her overgrown Indian and Colonial Empire.

The lust of territory I hold to be one of the great evils of American civilization. It has taken deep hold of the fervid imagination of this young and energetic people; and as yet the sober views of the wiser portion of the community have not availed to check the national folly. But it is needless for Englishmen to preach moderation, so long as we ourselves are extending our empire day by day, and loading with honours proconsuls who present us with 'four kingdoms at once,' and so long as a General setting out to steal an Empire can write: 'We have no right to seize Scinde, yet we shall do so, and a very advantageous, useful, humane piece of rascality it will be.' We must pluck this Indian beam from our own eye, before we can expect attentive listeners to our political homilies.

Returning to the subject of American disunion, I will not venture on any prophecy, but in the present fermentation of men's minds, no man, I hold, can foresee what even a day may bring forth. No doubt the feeling in favour of upholding the Union is immensely strong with all parties of Americans, if we except the anti-slavery fanatics of the

North and the pro-slavery fanatics of the South. But a victory or defeat of Walker in Nicaragua, an irruption of Missouri blackguards into Kansas, a slave insurrection, or another South Carolina brutality, in short, any striking or irritating event which passion or chance might occasion, would be sufficient to change the whole current of American affairs. Politics in this country have got beyond the control of politicians.

But though we cannot predict the future, we have at least an idea of the present. And here it strikes me that in a certain sense disunion already exists. A moral separation has already taken place. The two geographical sections of the States are even now arrayed against each other like two hostile camps. Instead of the brotherly affection which should bind together cognate communities, one hears nothing but contemptuous and even hostile and defiant expressions. In the South especially this feeling is very strong. A 'Yankee' is perhaps the most contemptuous name a Southern can apply to any man. It implies with him every dirty passion; cowardice, greed, hypocrisy, and every vile quality. On the other hand, Northern men regard their neighbours of the South as men degraded and debauched by their association with slavery, and they look down on them as their inferiors in every point of real culture, while they resent their supercilious and aristocratic airs. Now, what real union can there be between States so 'separated?' Can any federal bond make up for this moral disunion? To my mind it seems clear that unless some great change of sentiment takes place for the better, the dreaded disunion may be said to have been already accomplished. The slavery question has 'established a raw,' which will not be easily healed: which, on the contrary may be chafed to madness by the incessant friction of political strife. Even the present movement of the South in favour of independence will, if persisted in, give rise to much irritation, even among the prudent and calm-judging men of the North.

If this disunion were destined to continue, I do not see that an actual separation of North and South would make things much worse than they are. Of territory they have enough, and to spare, for two Empires; and, if we suppose them guided by common sense, the natural diversity of their productions would always ensure a free commercial interchange. But such speculations, I trust, are superfluous. I cannot but hope that the troubles of the Free and Slave States will be got over without any of those violent measures to which the fanatics on either side are hounding on the nation. No doubt chance or violence may precipitate a rupture; but it seems

LOVE OF SOCIAL DISTINCTIONS. 103

more probable that the strong feeling of the American people in favour of the Union, will preserve it long enough to give time for such social changes as will bring North and South into greater harmony with each other, and so ensure a real and lasting union ; a union of the heart as well as of outward relation.

I have been living a good deal with the American residents here, and have had an opportunity of observing them somewhat closely. I am amused, though not much surprised, at the very great store they set on social distinction. I was well aware that no mere political constitution could so far alter human nature as to extinguish the essential passions of our being, but I was hardly prepared for such devotion to rank and position as I find rife among our Republican cousins. The passion is *at least* as strong as among ourselves, only it varies a very little in form. It is almost identical with what we find so prevalent in the *parvenu* society of our mushroom cities. There is the same adoration of the ranks above us; the same uneasy straining after what is 'genteel,' and not a little of the same disdain of the grade below.

There is nothing very odd in this, after all, if we only consider that it is the same poor human nature which is playing its fantastic tricks here as with us. The only droll thing about it is the funny contrast all this gentility-hunting makes with the theoretical equality and simplicity of Republican institutions. But the truth of it is, that there is no equality in America, except as to the elective franchise; and that is perhaps the worst equality they could have.

The old families, principally Dutch, in New York State are said to be most determinedly exclusive. They are called the Knickerbocker society. The new-rich folks of New York, again, are called the 'Fifth Avenue' society, or, less respectfully, the 'Codfish aristocracy.' They revenge themselves for the Knickerbocker exclusion by excluding all the lower world of New York from their circle. It is quite the old French *noblesse* and the new Parisian aristocracy of the Bourse. The glory of Fifth Avenue is maintained principally by a lavish display of magnificence. The houses, furniture, and ladies' dresses are of fabulous costliness. Occasionally a magnate of the 'Avenue' trips and comes down; but is soon up again, and nobody is a bit the worse but his creditors. Lately, Huntington, the forger, fell from this social empyrean; and now, again, Mr. Jacob Little's brilliancy has been quenched for a time: but it is probably only a temporary eclipse. I have heard, on good authority, of Mrs. Little having purchased one lace dress for twenty thousand dollars. No wonder that Jacob failed.

This extravagance in the dealings of the men and the dress of the women is, perhaps, a natural consequence of the high profits consequent on the rapid development of the resources of the country. The fairy-like growth of wealth may well turn the heads of vain men and silly women : men's imaginations are heated, and the whole system of society is fevered with excitement. But as profits become more moderate, trade will become more sober, and the whole tone of society will be healthier. Then, too, a large class with superior intelligence and moderate desires will arise, to be the mainstay of the political fabric. I have no fears but that the follies and crudities of the present effervescent stage of American society will speedily pass away, and leave behind a large residuum of solid worth.

LETTER X.

MATANZAS, 11th January, 1857.

THIS island of Cuba is a little paradise. I do not wonder at the Americans casting a wistful look towards it. The climate, at least at this season, is exquisite; and I am told that, in summer, the heat never rises to any oppressive degree. It is the first time I have seen a tropical country, and everything has the charm of novelty. The most remarkable feature of the landscape is the elegant palm-tree, which is scattered all over the island, and which is generally left standing, even when they clear the forest for sugar plantations. They thus give a park-like appearance to the fields of sugar-cane, which would otherwise have a monotonous look. Here and there, too, there are groves of palm-trees, which are very beautiful. One of the finest sights I ever saw was the sun setting, as only a Cuban sun can set, behind such a palm-grove.

I have visited two sugar plantations, but I presume

they are *very* favourable specimens of Cuban slave-labour. The proprietors of both are men of highly-cultivated minds and enlarged views. One of them was educated in Germany, and has been much in Europe; the other lives much in America. Both speak excellent English. In neither estate is the lash used except on rare occasions; A——, I know, dispenses with it almost entirely, finding a system of small rewards and deductions more efficacious. D—— has given up night-work on his plantation for four years. The constant, unremitted labour, day and night, is, as you know, one of the great evils in the ordinary mode of conducting a sugar plantation. The slave has far too little rest during the whole crushing season, and is, consequently, soon used up. This leads to severe punishment during life, and to premature decay. D—— finds that, by stopping his works from ten p.m. till five a.m., he not only makes the work easier for his negroes, but, from their greater activity, more productive for himself. Last year he was unfortunate in losing a number of negroes by an epidemic; but even now he keeps up the number of his slaves, whereas on the island generally there is an average decrease of three per cent. annually. When I asked him why his neighbours did not adopt a system at once so humane and so advantageous, he pointed to a dog lying basking in the sun, and said, 'You cannot teach an old dog young tricks.' No doubt it is always difficult to get out of old ruts; and we must also remember that, in general, the Creole planter does not reside much, if at all, on his estate, but leaves everything to an administrator, taking no interest in anything but the pecuniary result. We see here, therefore, that the interest of the slave-owner does not always guide him sufficiently in the treatment of his slaves. No doubt man's interest, when intelligently followed, will, in the main, lead him to the same results as his moral sense; but men often fail in discovering their true interest, especially when it is at all remote; and they are frequently guided more by other passions than by a mere love of gain. This is particularly the case when they have to do with other men; and the interest which an intelligent slave-owner has in the prosperity, happiness, and consequent increase of his slaves, must not, by any means, be implicitly trusted to as a guarantee of constant good treatment. I insist the more on this point, inasmuch as it is one of the stock arguments of the slave party, as a proof of the benign nature of the system.

In Cuba, as in Louisiana, I have had the fortune, perhaps I should say misfortune, to see slavery in its very mildest form. This, however, has not altered my idea of the institution, which, as you know, is not founded on its external effects either on slave or owner, but on the spiritual nature and end of man. With all its alleviations from humane and enlightened administration, such as fell under my notice, Cuban slavery is still bad enough. A—— himself said the work was 'too hard.' Cane-cutting, especially, is hard and continuous work under a broiling sun; and this work is principally done by women. Another evil is the disproportion of the sexes. There is a scarcity of women in the island. Mr. Crawford, the English Consul, informs me that the decrease of the slave population used to be seven per cent. annually, but that it has now fallen to three per cent. This he attributes to the greater care of the slaves consequent on their increased value. Slaves are now nearly as valuable in Cuba as in the United States. Mr. D—— thinks the Cuban slaves are, as a rule, not so well cared for as those of the United States; he thinks they are neither so well fed nor so well clothed. This agrees with the statistical facts of their comparative increase. We must hope, however, that the excellent example shown to the Cubans by the more enlightened among their own countrymen will not be thrown away upon them, and that they will see it to be at once their duty and their interest to ameliorate the condition of their slaves.

I believe the abominable, benighted Government of Cuba is a great hindrance to any improvement in the system of slave-labour. The officials here have a horror of anything savouring of reform; and any man who should propose a change from the old, time-hallowed routine of evil, would be instantly set down as a dangerous character, and exposed to the hostility of the powers that be. The system of government seems to be the old, orthodox, Spanish-colonial system in all its mediæval barbarism. At this moment, for instance, flour is shipped from the United States to Spain, to be re-stowed in Spanish casks and brought here as Spanish flour. The duty on American flour brought direct is ten dollars. What the island thus indirectly loses no man can calculate; but in taxes and duties they pay 16,000,000 dollars annually, which is almost all eaten up by the army (25,000 men), navy, and civil expenses. When I suggested to a Creole friend that the inhabitants should offer a large direct contribution instead of indirect taxation, he stopped me at once by saying nobody would venture on any such proposition, which would be at once set down as *seditious!* As some wise man has said, 'the gods themselves can do nothing against stupidity.'

What a world this will be some day, when all these villanies and fatuities have been swept away, and an intelligent, virtuous race of freemen are cultivating Old Spain and glorious Cuba! What abundance is awaiting the magic touch of free labour, to spring forth in this paradise, and bless millions of men and women! And now Cuba produces, with infinite trouble and pain, a few boxes of clayed sugar and a few hogsheads of molasses; and in the scuffle between her and Spain great part even of this is lost. And Spain herself,—what a country that might, could, and should be! Travelling here, one cannot but remember, amid the wreck and ruin of her greatness, what Spain and Spaniards once were; nor can one help looking forward to what they will yet be. It is a noble country, and a noble race. For one, I cannot give them up. Assuredly the Spaniard will rise from the dust, and be a man such as he showed himself capable of being in the olden time. There is something grand and serious in his nature. The Spaniard is naturally heroic; and even in this, the day of his humiliation, I cannot but look with sympathy on his silent, stoical, unbending pride. There is always hope for the proud man; it is only the light, frivolous, vain man who can be an utter futility.

I have lately read a work in defence of American Slavery by one Fitzhugh. It is called *Sociology for the South,* and is a rambling, declamatory affair enough; yet it is interesting as indicating the state of public opinion in the Slave States. The scope of the author's argument is, that free society being an acknowledged failure, there is nothing left for us but to fall back on slavery, which he maintains, with reason, is the legitimate and consistent consequence of all Socialistic schemes. In support of his thesis as to the failure of free society, he quotes several English writers and publications of acknowledged authority, such as Carlyle, Kingsley, Alison, the *North British Review, Blackwood,* &c. As against these authorities, his reasoning is complete; and it would do a great deal of good in England if people saw the conclusions which slave-owners draw—and with justice too—from their communistic philosophy. The truth is, there are but two ways open to man: either the conditions of labour must be adjusted by contract, or they must be fixed by force. No doubt the former has its disadvantages, especially in the transition period from serfdom to freedom; but we must accept it with all its evils, or we must be prepared for the only possible alternative, with all *its* evils. If we prefer slave auctions, cow-hides, handcuffs, blood-hounds, and the other amenities of enforced labour, to strikes and combinations, and the wretchedness and sin of those workmen who abuse their freedom, well; but it is mere childishness to fret and pule at the evils of the one system, unless we are prepared to adopt the other 'for better for worse.' Fletcher of Saltoun, and Carlyle, have at least the merit of consistency; they would rather have well-fed slaves than hungry freemen. This is at least intelligible; but few even of those who rail at our present system would be willing to accept this alternative. Most of them dream of some impossible half-way halting-place, and would, no doubt, recoil with horror from the legitimate result of their own premises. They are, in general, men with more sensibility than strength of intellect, and are saved by an amiable inconsistency from the extremity of error to which their doctrines inevitably lead stronger minds.

Fitzhugh very properly commences by showing that the doctrine of '*laissez faire*' and free society go hand in hand; and he consistently maintains that the regenerate society which he proposes to build up on a foundation of slavery must begin by demolishing and denying the accursed science of political economy. Here again he seeks support from the authorities I have mentioned, and not in vain.

The great evil of free society, he maintains, in common with his Socialist collaborateurs, is competition, by which men are led to 'underbid' against each other until they are ground down to the veriest wretchedness. The error here lies in ignoring the twofold action of competition. The underbidding takes place on both sides; and in this sense, competition, far from being an oppression, is in truth a divinely-conceived mechanism for the prevention of oppression. It were better, no doubt, if the moral sense of society were so fully developed that men would treat each other well from motives of duty alone; but until this desirable consummation, which is probably yet far distant, shall arrive, Providence provides for the safety of the weak and poor by that curious mechanism of antagonist interests which we call competition. God governs us by the force of our passions, until we are able to rule ourselves by reason. But Socialists mistake the meaning and end of this complicated system of competing interests, and would sweep it away to make room for an artificial system of force, which, as Fitzhugh truly says, is, in its essence, slavery. Slavery, says he, is ' a beautiful example of communism, where each one receives, not according to his labour, but according to his wants.'

Fitzhugh says again (p. 47): 'The poor-laws and poor-houses of England are founded on communistic principles.' Most true; but is it fair, then, to condemn a system as a true exponent of free labour, which is so deeply tinged with communism? I believe that much of our misery and sin arises from our poor-laws and other aberrations from strict *laissez faire;* and yet all these social evils are most unjustly and unreasonably laid to the charge of our industrial system. Free labour has never yet had fair play. Let the labourer be really and truly a free man, and he will soon vindicate his claim to genuine independence and self-reliance; but it is at once cruel to him, and injurious to society, to set him to bargain for his labour, and at the same time emasculate his free will by demoralizing and degrading institutions.

At home we are now in a transition state from serfdom to freedom. It is scarce half a century since serfs existed in the collieries of Scotland. The wonder then is, not that the people have so slowly advanced towards rational self-government, but rather that they have made such astounding progress. It is childish to overlook the inevitable difficulties of such a transition, or to condemn a system on account of its attendant evils. Fitzhugh quotes Hume, on the abolition of monasteries, in a passage which may well be turned against himself. Hume says: 'There is no abuse in civil society so great as not to be attended with a variety of beneficial consequences; and in the beginnings of reformation the loss of these advantages is always felt very sensibly, while the benefit resulting from the change is the slow effect of time, and is seldom perceived by the bulk of the nation.' Does not that apply to the abolition of serfdom? The free labourer has not yet learned to turn his independence to good account; neither has he learned the law which overrules alike himself and his employer. But, at least, some progress has been made: the relation of capitalist and labourer begins to be better understood; the working man begins to feel, and in some instances to employ wisely, his independence; and in one or two generations he will be a truly self-relying, self-respecting citizen.

On the authority of *Blackwood's Magazine* and the *Westminster Review*, Fitzhugh brings the old charge against free society, that 'the rich are growing richer, and the poor are growing poorer.' Now, G. R. Porter, in a remarkable paper read to the British Association in 1850, proved, by irresistible statistics, that wealth is much more disseminated in modern times than it was of old, and that the tendency in England is towards an ever-growing diffusion of comfortable existence. Be this as it may, we must accept freedom with all its difficulties, wants, and evils. Freedom which, in our times, means mainly freedom of contract in matters of labour, is the appointed means of developing the powers of the human will. In this stern school, as in all schools, there must be much pain; but what of that? Man was not sent into this sweating, toiling world to be saved from pain, but by pain to be ennobled. The modern world of free industry presents much wretchedness, it is true, but it also presents a scene of more rapid progress, of more true and widespread culture, than the world has yet seen; therefore I admire it. Ancient civilization may present us with more noble specimens of individual men, but modern society is preeminent for the diffusion of an ennobled humanity over a large surface of the world. In this view I cannot regard modern free society as 'a failure,' still less would I consent to return to any modification, more or less complete, of forced labour; and I cannot but look on those who advocate such measures as false to the great work which was given them to do.

I have also been reading a work on 'Liberty and Slavery,' by Dr. Bledsoe, of Virginia University. This is a more ambitious, and more artistical work than Fitzhugh's rhapsody. The Doctor writes with considerable logical acumen, and some depth; but, after all, what do such weapons avail against the common sense and moral sentiments of mankind? He begins by metaphysical considerations of the nature of society and liberty. There might be much said on these heads, but it is needless; because the question of slavery will assuredly never be settled by metaphysics. It is a question to be decided by the moral sense of man; and, therefore, all metaphysical refinements are utterly irrelevant. No doubt, they may lay the foundation for a philosophical judgment of the matter, but they can have no weight in the popular decision. The conclusion which Dr. Bledsoe arrives at is one quite opposed to mine: he holds that the root of society is a consideration of the public good, and hence he appeals to expediency as the ultimate guide in all questions of disputed policy. From this he deduces the right to enslave negroes, inasmuch as they are men incapable of self-government, and it is both for their good and the public good that they should be subjected to the rule of a superior race, in the same way as we subject children and malefactors to external control.

It is needless to unravel all this tissue of sophisms, nor to point out the *non-sequitur* implied in the reasoning by which he arrives so easily at domestic slavery. The whole fabric rests on an erroneous foundation: no expediency can justify an unrighteousness. The man, as man, is an end unto himself, and it is unjust to make him a means to the ends of another. Any pretence of consulting his own good is but the sophistical *ex post facto* defence of a manifest wrong. Bledsoe admits that formerly the moral sense even of the South was more distinctly opposed to slavery than it now is. They have set about finding excuses for their system, and have succeeded in throwing dust in their own eyes. For what absurdity and what enormity may not be defended by metaphysical sophistry? When we go back to first principles, ideas are so very vague and intangible, that it is an easy matter to find one which may be worked out to any desired conclusion. In such cases we are much safer to trust to our moral intuitions than to refined ratiocinations. This is especially true of common minds.

No doubt the agitation of the slavery question has confirmed the South in its slavery prepossessions, and made it more than ever fanatical on the subject. Bledsoe says—'We owe at least one benefit to the Northern Abolitionists. Ere the subject of slavery was agitated by them, there were many loose, floating notions among us, as well as among themselves, respecting the nature of liberty, which were at variance with the institution of slavery. But since this agitation began, we have looked more narrowly into the grounds of slavery, as well as into the character of the arguments by which it is assailed, and we have found the first as solid as adamant; the last as unsubstantial as moonshine.' In other words, the spirit of controversy has led them to destroy their own moral convictions by specious argumentation. There is more truth in the Doctor's statement than he is perhaps aware of.

A large portion of Bledsoe's book is devoted to the Scriptural argument in favour of slavery; and here, I must confess that, as against his opponents, the orthodox Abolitionists, he is perfectly triumphant. The express recognition of slavery, both in the Old and New Testaments, the rules for its regulation in Leviticus and Exodus, and the precepts for the behaviour of masters and slaves (mistranslated 'servants' in our version) in the Epistles of Paul and Peter, are irresistible proofs that the institution was recognised by the founders both of Judaism and Christianity. How those who adhere to a literal interpretation of the Bible, and consider every direction contained in its pages as applicable at all times to all men, are to reconcile these facts with modern anti-slavery notions, it is, thank goodness, no business of mine to find out.

Another large portion of the Doctor's work is devoted to show the inexpediency of abolition, from the ill-success of the experiment in the British colonies. Here we must grant his premises, though we deny his inference. No doubt the 'prosperity' of Jamaica has suffered in consequence of negro emancipation. There is less sugar and rum produced than before; and if the end of human existence were the production of rum and molasses the argument would be triumphant. But this is not a question of rum, but of right and wrong. As an industrial measure, emancipation may have been ruinous, it may even have been inadequately and unjustly executed; but, as regards the rights of the slave, there can be, for English freemen, no question or doubt; and no ruin, even though the British Empire had fallen with Jamaica, could cloud the glory of that great act of national justice.

The indolence of the free negroes of the British Colonies is to be regretted, though I have doubts of the alleged fact that they are fast lapsing into barbarism: but, even were it so, it does not follow that the negroes of America would refuse to work if liberated. They would have no means of existence except by labour, and they certainly would prefer labour to starvation. The free negroes of the North, and also of the South, labour, and that under very discouraging circumstances; why should not the present slave population do so also, if manumitted, especially if freedom were gradually bestowed on them, and in proportion as they were fitted for it? I grant all the practical difficulties of emancipation. Foremost among these is the great value of the slaves. A no less troublesome element is the hostility of a slave-owning class to a freedman class. The transition period would doubtless be very difficult, but, on the other hand, there are difficulties, and dangers too, in the *status quo*. The numerical increase of the slaves is preparing a revolution that cannot long be delayed. A slave-owner said to me—'It is all very well just now, but I do not know what is to become of our children, or at farthest, of our grand-children. They will need an army to keep their slaves in order.'

I believe these difficulties and dangers perplex and torment the minds of slave-owners, and, unconsciously to themselves, produce irritation and resentment. We must confess their situation is painful, placed by hereditary accident in a false position, and in antagonism with the enlightened opinion, not only of civilized Europe, but of their own happier countrymen. In view of these unhappy circumstances I should be disposed to make great allowances for the irritability of the South, and sincerely to commiserate their situation, if one only saw the remotest desire on their part to acknowledge and to remedy the crying evils of the institution. But at present the tone assumed by the South is rather one of defiance and contempt for free institutions, combined with a determination to spread still further the evils of slavery. This naturally leads to active antagonism.

With all his loud assertion, I do not believe that the slave-holder is thoroughly persuaded in his own mind of the truth of his doctrines. His creed, like many other creeds, is reiterated all the oftener and the more loudly from a lurking doubt of its perfect truth. The slave-owner defends his position ostensibly against the Abolitionist; but in reality against his inner self. Hence, too, his impatience of contradiction; his faith is all in all to him: therefore to doubt it is to wrong him. Heresy is not only a blunder, it is a crime. And yet slave-owners cannot avoid the subject. They eternally introduce it. They are ill at ease, and must try to convince.

LETTER XI.

NEW ORLEANS, 22nd January, 1857.

ONE cannot help being struck with the difference between the tone of society in Cuba and that of the Southern States of America, especially with regard to slavery. There all is stagnation and contented nonchalance; here all is fermentation, unrest, and propagandism. The Spaniard takes slavery as a matter of course, and the Creole looks on his negroes merely as useful sugar machines. Nobody thinks of disputing the propriety of the institution, and therefore no one takes the trouble of defending it. In Cuba there are no Abolitionists, and no Pro-Slavery fanatics; no Stowes or Garissons, and therefore no heroic Brooks. The whole system is received as a piece of the ordinary working world, and nobody thinks of praising it as a boon from heaven, or cursing it as a gift of the devil. Here, on the contrary, every man is either for or against; there is no neutrality, no indifference. You must be a true believer or a heretic. Fanaticism

LOUISIANA.

and violence, on one side or the other, are expected of every true citizen; and it is well it should be so. I honour this energy of thought and feeling in the American people, and sooner or later there will go forth from this fermentation a purer and better social state than the present. Anything is better than the blank desolation of besotted ignorance; and in spite of the striking exceptions which came under my notice, the Spanish colonial system must needs be characterised as one of utter stagnation. Here, on the contrary, there is at least progress,—progress 'under difficulties,' it is true, but still progress; and the very violence which characterises its march is a proof of a great, though as yet misdirected, energy. Energy is the soul of American civilization; and as it is the energy of youth, we must not wonder that it is sometimes heady. We must not, on that account, despair of its ultimate success.

Louisiana seems to be somewhat unfortunately situated in regard to climate, in a productive point of view. It is too far South for cotton, too far North for sugar: between these two stools its prosperity is in a doubtful position. The range for cotton culture is a peculiar, and therefore necessarily a limited one. Cotton requires a climate where there is little frost, and, on the other hand, no tropical rains. It can, therefore, only be cultivated with success on a narrow range between the temperate and tropical zones. Tennessee is becoming too cold for cotton, frost having of late years become more frequent and severe. On the other hand, Louisiana has too much of the tropical rains for its successful culture. Then, as to sugar, Louisiana is too far North. The cane does not yield so much saccharine matter as in Cuba, neither does it last so long. Three years is the usual duration of the Louisiana cane, whereas in Cuba I saw canes growing luxuriantly which had been cut fifteen years in succession. Then the frosts which occur in Louisiana are severe enough to injure the cane, so that the crushing has to be hurried over before the cane arrives at maturity. Sugar-crushing is generally finished about the end of the year in Louisiana, which is just the time when it commences vigorously in Cuba. The result of all this is, that sugar in Louisiana is at best a very precarious production, and, on the average of years, cannot be a very profitable one. The large outlay of capital, and the large amount of labour it requires, are also serious drawbacks in a country where both are scarce and dear. And again, the severe nature of the labour on a sugar plantation, during the crushing season, is objectionable both in an economical and social point of view. On the whole, I am inclined to think the sugar planting of Louisiana to be a mistake; and, should low prices of sugar prevail for some years running, I should not be surprised to see many of the sugar estates abandoned.

Under these circumstances one cannot wonder that the Louisiana sugar-planter should cast many a longing glance towards the glowing Cuba. There he sees, only 600 miles away, an island, the paradise of sugar-planters, whither two days' sail would bring him and his slaves, and where rich and sure crops would reward his capital and labour. At present an old despotic power is playing the dog in the manger, and our energetic Louisianian may flatter himself, without much exaggeration, that he would be conferring a benefit on the world at large at the same time that he was filling his own pockets. This is the *fair* side of filibustering; of the *foul* side I shall say nothing just now. Indeed, there is not much need of saying anything against ' private stealing.' When stealing is to be done at all, it should be done in public, and on a large scale; then, like murder, it acquires a certain dignity: as witness our East Indian thefts of a kingdom at a time. But one thing seems clear to me : England is not the constable of the world, and if thefts do take place in the Gulf of Mexico, it is no business of ours. Whatever Spain cannot keep, she deserves to lose. We can have as little sympathy with an effete despotism as with a filibustering democracy.

One thing it specially behoves Englishmen to remember, viz., that filibustering is essentially a thing of the South. It is especially in the interests of slavery and slave-extension that Cuba and Central America are coveted. In the North this policy is only adopted by the Democratic mob. Among the wise and honourable Republicans of the North ' filibustering ' is a term of even more indignant reproach than among Englishmen. They abominate it on two grounds—first, as tending to strengthen slavery and the slave-interest; and, secondly, as casting an undeserved slur on the American nation at large. We should never forget, therefore, that in all matters connected with Southern aggrandizement, the best, truest, and most powerful ally of the English nation will be the noble people of the Northern States of America themselves.

There is a subordinate view of filibusterism which should not be altogether overlooked. Many respectable Americans look on such adventurous expeditions as a useful ' counter-irritant' to draw off the peccant humours of the body politic. In the States, and especially in the South, there is always a considerable floating population, made up of the restless and worthless spirits of the whole world, ready for any mischief, and a nuisance to every well-ordered society. These are the men who recruit most largely the ranks of armies such as Walker's; and sober citizens are not sorry to see them depart on any desperate enterprise. They think them good food for powder, and good for nothing else. It was of these desperadoes mainly that the famous 'Border-ruffian' band consisted; and since the return of something approaching to law in Kansas has deprived them of their occupation there, many have taken their departure for Nicaragua; a circumstance which augurs well for the future peace and welfare of Kansas, whatever mischief it may do to Central America.

I crossed from Havana with a distinguished Southern lawyer, a man of great talent, who, was born in France, and educated in Germany, and who, having resided thirty years in the States, may be supposed to be sufficiently cosmopolitan in his views. He considers, in common with most intelligent Americans I have met, that the plague of this country is her universal suffrage. The worth and intelligence of the nation have not their due weight. But how is this evil to be remedied? There's the rub. You cannot unliberalise political institutions. The evil influence which you deplore is an insurmountable obstacle to its own reform. Some trust for a remedy in the 'common schools:' I do not; for I do not believe that any mere book-learning, however thorough, can educate men to an intelligent use of political institutions. How much less need we look for political salvation from the horn-books and pothooks of a primary school? If America had nothing but her common schools between her and ruin, I should tremble for her fate: and some very intelligent men do tremble for her fate. Some look to a military despot as the most probable *Deus ex machina*. For my part, I have still good hope of the future of the States, especially the Northern ones, although I do not see how Reform is to be effected. I put my trust in the inborn worth, intelligence, and energy of the people. These admirable qualities have hitherto helped the Republic over all her difficulties, and I trust to them to overcome the difficulties yet before her. It is the struggle with difficulties that makes the man, and I believe that the Anglo Saxon of the New World, like him of the Old, will be strengthened, not overcome, by his painful wrestling.

The gentleman to whom I have referred told me that Europeans can have no idea of the extent of corruption in this country; and really the evidence which is forced upon me of corruption, both in municipal and general government, is such that it is impossible to resist it, even making all due allowance for the exaggeration of party statement. This evil, too, I believe, has its root in the ultra-Democratic nature of American institutions. The populace is the source of all authority, and those only can arrive at power who are willing to propitiate the populace even at the expense of principle. Hence a race of trading politicians, who live by pandering to popular whim and prejudice, while men who respect themselves and insist on the luxury of 'keeping a conscience,' are, as a rule, shut out from all participation in public affairs. A politician here, as my informant said, is more thoroughly tongue-tied than in the most despotic State of Europe. He dare not, for his life, express an opinion hostile to that of his constituents. The first moment of his independence would be the last of his power.

This is a lamentable state of things in a country that calls itself free; and yet, both from my own private observation, and from the public and too striking proofs which the South has lately afforded of its intolerance of contradiction on points of essential moment, I believe the statement to be true to the letter.

The experience of America in this matter should

not be lost on England. I hold that universal suffrage would be desirable, if with universal suffrage we could have good government; for the broader the basis of the social structure the better. We must not, however, sacrifice the end to the means. Good government, by which I mean a government which ensures substantial justice, is the end of all society, and to sacrifice this to any theoretic fancy whatsoever, is at once the shallowest, the most pedantic, and the most fatal of political blunders. This blunder, I conceive, has been committed by the Democratic party of the United States, and while I would point out to our countrymen American clippers as a model of imitation, I would no less earnestly point to American polling-booths as a beacon of avoidance.

I am sorry Villiers did not accept the office of ambassador to America. I know him from the old Anti-Corn-Law times, and should gladly have seen a man of his calibre and attainments, as well as station, representing the English nation in the American capital. The Americans complain, and, as I think, most justly, of the class of men who have hitherto been sent as ambassadors to their country. They send us, they say, their best men, while we have as yet sent only second-rate mediocrities of the Foreign Office. It seems to me they have just reason to complain of this usage, and that it is as suicidal on our part as it is uncourteous to them. The United States are now, without contradiction, one of the greatest nations of the earth; certainly they are the most progressive: they are a free nation, and they are bound to us by the intimate ties, not only of blood, language, and laws, but also of a continually-extending commercial intercourse; and yet to this great and nearly-connected people we send representatives whom we should blush to send to a paltry Grand-Duke or the tyrant of Naples.

This is a matter of more importance, I believe, than is generally understood at home. The Americans are a very sensitive people, prone to fire up at the least appearance of insult, or even slight; but at the same time remarkably open to every sincere expression of respect and affection. And why, in God's name, should we not give them every assurance of the sincerest respect and affection? Are they not our children? blood of our blood and bone of our bone? Have they not the same old English manly virtues, with perhaps the same tendency to the old English love of power and dominion? Are they not a free nation like ourselves? and a progressive nation like ourselves? And to sum up, are they not our best customers? To whom, then, in the name of common sense, have we more reason to send our very best men, to cultivate their good will, smooth down paltry irritations, explain away foolish differences, and, in a word, be the friend and peacemaker of both nations?

A year ago we were within an ace of war with America. That 'difficulty,' I am persuaded, would never have arisen, certainly would never have reached the insane height it did, had we been represented by a gentleman of the standing, character, and capacity which should distinguish every English minister in this country. Of this fact I have been assured in private, and have seen proofs in public; and it entirely agrees with my own convictions in the matter.

The ambassador to the United States, too, should be a man of high position in the social world. I do not mean by this that it is necessary to flatter the American love of aristocracy and title; but rank with us is, after all, the 'guinea-stamp,' and though it may no doubt be impressed on base metal, yet to strangers it does indicate a certain presumptive value in social appreciation at home. To foreigners, therefore, it has a certain introductory value; and though rank will certainly not ensure the respect of Americans for an ambassador, it will at least prove a valuable passport to their good will. The finished manners, too, of the English nobleman will not be without their weight in this country. No nation of the world, I believe, has a stronger appreciation of refined manners than the Americans; and they have a high admiration of the genuine courtesy of the really high-bred English gentleman, as indeed they should, for the refined and high-toned manners of our aristocracy (at least such of them as are really noble) are but the outward presentment of an inward grace and refinement. Manner is an outward thing, but it takes shape and form from the inward man.

Lastly, the English ambassador to America should be a family man; the last three have been bachelors. Now, anywhere this is wrong; but in America, where every man marries at twenty-one, and where every bagman carries his wife with him on his business tours—where, in short, celibacy is a reproach, and women are the 'masters of the situation,' a bachelor ambassador is singularly out of place. The charm of woman is great; and it is not easy to calculate the effect of a thoroughly well-bred, and it may be high-bred English lady in such an embassy as ours at Washington. With such an ally in his wife, an ambassador, such as he should be, might do much to unite the two nations. Members of Congress from all parts of the Union, as well as other men, eminent in different ways, meet at Washington. How great might be the influence of an enlightened, prudent, well-bred gentleman in the high position of ambassador, in such a situation, especially if aided by the good sense and good manners of a really noble Englishwoman. After all, the only true natural ally of England at this moment is America; we have every reason to be friends, and, if we were truly united, we might defy the world in arms. No alliance with any despotic power can be lasting; it never can be more than a political expediency, or at most a state necessity. But an alliance with the free Republicans of America, our own blood-relations, who speak our tongue and think our thoughts, this is a political arrangement based on the deepest natural sympathies. And notwithstanding the many little rubs which from time to time fret the two nations of England and America, and in spite of their occasional boastful sallies, I am convinced, profoundly so, that at the bottom of their hearts the American nation loves the English. Most indubitably the best Americans do so. They resent our haughty nationality, and have not forgot our domineering ways—although they begin to see we have repented of those sins of our youth—but at the same time they honour our sturdy honesty of purpose, and are proud of our greatness, while hoping, by-and-bye, to overtop us. I am persuaded it is the fault of the English if the Americans are not their friends and allies. It only wants a little kindness and cordial appreciation on our part, not condescending patronage, for they have outgrown that, but a true, manly, sensible recognition of the American people, as an equal, and honoured ally in the march of human progress.

One more little remark before finishing my subject and my sheet. The community of language is a strong tie between nations; but it is also the source of no small difficulty. Whatever is written or spoken on one side of the Atlantic is read on the other. Hence every little word that in a foreign tongue would be passed unheeded and unknown, may here be the cause of much national irritation. This is particularly true of the English press, and more particularly of the London *Times*. Every article in that great letter-press ruler of England bearing on America and Americans, is republished in every State of the Union, and perused with interest, not to say avidity, by all American men and women, boys and girls, from New York right across to San Francisco. Judge, then, how any sarcasm, any stinging word, or contemptuous expression is burned into the American mind. I have been assured, and can well believe it, that the effect of such diatribes remains on the mind of the American people sometimes for years; long, long after the whole matter in dispute, it may be, has passed from the thought of the British public. It behoves, then, every sincere friend of the American alliance, and that means every friend of human progress, to consider well what he writes and publishes on American affairs and people.

LETTER XII.

NEW ORLEANS, 27th January, 1857.

THERE has just appeared in the public prints a most remarkable document, entitled an 'Extract from the Report of the Attorney-General' of the State of Louisiana on the state of 'Crime in New Orleans.' From this extraordinary paper it appears that, in the year of grace 1856, crime was the ruling element in New Orleans society. Not only were frequent crimes committed, but peaceable citizens did not dare to accuse, nor magistrates to convict, criminals ; and, as a natural consequence, we find the first law-officer of the State not only hinting at the possibility of Lynch-law, but absolutely suggesting apologies for the proposal. The following is a list of *some* of the crimes committed in New Orleans. He says :—'On the docket of the First District Court there are now pending—

Cases of Murder 14
   „   Manslaughter. 3

Cases of Assault with a dangerous weapon   34
,, Assault with intent to kill . .   18
,, Stabbing with intent to commit murder   10
,, Shooting with intent to commit murder   6
                                                                    ——
                                                                    85

Another portion of the Report states that 'there are three hundred and forty assault and battery cases pending before the First District Court.'

Notwithstanding this formidable list, the Attorney-General tells us that 'a large number of homicides are committed by persons unknown, and many by parties known, who escape arrest.' Now this appalling amount of atrocious crime was committed in a city which, in 1856, had only 116,375 inhabitants. The proportion of crime to population is, to an European, perfectly astounding.

But worse even than the mere amount of crime (and in part accounting for it) is its seeming impunity. We learn from the same authoritative document, that the fear of criminal vengeance is much stronger than the fear of the law. 'It is well understood,' says the Attorney-General, 'that no affidavits are filed against the offenders, from an appre-

THUGGISM IN NEW ORLEANS.

hension that any attempt to bring them to justice would lead to the sacrifice of the affiant's life. A general sense of insecurity prevails in the community, and a conviction exists in the minds of many persons, who have been grievously beaten, that it is better to endure present evil than, by lodging a complaint, take the risk of assassination.' Had ever a poor Attorney-General so humiliating a 'Report' to make? Peaceable citizens, 'grievously beaten,' dare not appeal to the law for protection, because the villains are stronger than the law! Is this savagery or civilization?

The Attorney-General does not state, what I have learned from private information, that the lawless state of New Orleans is more or less connected with its political organization. The Know-Nothing party, which is here in the ascendant, have possession of the municipality; the magistrates, if not the creatures of the Know-Nothing organization, are at least devoted to their interests, and inclined to wink at their enormities. During the late election this organized body prevented all free voting, except at one polling-booth, where a dozen bold young men of the opposite party marched up, with a pistol in each hand, and threatened to shoot down the first man who should obstruct a voter. Since the election the same terrorism has continued, principally directed against the foreign portion of the population. The ruffians who perpetrate these unprovoked and murderous assaults are called 'Thugs;' and the social state of New Orleans is little better than a Reign of Terror. I cannot see, however, that there is any political principle involved; and I am inclined to think that the name and form of a political organization are adopted, to cloak villanies of quite a personal and private character. I am confirmed in this opinion by the suggestion of the Attorney-General in his 'Report,' that violence may be directed against property rather than the person, and that 'plunder, not blood,' may become the object of New Orleans Thuggism. You are perhaps not aware that Know-Nothingism was essentially a secret organization, and was therefore, by its nature, well adapted for those who 'love the darkness better than the light.'

Such has been the persevering and systematic terrorism of the Know-Nothing Thugs of New Orleans, that many foreigners have resolved to leave the city; and the value of property has, for the moment, been sensibly depressed. Indeed, to such a pitch has the insolence of crime proceeded, unwhipped of justice as it was, that serious intentions were entertained of organizing a Committee of Vigilance; and it is probably to the knowledge of this circumstance that the present momentary lull in the violence of the Thugs is to be ascribed. They know well that a Committee of Vigilance, composed of energetic and angry foreigners, would make short work both of them and their protectors in the magistracy. Certainly, the Report of the Attorney-General throws no obstacles in the way; on the contrary, this legal authority tells the men of New Orleans that 'it is the universal sentiment, in our country, that when Government is a mere oppression or tyranny, revolution is just. So also, it is said, as we relinquish the right of self-protection for a consideration promised by the law, that the law will protect us, and the law fails to protect us, then the same reason that justifies revolution sanctions what is equivalent to revolution—summary justice on the criminals whom the law is unable to reach, or who, possibly, represent the law.' True enough doctrine, I believe, though it sounds queerly from an Attorney-General. The hint, too, in the last sentence to the Mayor and his brethren in office, as to the 'possibility' of a vigilance halter, hovers in a singular manner between the comic and the terrible.

On the whole, one cannot help asking, is all this real, or is it a phantom of some diseased Abolitionist imagination?—is this really a city of the Model Republic—a fair sample of the 'first great experiment of self-government'—a sample-brick of the glorious fabric of modern Democracy? At bottom it is rather a pestilent symptom of the gangrene of ultra-Democracy: it is a natural fruit of mob-government, of universal suffrage in a community not yet wise and virtuous enough to use it well. The Attorney-General tells the people of New Orleans they have themselves to thank for this plague of rowdies: but who are the 'people?' Here the governing 'people' are precisely the criminals who are to be coerced. The populace makes the magistracy, and the magistracy winks at the iniquities of their constituents. There is nothing wonderful in that: nothing that should stir the bile or excite the wonder of a philosophic Attorney-General. Given a dynasty of cut-throats, must we not logically expect our throats to be cut? The Attorney-General, instead of jeering at the oppressed respectabilities of New Orleans, should reserve his sarcasms for his next Fourth of July oration, when he has to descant on the glorious experiment of self-government in this world's wonder of a Republic. Meanwhile, may not the Republicanism of Louisiana be characterized as a despotism tempered by Lynch-law halters?

The Attorney-General speaks more to the purpose, when he attributes the disorders of the city to an 'inefficient police;' he might have almost said to the want of a 'police;' for no force deserves the honourable appellation of a 'police' which tolerates crime, nay, connives at it. It is not the badge or the button that makes a policeman, but the sacred character of his calling as a peripatetic embodiment of the law. A policeman, where there is no law, is at best a miserable scarecrow, a sham representation of what he pretends to be. This matter of an efficient police goes deeper into the philosophy of government than some folks imagine; and there is perhaps no point where the difference of English, American, and Continental civilization is more strongly marked than in that of their police. The London policeman is the best representative of English civilization. Neat, civil, alert, and imperturbable, he is the very embodiment of order. He is the law made visible. There is something grand even in his want of arms. Not even a cane soils his clean white gloves. His authority is wholly spiritual. He is strong in the love of law that dwells in every worthy citizen's heart. There's a divinity doth hedge him, for every man feels that he is the representative and minister of justice; and he is a base Englishman, indeed, who will not fly to the policeman's aid when he is obliged to use force to carry out his sacred mission. The English constable is essentially the people's friend, and is no less the pet of the people.

Very different it is with the foreign gendarme, half spy, half bully, armed to the teeth, the creature and tool of some prefect of police, the hated agent of an oppressive Government. Such a functionary has nothing sacred in his character, nothing noble in his mission, nothing popular in his nature. He is simply the lowest and most contemptible instrument in the organization of despotism. As such he may be feared, but can be neither loved nor respected.

In America, again, the impatience of authority, which is the characteristic of the political sentiment of the nation, leads to a contraction of the power and a disregard of the authority of the police. The constable here is regarded less as the embodiment of the law than as the instrument of a meddling, despotic Executive. 'Every man his own policeman' is the motto here. Any universal and overruling authority is an idea very foreign to the Democratic mind: still less can the American venerate, as the representative of such a spiritual power, the Irishman with a badge at his button-hole whom he calls a policeman.

In no city of the Union have I seen any appearance of an efficient, well-organized body of police. Any stray policeman you may encounter seems a poor, isolated, dispirited creature, half ashamed of himself and his office, and utterly inefficient for any public good. At public meetings, at jams at a theatre-door, or wherever else rows and crushes are to be expected, you see no six-foot, uniformed peacemaker. On the contrary, you have the uneasy sensation that, if the floor falls, or a row is got up, you have no chance of safety but from such innate love of order as may dwell in the hearts of the assembled rowdyism. Nothing in all Canada reminded me so much of Old England as meeting a smart, blue-coated, buttoned-up policeman in the streets of Toronto. Although it was but a plank pavement on which we met, I could hardly fancy we were four thousand miles from home. In the States the policemen wear no uniform. In New York they wear a badge dangling from a button-hole. Their principal occupation in that metropolis, as far as I could see, was handing ladies over the crossings in Broadway. Reverence for the law only becomes a practical principle of conduct in the States when backed by the national chivalry towards the fair. Even the American will tolerate law and law-administrators where a lady is concerned.

To an Englishman it is quite distressing to have before him daily proofs of the inefficiency of the criminal police of this country in detecting and arresting evil-doers. Scarce will you find one of the numerous records of violence that fill the daily papers which does not end with some lackadaisical lament over the escape of the homicide, or a feeble hope that he may some day be brought to justice. Judging from newspaper reports of crime, it would seem that the capture and punishment of the offender is the exception, the rule being his temporary absconding and ultimate return to the bosom of benignant society. It is not to be wondered at that crime, thus benignly treated, should at times run riot, and universal license culminate in some such miniature Reign of Terror as lately disgraced the city of New Orleans, and roused from his official apathy even a Louisiana Attorney-General. Still less should we wonder that our philosophic functionary, in discussing the causes of crime, should at last awaken to the evils of 'an inefficient police.'

The St. Charles Hotel, at which for the present we have pitched our tent, is a characteristic picture of American life. The hotel is quite a 'peculiar institution' of this country. Various causes contribute to this. The first and chief is, probably, the difficulty of procuring good servants, and the great expense connected with them. An Irish cook or housemaid is not only an expensive luxury, but she will only engage by the week; and during the week she stays, she insists on being mistress of the house. Native-born Americans are a degree more expensive and more domineering. Under these trying circumstances, it is natural that the American matron of seventeen or eighteen should seek refuge from this domestic terrorism in the gilded saloons of the St. Nicholas or St. Charles, or whatever other Saint may offer his protection for two and a half dollars a day. The saving of money is considerable, even in these money-making, money-spending regions; and the saving of temper and nerves is infinite. Here, then, is one great efficient cause of hotel-boarding. It is a refuge from ruinous and vexatious housekeeping

The feebleness of the domestic tie between parents and children is another cause. So soon as young America is able to support himself as a clerk in a store, or a subordinate reporter in a newspaper office, or as a semi-speculator, semi-swindler in Wall-street, he straightway emerges from the paternal mansion, and takes up his abode in a neighbouring hotel. Here he is, if possible, more his own master; is rather nearer to the bar; and can more conveniently make love in the corridors, and so prepare betimes for matrimony against coming of age.

But besides the permanent boarders of an hotel, there is a vast deal more of temporary sojourning in distant places among the Americans than with us. They are essentially a migratory people. There is a constant swaying to and fro, a flux and reflux of the whole population. Like migratory animals, they move north and south, east and west, at certain periodic seasons, in whole masses; and to provide for their entertainment establishments are required of corresponding magnitude. In the heats of summer, the whole South, that can afford it, moves Northward. Then you find the hotels of New York, Saratoga, and Newport, overflowing with planters and their families, and absorbing the proceeds of the last rice and cotton crop. At the same time, the people of the Middle and Northern States journey still further northward, to Niagara, Canada, the Catskill, or White Mountains. With the approach of autumn the great wave of population recedes; and now the Northerner seeks a milder climate in South Carolina, Florida, Louisiana, or even Cuba.

Besides these great popular migrations, there are various subordinate and local movements, the population of a State or region being attracted towards some great centre of gaiety and business, shopping and flirtation. Such is the winter gathering of the South-Western planters at New Orleans. From all the neighbouring States the planters come in with their wives and daughters, and spend one or more weeks, or even months, in dancing, fiddling, flirting, smoking cigars, and abusing Abolitionists. When their money is spent, they go home. A joyous, sociable, fiery set; somewhat prone to gin-sling, and as apt to 'go off' as one of their own hair-triggers.

No doubt the migratory nature of the American people is greatly owing, not only to the climate, but also to the manner in which the population has been scattered over the surface of the Union, in the natural course of its industrial development. Not one man in ten resides in the place of his birth; and it is a fair bet that he comes from a different State from that in which you find him. The proportion of 'foreign born' by the last census was 11.46, and of those 'born out of the State, and in the United States,' 21.35, making together, as born in strange localities, 32.81, or nearly *one-third* of the whole population. It can be easily conceived what a network of relationship this makes all over the Union, and how much travelling to and fro this must give rise to, especially among a people in whom the domestic affections are so strong as the Americans.

You will now be prepared for some details of the magnitude of the caravanseras which such a state of matters demands. They are, indeed, more of the nature of huge barracks than of the cosy place of entertainment, in which an Englishman delights to take his ease. In the St. Charles Hotel, New Orleans, this season, the greatest number of guests sleeping on any night was 725; the greatest number dining on any day was 850. There are 650 beds, and 270 servants. About one-third of the guests are permanent boarders, who remain from three to five months. About one-third of the boarders and guests are planters and their families. The remainder are principally business people, and a small proportion are ordinary travellers. The servants of the establishment do not sleep or eat in the house, and are not included in the above numbers as sleeping or dining in the hotel.

The 'United States' Hotel at Saratoga, with the connected premises, covers six acres of ground. It contains 800 beds. There are 175 male and 75 female servants; and it occasionally accommodates as many as 1200 guests at one time.

I should mention the provision against fire at the St. Charles. There are six watchmen who perambulate the house during the whole night. Their beats are so arranged that, as soon as one finishes his tour of inspection, another commences; and as they have to communicate from above with the office, on every tour, by a voice-conductor, there is a perfect check on the efficiency of their inspection. I made the discovery of this arrangement one night, while watching from a corridor the progress of a fearful fire in a neighbouring street, and I slept the more comfortably afterwards for the discovery.

The capital required for building and conducting such an establishment as the St. Nicholas or Metropolitan at New York must be enormous. An hotel in Broadway, to hold 1000 beds, cannot be built for less than 2,000,000 dollars, for house and furniture; and then there are the current expenses of servants, food, &c., to provide for besides. Most of the large hotels have been losing speculations for the original projectors, though some of them have realized handsome profits for the lessees, or purchasers from the original proprietors.

In connexion with this matter, it only remains to ask, what may be the effect of this hotel-life on those who habitually lead it. In every sense I think it bad. It destroys all sense of domesticity, and increases that excitement which is the bane of American life. It tempts the men to loaf about the lobbies and bars, smoking, dram-drinking, and disputing. In the women it encourages an idle, gossiping disposition, even where it does not foster a love of still more dangerous excitement. And as for the children, the poor children! for them it is sheer ruin. What can possibly be conceived more pernicious for a precocious, excitable American child than the glare, hurry, noise, and dissipation of a New York or New Orleans hotel? The poor infant is *blasé* before it is well born; corrupted and used-up before it has left its nurse's apron-string. I have seen infants of three and four years of age playing about the corridors of a New York hotel till nine and ten at night, while their parents were perhaps absent at a ball or an opera, and their black nurses were philandering with the Irish waiters. Need we wonder that the precocious *roué* takes to drams and cigars while yet a boy, and dies of old age before he reaches manhood?

I sincerely hope, for the good of the American people, that they will ere long find some remedy for the difficulties, which have forced them into the pernicious dissipation of hotel-life. The Americans have strong domestic affections. They love their wives and their children. Their want of domestic life is a necessity forced upon them by external circumstances; not, like the coffee-house life of the French, the result of lax domestic ties. We do the Americans a grievous wrong when we accuse them of a want of domesticity. On the contrary, with the exception perhaps of the English, I know no people with stronger domestic affections. The American marries young; he loves his wife and his children, and he passes his life with them. The American pioneer carries his family with him to the

AMERICAN DOMESTIC AFFECTION.

Far West; the American bagman scours the country in company with his wife. All over the Union I have seen striking instances of domestic affection. I have met a young mother and her children journeying in the bleak fall from Minnesota to New England, to visit 'grandpapa and grandmamma.' I have fallen in with a rough Texan, on a long pilgrimage, through swamp and forest, to stand by the death-bed of an aged mother; and I have travelled hundreds of miles with an old couple, on their weary way from Philadelphia to the Mississippi, to see a darling son. On this point it were ungrateful not to add our own experience. We have every reason to speak well of American hearts and homes. Both North and South we have met with friends who made their country almost seem a second home to us; and when, alas! occasion called for it, we experienced even from utter strangers an officious sympathy, that could only come from hearts nurtured in the daily practice of domestic virtues.

Everywhere since I came to the South I have been struck with evidences of the want of capital. This is the case also in the North, but in the South to a much greater extent. One necessary consequence is the want of that division of labour among retailers which enables you easily and satisfactorily to supply your wants. Shopping is a sad business, even in

New Orleans, the capital of the South. It is sad, because you cannot get what you want; and still sadder because you must pay extravagantly for the substitute that is forced upon you. The retailer cannot afford to keep stocks, because he must keep so many heterogeneous articles; and keeping all manner of things, they are bad and dear. In a shop-window in St. Charles-street I noticed yesterday guns, shovels, fiddles, and boxing-gloves, besides a host of other miscellaneous knicknacks. Why this is as bad as the old Canongate sign of ' Mousetraps, tripe, and other sweetmeats.' I wandered about to-day in vain looking for a brass watch-key, and my sister was in half-a-dozen shops in search of a bit of ordinary tape. These trifles mark the point of material development attained as correctly as the most elaborate statistics. Division of labour is one great instrument of civilization, and its absence is not to be overlooked as a social indicator. There is something very striking when one compares the shops of London with the stores of American cities. In the former a minute subdivision of labour has given rise to the most microscopic specialities; and the consequence is, that everything is supplied to the purchaser that the most extravagant imagination can desire; nay, the most capricious fancies are anticipated, and the wayward buyer finds that human skill and fancy had been secretly labouring for him in advance. In the States, on the contrary, there is a striking want of those thousand and one knicknacks which are almost necessaries in an old society. In New York you may procure all the essentials of civilized life ; but the pleasant little trifles which to us are necessaries are to be got only in London or Paris. This is partly owing to the want of demand natural to a people only passing into luxury, partly to the insufficient supply resulting from an imperfect division of labour.

In literature New Orleans seems sadly deficient. I spent a considerable time in search of some works, which had been recommended to me in connexion with the question of slavery; but even those which adopted the views of the South I could not procure. Some they did not know, even by name. The life of the great Southerner, Clay, by Colton, for instance, had never been heard of in New Orleans. Truly the South has much lee-way to make up, before she can expect to carry out to a successful issue her ambitious project of a 'Southern literature.'

The ladies of New Orleans, like their sisters of New York, are great dressers; indeed the dresses of American women generally, at least of the new-rich class, are something fabulous in expense, taking into consideration the rank and fortune of the wearers and their husbands. The dresses of ladies in New Orleans, I am told (and by New Orleans people), often equal in richness and expense those of our crowned heads in Europe. What do you think of a creole lady's dress powdered over with diamonds? her husband probably a cotton broker! Ladies here think nothing of expending a large proportion of the profits of a year's trade in a few dresses. Of course we must suppose that this is, in most cases, done with the knowledge and approval of the husband. He works, or speculates, and his wife wears the *spolia opima*.

There is some excuse, or at least explanation of this, to us, astounding extravagance, in the circumstances explained above of American housekeeping. As a rule, the inhabitant of an American city does not keep house. He has no opportunity, therefore, of displaying his wealth, as our parvenu merchants and manufacturers do, in fine houses, plate, and equipages. Neither is there the same passion for landed estates in America as with us. With land at five shillings an acre, its possession cannot confer social distinction. The New York stock-jobber does not lay out 100,000*l*. on land at two per cent. to give him the *entrée* to the houses of half-a-dozen neighbours, who drink his claret and laugh at him. He is making probably 50, perhaps 100 per cent. per annum on his capital; and all this fast-gotten gain he can only display to the public in one way, by clapping it on his wife's back. An American's wife is the peg on which he hangs out his fortune: he dresses her up that men may see his wealth: she is a walking advertisement of his importance, the 'sandwich' announcing to Broadway or Canal-street that her husband is a man of money and station. All this is very sorry work, but I do not see that it involves any greater absurdity than those displays of plate and upholstery, by which our rich vulgarians announce their wealth and hide their want of real refinement. If a sham gentility is to be set forth, it matters little whether it be done through the instrumentality of the upholsterer or the milliner. The Englishman loves his house, and he decks it out when he makes money; the American loves his wife, and decks her out for want of a house. Neither have much to boast of over the other; it is the same vulgar ostentation in different forms.

We have met with much kindness here from some of our Southern friends. They know that, as English folks, we do not sympathize with their pro-slavery feelings; yet that does not seem to prevent their friendly dispositions, so long as we do not obtrude our notions offensively on them. In this respect they seem to regard us more favourably than they do their countrymen of the North. They have no patience with the Yankees, though they can tolerate, and even hospitably entreat, the Abolitionist Englishman. It pains me to think that this plague of slavery should stand between us and the cordial affections of this kindly, and, at bottom, noble Southern people. But for this one hateful ground of quarrel, we should be the best friends in the world with the South. But the idea of a tabooed subject throws a spell over all intercourse with Southern people; and, unless one can conscientiously coincide with these views on this all-important subject, there is always a certain restraint and awkwardness in one's intercourse with them. I regret it extremely. I feel very grateful for the kindness, I may say friendship, we have received at their hands; I respect the intelligence and energy of the able men whose acquaintance I have made; I recognise the difficulties, the enormous difficulties, of their position; but I cannot sympathize with them in their love of slavery, nor in their hostility to the Free North. I am grateful for their kindness, and in return would give them anything but my opinions.

I hear a good deal here of Texas, but the future of that State, or rather series of States—for they talk here of making four States of it—seems to me somewhat problematical. No doubt it is rich in soil, and varied in climate; but, besides labouring under the curse of slavery, it lacks one great natural element of progress, easy means of communication; and the titles to the land are bad. The position of the country, on a slope from the Rocky Mountains, is adverse to a regular river navigation. The 'Report of the Southern Pacific Railroad' says—'The entire State may be said to be an inclined plain, stretching from the Rocky Mountains to the Gulf of Mexico, with sufficient declivity to give a rapid current to the large rivers.' They consequently 'flow, when full, with great rapidity, and remain in a navigable state but a short time and at uncertain periods.' The rivers, therefore, are not available as means of transport; and the rich, tenacious soil makes the roads almost impassable in wet weather. The consequence has been a tardy development of the country. This want it is now sought to supply by a railroad; but railroad-making is a slow process in a Slave State; and even if they had one or two trunk lines, what would that be to so immense a territory? The doubtful title to the land, arising partly from its old Spanish connexion, is also a serious hindrance to its prosperity. Litigation is a frequent accompaniment of Texan settlement; and a worse it could not have. It is no joke to eject a squatter armed with a Sharpe's rifle in lieu of a good title.

The Texan State Legislature, following up the lead of the Illinois Central Railway, has made immense concessions of land in aid of the 'Southern Pacific,' which is to cross the State from east to west, and ultimately, it is hoped, to reach the Pacific. The Illinois Central got 2,595,000 acres for 704 miles of road; the 'Southern Pacific,' supposing only the 783 miles across Texas are finished, will be entitled to 8,017,920 acres. To be sure, land, even by the million of acres, is no great boon when there is no access to it, barring the railways yet *in nubibus*, and no title but what has to be fought for in a court of law, or at the point of the bowie-knife. Then, in its further progress towards California, the 'Southern Pacific' encounters a desert, where no rain ever falls, but where, 'it is hoped,' water may be procured by Artesian wells for the thirsty engines and passengers. The Rocky Mountains would be crossed, we are told, at a height of *only* 5000 feet; the more Northern lines crossing at 10,000. All this is mere hearsay and loose talk. A vast mass of information has been collected by the Government surveyors and reported to head-quarters as to the capabilities of the Pacific routes, but nothing has been published. Nothing is *known*, so believe as much or as little as you like as to Pacific railways.

LETTER XIII.

MONTGOMERY, ALABAMA, 2nd February, 1857.

OLMSTED gives a very poor account of his fellow-passengers on the Alabama river. He says they were 'a rough, coarse style of people, drinking a great deal'— 'very profane'—' often showing the handles of concealed weapons about their persons;'—and gambling during the whole passage, night and day, except on Sunday. My experience of Alabama river life was very different. The passengers seemed a very quiet, respectable class of people. There was no swearing or profanity to be heard, and no gambling to be seen. The only appearance of intemperance I noticed was in the case of a genteel-looking young man, who came on board at Mobile in a state of intoxication. I allude to this contrast, not only because it shows how careful a traveller should be in drawing general inferences from his partial experience, but because it illustrates the different waves of population that surge up and down this country.

Mr. Olmsted's fellow-passengers, he says, 'were generally cotton-planters going to Mobile on business, or emigrants bound to Texas or Arkansas.' Those who ascended the Alabama with me were mostly, I understood, business-men from New Orleans or Mobile, going north to make their Spring purchases, or Northern men returning from a business tour to the South. In manner they were a little reserved, but perfectly gentlemanly, and it gives me pleasure to be able to qualify so far the severe judgment of an American observer.

I have just seen in the New Orleans papers a memorial from a number of property-holders in that city, by which it appears that the tax-paying portion of the New Orleans community is in abject subjection to the tax-levying portion. Property may here be almost said to be a disqualification. The penniless multitude lays on the tax; the powerless few pay it. The absurdity of such a system is too gross to need any enforcement. It is equally bad in a moral and a practical point of view. It is equally inexpedient and unjust, and I do not wonder that the plundered respectability of New Orleans should revolt against so outrageous an abuse; rather, I wonder that any set of men could for a moment submit to it. Bad enough to be highly taxed, as we are, for good water, good gas, good police, all controlled by tax-paying committees; but to be highly taxed by a band of desperadoes, for their own pecuniary benefit, and to have in return streets ill-paved, ill-lighted, and worse cleaned, while, instead of policemen, you have gangs of assassins,—that surely might stir the wrath of less bilious mortals than the Thug-oppressed inhabitants of New Orleans.

The memorialists speak of the misrule of New Orleans as a thing which has existed 'for years past.' It is, therefore, no passing evil, produced, as might be supposed, by the excitement of the Presidential election. The lawlessness of New Orleans is a chronic disease, and its virulence may be estimated by some of the symptoms enumerated by the memorialists, such as 'the depreciation of real estate, the withdrawal of capital, and the retardation of increase of population.' Misrule must have been carried to a high pitch, to produce such effects in a city so favourably situated as New Orleans, for profiting by the rapid development of a large portion of the North-Western and South-Western States.

The truth is, I believe, that throughout the States, both North and South, Old and New, the rule is, that the pauper populace puts its hand into the pockets of its richer neighbours and helps itself; and that liberally. That this legal confiscation should be submitted to quietly, by a people that owes its independence to impatience of 'taxation without representation,' has always appeared strange to me; but as the New Orleans memorialists remark, this is nothing compared with the iniquity of representation without taxation. One great source of the French Revolution was the exemption of the privileged classes from the taxation that ground down the commons. In America you have the same oppression with reversed circumstances, a privileged and exempted populace bleeding the holders of property. There is this difference, however, between the two cases: a people cannot go away; property may be removed. As we see already, the natural consequences of oppressive taxation is found in 'the withdrawal of capital;' and that withdrawal will tell heaviest on the poor blockheads who have banished the capital that fed them. Unjust taxation may not lead here, as in France, to a Reign of Terror, but it will assuredly tend to the impoverishment of any community which is long guilty of it. No injustice—least of all, unjust taxation—can escape retribution. The pocket is the most sensitive part of a man. 'Take lives, take wives, take aught except men's riches.' A coarse truth; but not the less, I fear, a truth.

The memorial very naturally and truly, as I think, traces the bad government and unjust taxation of New Orleans to the state of the elective franchise. 'In the existing condition of things,' say they, 'our most responsible citizens, those who bear the heaviest burthens in the form of taxation, are the class who have the least agency in directing public opinion, or in controlling public affairs.' That is it: universal suffrage prevents the worth and intelligence of the community from having its due weight; for we must remember that property does afford a rough, but in the aggregate, sound measure of worth and intelligence. The pauper, as a rule, is the least worthy and least intelligent man in the community; wherefore a government of paupers is necessarily an ochlocracy.

A suffrage based on property alone would give a despotism of the rich; a suffrage based on population alone gives a despotism of the poor; a suffrage based, like ours, on mingled elements of property and population is the most likely to give a representation, which will embody the mass of national virtue and intelligence.

Universal suffrage in America is in some respects less dangerous than it would be in England. The great safety of the States under their present constitution is the industrial condition of the population. There is less proletarianism than in England. In the Northern States an independent, property-holding yeomanry forms a sufficiently large proportion of the community to control the public decision of affairs. It is only in the larger cities and manufacturing districts, that the proletarian populace has a dangerous predominance. In the South, again, the servile condition of the great body of the labouring class materially modifies the Democratic tendencies of universal suffrage: the slave representation, nearly one-third of the whole Southern representation, being based on property rather than population.

I came down the Mississippi with a gentleman from Nashville who had been at school with General Walker, and who confirmed, in the strongest manner, the accounts of his reserve at school. Indeed he said Walker was the puniest, quietest milksop of a boy he had ever known; so much so, as to be an object of derision to his schoolfellows, who called him 'honey,' 'missy,' and other similar contemptuous names. Walker never joined the other boys in any athletic games; the only thing by which he distinguished himself was that he always knew his lesson better than any boy in school; and the moment school was over he ran home to his mother. In his leisure moments his favourite pastime was reading the Bible. Indeed there is little doubt that Walker possesses one of those peculiarly organized, imaginative minds which seize all objects in a strong and original manner, and to which, at one time or another, theology is sure to be a source of irresistible attraction. Walker first of all studied divinity, and it was probably only in consequence of the doubts and perplexities, that so often disturb the studies of our young theologians, that he abandoned that study for medicine. This, too, for some reason he gave up after a time, and took to law, which, as you know, is in this country often synonymous with taking to politics. In New Orleans he connected himself with the press; but here, in addition to law and physic, he also had an episode of love, which, though not mentioned in the public accounts of his career, had, I believe, a great effect on his fortunes and character, and the story of which I had from a source in which I can put every confidence. At New Orleans he became acquainted with a young girl, very beautiful and intellectual, but deaf and dumb. Walker was at first attracted to this young lady by sympathy for her melancholy privation, but tenderer feelings soon arose, and on her part the young lady became passionately attached to Walker. Indeed, not being aware of the usual restraints which the conventionalities of society impose on females under such circumstances, she even displayed her affection in a more open manner than was pleasing to her friends. This led to some restraint, and misunderstanding, and estrangement; and the poor beautiful, but speechless girl, thinking herself deserted, sickened and died. From that moment Walker was a changed man. He went to California, fought a duel, and then joined a band of desperadoes. Thenceforth the sickly, studious milksop was the stern and daring adventurer. The story sounds romantic, I confess; but it is the only intelligible clue I have yet received to the strange revolution, which is admitted to have taken place in this man's character. It must have required some great mental shock to transform the sickly, 'yellow-haired laddie' of Nashville into the stern Nicaraguan filibuster. Why should it not be blasted love, and the vision of his broken-hearted deaf-mute, dead for love of him? To an imagination such as his must be, a vision like this may well become a permanent and powerful reality, casting its dark hue over his whole career and character. One thing in Walker I do admire: I mean his silence. For I agree with Carlyle, that 'silence is great.' In an age of babblers, it is much to find a man that can hold his tongue.

Here in the South a most exaggerated importance is attached to the value of cotton—'King Cotton'—as the basis not only of all American, but of all European industry. However indispensable its cultivation may be to the prosperity of the South, it forms but an inconsiderable portion of the industry of the Union at large. A few figures will set this in a clear light. By the census returns of 1850, the value of the total agricultural products of the preceding year was 1,311,169,326 dollars, of which amount only 98,663,720 dollars, or seven and a half per cent., were due to cotton. The values of the four principal agricultural products stood thus:—

	Dollars.
Indian Corn	296,035,552
Wheat	100,485,944
Cotton	98,603,720
Hay	96,876,494

The value of the Indian corn produced was therefore three times greater than that of cotton. Wheat exceeded cotton by nearly two millions of dollars; and even the ignoble hay crop, which nobody boasts of as a pillar of American power, was only some million and a half dollars behind the regal cotton crop. Equally unfounded is the idea, that cotton is the main support of the external commerce and naval power of the Union. The value of the total exports from the United States in 1855 was 246,708,553 dollars, of which only 88,143,844 dollars, or about thirty-five per cent., were represented by cotton. As yet, then, cotton is no 'king;' though, with wise and virtuous statesmanship, its empire may indeed become kingly.

But it is especially the importance of cotton to England that the philosophers of the South delight to dwell on. What would mankind do without us and our slaves? they ask triumphantly. But for our productions, the mills of Lancashire would be shut up, and the Chartists of England would revolutionize the country. There is some truth, and much nonsense, in this statement of the question. No doubt, when an extensive division of labour has taken place, and one country supplies the raw material which another works up, the production of the former may be regarded as the initiatory and indispensable condition of the whole industrial process. But philosophic cotton-growers need hardly be reminded that the relation here spoken of is two-sided. If demand is vain without supply, so supply is ruinous without demand. Manchester is no less needful to New Orleans than is New Orleans to Manchester. Nay, if there be any difference, it is in favour of the latter. Not only can cotton, at a certain price, be furnished by other countries than the Southern States, but the cotton manufacture might be abandoned without the destruction of England's industry. No doubt it is an important element of our national riches, but it is hardly half a century old, and cannot, therefore, be essential to our industrial existence. The loss of our cotton manufacture would be a severe check to our prosperity, but it would not extinguish it. Our capital and labour would be transferred to some other pursuit, and men and women would wear some substitute for cotton shirts and gowns. But the cotton culture is the one possible production of the cotton-growing States. Take cotton from the South, and you extinguish her industrial life. She cannot change her soil and climate, as we may change our machinery. She is a cotton-growing country, or she is nothing. It is not for her, then, to speak of forced changes in international relations of trade; any such change would be a loss to us, but death to her.

But all this sort of talk is mere childishness. The simple truth is, that both countries need each other's productions, and that an interchange tends infinitely to the advantage of both. Of what possible advantage, then, can it be to provoke discussions as to the possible evils which one country might inflict upon the other? A much more philosophic spirit it would imply to remove, if possible, any lurking irritations from the minds of either nation, and to bind by still closer and more enduring ties communities so indispensable to each other's welfare. This, I am persuaded, is the view of all wise and liberal Americans; and we must not be led astray by the carping futilities of the small fry of Southern Democracy, who look on all Englishmen as leagued together for the twofold purpose of freeing niggers and beating down the price of cotton.

For my part, I desire to see the cotton trade between England and America more and more extended, and so the two nations bound over in yet heavier penalties to keep the peace. I have no sympathy with the twaddle at home about 'dependence on foreigners.' We must be, and should be dependent on foreigners. The very essence of modern civilization is the interdependence of nations. If India, or any other country, can produce cotton, by private enterprise, either cheaper or better than America, by all means let us take our cotton supply from it. But hitherto the whole course of trade has gone to prove that Nature has given the Southern States of America a practical monopoly of cotton culture, if they have only the virtue and wisdom to profit by it. Let them only give themselves fair play, by setting labour free, and they will produce cotton at such a cost, and in such abundance, as will baffle all competition. There are some 400,000,000 available cotton-lands in the South. Of these about 28,000,000 are cultivated, the rest is a desert; there are no hands to till it. Now, by adopting free labour, the South would not only double the effective force of her negro population, but would turn into her territories that stream of emigration which is now enriching the prairies of the North-west. The association with the noble free labourers of the North would be the best education for the freed negroes, and together they would build up a prosperity of which the South, as yet, has not the faintest conception. A generation would convert her waste cotton-lands from a howling wilderness into a garden-land.

The slave-holders of the South, in their argument in favour of slavery, derived from cotton as a power in the world, assume that slavery is indispensable to cotton culture. That this is not he tcase we might know from the latitude most favourable to the growth of cotton. Cotton is not a tropical production, even were it proved that negroes alone are capable of tropical labour. But we have more than a general inference to go upon: in these very Slave States cotton is cultivated by free labour. In Texas it is raised by the free labour of Germans, and the quality is confessedly superior to that produced by slave labour. And even in Alabama the small farmers, who are too poor to own slaves, produce, with the help of their families, two, three, or five bales per annum. Therefore, even granting the importance of cotton,—granting, too, the indispensableness of American cotton,—it yet remains to be proved that slavery is either a necessity or a good. The onus lies clearly on the slave-owner.

One thing is certain, no need of cotton or any other supposed necessary of life will ever induce the English nation to relax one tittle in its antipathy to slavery. This is with us a settled conviction, which neither gain nor argument can disturb. Cotton is great, but conscience is greater; and in any question where these two powers may come in conflict, the issue for the English mind will be nowise doubtful.

LETTER XIV.

MACON, GEORGIA, 4th February, 1857.

EVERY step one takes in the South, one is struck with the rough look of the whole face of civilization. The country is nowhere well cleared; towns and villages are few and far between, and even those which you see have an unfinished look. An Englishman, accustomed to clear fields, trim hedge-rows, and regular plantations, can hardly conceive the condition of a Southern State. Notwithstanding the rapid prosperity of the South, and especially of the Gulf States, during the last twenty years, they have, on the whole, a very wild appearance. During my whole course down the Cumberland and Mississippi rivers, up the Alabama, and across by rail from Montgomery to Macon, a distance of some 2000 miles, I have been travelling, for the most part, in sight of the primæval forest of the continent. The cleared portion of the country is trifling compared with that which is yet unreclaimed; and even where the cotton-planter has put his plough into the virgin soil, his plantation is fringed with the ancient forest; and even his cultivated patch is, in many places, disfigured with stumps, or what is still more unsightly, girdled trees, which rise like great naked, death-like poles, all over the surface of the ground. During our passage of 430 miles up the Alabama River, we hardly saw a single village; and the one or two towns which it boasts we chanced to pass during the night. The whole scene, therefore, was one of impressive desolateness. Two days and two nights toiling up the muddy river, and on either hand the great, silent, tangled woods. As you advance the banks are more and more cleared; a narrow margin of plantation lines the river; a cotton-press is seen here and there; and, more rarely, a planter's cottage.

Even on our land journey hither, few evidences of an advanced state of cultivation met our eye. Few towns or villages are to be seen even at the stations of the railway; and planters' houses are also unfrequent. How different from the face of a New England State, dotted over with neat farm-houses. And how different a social and political condition of the community does this outward state of things infer.

The towns, and even cities, which I have seen in the South, are ill-paved, and utterly in want of

BACKWARDNESS OF THE SOUTH.

sewerage. New Orleans has nothing but open gutters to carry off its putrescent waters, and this in the City of the Plague *par excellence*. The want of scavengering is also atrocious. Even in the immediate vicinity of the St. Charles Hotel heaps of garbage and unmentionable filth are suffered to accumulate, in strange contrast to the marble grandeur of that imposing edifice. Mobile is, with the exception of Quebec, decidedly the muddiest town I ever saw; even to get from the hotel to the steamer, a distance of some few hundred yards, we were forced to hire a carriage, for fear of being 'mired.' The streets of Montgomery, Columbus, and Macon, are unpaved, not even planked; and the sewerage consists of huge ditches cut in the sand at each side of the streets, or down the middle. The absence of stone is some excuse for the want of paving; but why can the Southerners not have plank causeways and pavements as well as Northerners and Canadians! Surely they have pine enough! Yes, they have pine enough, but they lack that high spirit of civilization which is the soul of the North and of Western Canada. What capital they save, and that is not much, they lay out in niggers. Niggers and cotton—cotton and niggers; these are the law and the prophets to the men of the South.

Another criterion of civilization is roads. Judged

by its roads, the South is far behind. In Kentucky I saw some good roads. In Tennessee they have some 'pikes' (turnpike-roads), and some ' mud-roads.' In Louisiana, Alabama, and Georgia, I have as yet met no well-made road. In the town of Montgomery I saw a country wagon with six mules, and the spokes of the wheels plastered over up to the very naves with thick tenacious mud. And Montgomery is the capital of the State! Such deficiencies in Minnesota did not surprise me: that was yesterday but a forest; but Tennessee dates from 1796, Louisiana from 1812, and Georgia is one of the original thirteen. She, at least, might have got clear of ' mud-roads' in the sixty-eight years of her independence.

The want of enterprise or of capital in the South, as compared with the North, cannot better be illustrated than by a comparison of the railways they have constructed, taken in relation to the amount of their population. From statements in De Bow's census, I find that, in 1854, the railways in operation stood as follows :—

	Miles.	Population.	Miles.	Population.
14 Free States	13,105	13,150,111,	or 1000	per 1 million.
12 Slave ditto	3,991	8,418,857,	„ 500	ditto.

Railways, in our day, are recognised as one of the most important means of industrial and social improvement, and nowhere is this conviction more decided than in the United States. We may, therefore, take it for granted that every State has strained to the uttermost its capital and credit, to procure this necessary of modern civilization; and on this life-and-death struggle the North beats the South two to one. Nay, this is understating the matter; for some, and I believe much, of the Southern railway capital has been contributed by their Northern neighbours.

Another and more searching test of the comparative development of the Free and Slave States is the density of their population. In 1856 the density of the former was 21.91; of the latter, 11.35. The density of the 'South-Western' States, under which De Bow includes Alabama, Mississippi, Louisiana, Texas, Arkansas, and Tennessee, was only 7.00. After all, King Cotton has hardly, as yet, taken possession of his kingdom. He has done little more than unfurl his flag on it. Why, even barbarous Russia (in Europe) has a density of 28.44, and moribund Turkey (in Europe) of 73.60!

The two staples of the South, cotton and sugar, have the evil in common of being precarious productions. This is a serious misfortune to the planters engaged in their culture; for a precarious growth necessarily involves a fluctuating price; and the more uncertain the results of an industry are, the more nearly it approaches the nature of gambling, and the more injurious is its effect on the character of the producer. The imagination naturally fixes on the result of the best years, just as the gambler's mind dwells on his last great success: his expenditure is calculated on the profits of good crops and high prices, and when bad times come, he is a ruined man. This I believe is the secret of the notorious 'indebtedness' of the Southern planters. Not one in fifteen, I am assured, is free of debt.

But sugar-planting in the States has another, and perhaps worse, bane to contend with; it is based on Protection. Cotton culture is, at least, a natural and legitimate industry. It has not, like sugar-planting, to fear the breaking down of a rotten foundation. I believe that cotton-growing in the Gulf States can defy all competition. The perfect adaptation of soil and climate, the ready access to the ocean, and the comparatively short transit to European markets, must always ensure for it vast facilities. The one thing which in my view may yet expose the South to a dangerous competition (however paradoxical it may sound here) is her slave-labour. Within the last ten or fifteen years the value of slaves has risen fifty per cent. at least. During the same time the price of bacon has risen

100 to 200 per cent. Let this process only be continued for ten years longer, and where will be the profits of the cotton-planter? And here we may perhaps find the long-looked-for solution of the Nigger question. When slave-labour becomes unprofitable, the slave will be emancipated. South Carolina herself will turn Abolitionist, when slavery ceases to pay. When she finds that a brutalized race cannot and will not give as much efficient labour for the money as a hired class of superior workers, it is possible that she may lay aside the cowhide, and offer wages to her niggers.

The chances of the continuous prosperity of sugar-planting seem poor indeed. Resting on artificial props, it has to fear social and political disturbance as well as natural calamities. The progress of Free Trade notions may destroy it. So would the annexation of Cuba, the duties being equalized; for those planters only who could transfer thither their slaves could continue the production. Planting in Louisiana must at once cease. This is already seen by the more long-headed among the planters, although the senseless crowd halloo for Filibusterism as lustily as if its success were not their certain ruin.

LETTER XV.

Macon, Georgia, 7th February, 1857.

The great difference between English and American civilization is the greater thoroughness of the former. This arises, I conceive, from the greater age of society with us, and the greater concentration of our energies. The civilization of the United States, on the contrary, has had but a brief duration, and is extended over a vast surface; hence, both in its industrial and intellectual aspect, it is essentially superficial.

The distinctive characters of English and American civilization are represented, to a great extent, by the comparative density of population in the two nations. The density of population to the square mile was, in 1850, in the whole territory of the United States, 7.90; in Great Britain and Ireland, 225.91. In Great Britain, 18,720,394 persons are concentrated within 121,912 square miles of territory; whereas, in the Free States of the Union, 13,434,912 inhabitants are at work on 612,597 square miles; while in the Slave States 9,664,656 people undertake to cultivate 851,508 square miles. Thus, a people little more numerous than that of Ireland is struggling to develope the resources of a territory as large as Austria, Prussia, Germany, France, Spain, and Portugal combined (867,291 square miles)!

Emerson praises the thoroughness of the English worker; and with reason. The minute division of labour and the intense competition which characterise our industrial system, enforce thoroughness. Hence it is the pride of the British worker to do well what he does: to make a sufficient job. The greatest reproach you can make to an English workman is to tell him his production is 'unworkmanlike,' as 'unbusinesslike' is the reproach most feared by the English business-man.

In passing, I must regret that Emerson, notwithstanding this frank recognition of the excellence of English workmanship, should inconsistently, as it seems to me, join in the shallow objection to division of labour as deteriorating the capacity of the workman. This contradiction cannot exist. A system that produces a national thoroughness of production cannot undermine the capabilities of the people; nor is it conceivable that an organization which is indispensable to the progress of industry, should be necessarily destructive of the human powers. Such contradictions have no place in the Divine economy. Without entering on intricate considerations, it is enough to point to general results. The most enlightened and generally cultivated communities are those in which division of labour is most developed; and in the interior of a nation those occupations are the most elevating, in which division of labour is most systematically carried out. Compare a Manchester artizan with a Dorsetshire labourer, and you will have some measure of the elevating power of a minute division of labour. Or, compare one of Napier's engineers with a Highland blacksmith, and see which is the more cunning workman and intelligent citizen.

Workmanship in America is mere surface-work. There is no sufficiency, no thoroughness in it. The American workman displays energy, ingenuity, rapidity to a surprising degree, but he lacks utterly the care and completeness of the British tradesman. His work is thoroughly 'unworkmanlike.' It bears all the marks of haste and imperfection; has no appearance of finish or minute care about it. The marble-veneered palaces of New York often come down by the run. The clippers of New England sail well, but leak and damage cargo. They are splendid models, but slim in construction. Twenty-five thousand miles of railways intersect the American continent—they cross swamps and mountains, the St. Lawrence and the Mississippi—but their frail tresselwork is continually coming down; their bridges are crazy, their roads often unballasted, their whole apparatus flimsy. The consequence is, you enter their cars with fear and trembling, and thank God at your journey's end. I need not dwell on river and lake steamers; a prudent man makes his will before he goes on board. And so it goes on, down to the minutest article of domestic use throughout this country. There is not a lock that catches, not a hinge that turns; knives will not cut, and matches will not light. The doors will not shut, the windows will not open: and all this is made more striking and provoking by its contrast with the pretension to finish and refinement. You sit down on a fine velvet sofa, and are startled by coming down on a spring as hard as a cricket-ball. The hotel whose doors are creaking and windows gaping, is gilt and carpeted like a palace; and the Mississippi steam-boat, on which you are snagged or blown up, is gilt and painted, and goes twenty miles an hour: you cannot sail to destruction in greater luxury or at greater speed.

The Americans are very fond of the word 'reliable.' Everything is 'reliable'—information, railway connexions, politicians. But, alas! it is *lucus a non lucendo*. At least, in matters of workmanship, you cannot rely on the American: he is not a trustworthy workman. It is not that the American is less conscientious than the Englishman; in point of morals and intelligence the free labourer of the North is at least the equal of the Englishman. But the necessities of his position force on him haste and imperfection; he is too much a Jack-of-all-trades, and has neither time nor opportunity for making himself so fully a master of his trade as his English rival; neither can he bestow on the work in hand the patient and minute care which characterizes the workmanship of the British artizan. The 'accidents' by flood and field which are so frequent here, arise, I have no doubt, in a great measure from hasty and inferior workmanship. The success and safety of the Cunard Line is no chance affair: much of it is owing to the thorough workmanship of our Clyde mechanics.

The superficiality of American civilization is the natural result of their impetuous energy. The Englishman undertakes only what he can do well; the American flies at everything. 'Go ahead anyhow,' that is his motto. The characteristic of his civilization must, therefore, necessarily be extensiveness rather than thoroughness. The American people —a people scarce half a century old—diffuses itself, its energy, and its capital, over a whole continent. Must not its work, of necessity, be imperfect and superficial? In this fast and furious race of civilization every element of deep and thorough effectiveness must be a-wanting. There can be no minute division of labour, no long accumulation of capital, no strenuous competition among labourers or among capitalists. A people that goes ahead at the American pace, cannot stoop to minutiæ. It goes ahead 'anyhow.'

The superficiality I have remarked in the material civilization of the Americans extends, I believe, and for the same reasons, to their intellectual development. There is a certain superficiality in their thought as well as in their work. There is vivacity, originality, power in their manner of viewing things, but I think there is a want of profundity.

In a community of recent origin, where accumulation cannot exist to any considerable extent, and where, consequently, there is no large leisure class at liberty to devote itself specially to the pursuit of study, the conditions of deep and concentrated thinking are a-wanting; for thinking is a business which, like every other business, can only flourish under certain necessary conditions. Without an extensive accumulation of capital, and a consequent division of intellectual labour, there may be strong individual thinkers—for genius breaks through all rules—but there cannot exist a class of profound scholars, and the tone of popular thought is necessarily light and superficial. In the middle ages the church supplied this scholarly leisure class, fanaticism affording the necessary accumulation of wealth; and in Germany the University system provides for an extensive division of intellectual labour; but neither of these modes are open to the United States. As an industrial and free community, opposed to all guilds and corporations, America, like England, must look to an enriched and easy class to supply her with thinkers. When this class shall have been sufficiently extended here to organize a minute subdivision of intellectual pursuits, the resistless energy of the national mind will, no doubt, manifest itself as conspicuously in the depth of its intellectual researches, as it does in the vigour of its material enterprises.

Besides this industrial condition of the States, their political organization leads to superficiality in matters of thought. There is a levelling tendency in Democracy, even in matters intellectual. The uneducated or half-educated multitude is predominant, and their no-thought gives the tone to the general mind. No man dares to think for himself. To differ from the popular opinion is treason to the popular power. Men think in masses, and the sophistry of the day is the universal rule for the national mind. A certain shallowness is, therefore, natural to Democratic communities where popular opinion necessarily prevails. Under Democracies intelligence is widespread, but superficial; there is diffusion, but not depth.

On the whole, then, the great want of American civilization is concentration. Yet here, as everywhere, the law of compensation is at work. If, on the one hand, the expansive nature of American civilization tends to superficiality in thought and deed, on the other hand it developes more and more that impetuous spirit of enterprise which is the soul of American progress. The American does not stop to polish his work; but neither does he quail before any work. He has no taste or time for filing; but his axe and plough are irresistible. On the whole, he does his work nobly; and every new day finds him stronger and readier for the day's work. Such is the right temper of the Pioneer of Progress, and so he is trained up to subdue the wildernesses of the Western world, and make it the fit abode of a new-born civilization.

One word of limitation before I leave this subject.

When I attribute superficiality to American civilization, the charge does not apply equally to all parts of the Union, and its applicability to any part varies from day to day. This qualification, indeed, should modify every judgment on American affairs. It is this varying aspect of the social phenomena of America that makes it so intensely difficult to form an accurate estimate of her progress. Everything varies, and everything is in flux. The phenomena change with every step you take, and with every hour you continue your observations. The East differs from the West; the North differs from the South; and all are different to-day from what they were yesterday, or will be to-morrow. You have to daguerreotype a scene that is at once a moving panorama and a dissolving view.

Last night I attended a Free Trade meeting, a sorry one, but interesting to me as the first symptom of movement on this vital question which I have encountered in my long peregrinations. I have indeed been struck with the apathy and ignorance of the Americans on all economical subjects. I have not met half-a-dozen sound and hearty Free Traders in the United States. Neither have I perceived in the newspapers any appearance of interest or intelligence on matters connected with political economy. Some men there are in the States, such as Senator Hunter of Virginia, who are thorough masters of economical science, but as yet they have not succeeded in impressing their views on the popular mind. The prevalent fallacy here, as on the continent of Europe, seems to be, that an infant industry needs nursing. Free Trade, they say, may answer in England, where manufactures are firmly established, but we need Protection here, till our industrial enterprises are fairly set a-going. They never seem to consider that Protection is most hurtful precisely where it is most needed, and the more weak and rickety an industry is, the less desirable it is to foster it at the expense of healthier undertakings. The want of even the elementary notions of economical knowledge in the ruling portion of the American people is sufficiently manifested, not only by their restrictive and protective laws, but by their legislative bounties and their usury laws, remnants of barbarism which have ceased to disgrace the English statute-book. It is true the Democratic party affects Free Trade principles, but it seems to me a mere pretence; it is a mere political movement, a policy of circumstance, not of conviction. In private, I have not found the Democrats one whit better informed or more zealous in the matter of Free Trade, than their Whig or Republican opponents.

Neither is the South serious or consistent in its

Free Trade movement. The ablest and most powerful organs of public opinion in the South are outrageously wrongheaded on economical questions; and the Southern commercial conventions are unanimous in their adhesion to Protective principles; and yet, if there is a country on earth where Free Trade should find acceptance, it is here. This is a young nation, without superannuated institutions or traditionary prejudices. It started on its unembarrassed course at the close of the eighteenth century, when economical science had already risen on the world, and a shock had been given to ancient fallacies. There were no old monopolies to bolster up, no vested interests to conciliate. The country was a *tabula rasa*, fitted beyond all others for building up a free system of industry. Moreover, there are strong reasons against a Protective policy in the States. There is a dearth of capital; and therefore here, less than anywhere, should it be wasted on unprofitable enterprises. There is scope enough, and to spare, for industrial enterprise; and there is, therefore, none of that fancied need of opening up 'new fields' of industry, which misleads less favoured nations. Nature herself, too, by the manifold facilities she afforded for agricultural and maritime purposes, clearly pointed out the industrial course of the young nation. Neither were political reasons wanting, to back these urgent economical inducements to eschew all restrictions on the natural course of industry. A Protective policy naturally creates jealousies and heartburnings between the different sections of the country. Next to slavery, Protection has been the worst enemy of the Union. Abolitionism is doubly hateful to the South, as coming from the 'protected' North. If Abolitionism has its disunion, the Tariff had its nullification.

Again, Protection in this country fosters corruption, the reproach and bane of American administration. An 'overflowing treasury' becomes a curse, when it engenders a brood of greedy political adventurers. At this hour the surplus revenue wrung from the consumers of the nation, to the great discouragement of industry, is a premium held out to political scoundrelism, and so long as such a prey exists every administration will be a 'spoils-administration.' Where the carrion is, there also will be the vultures. Finally, Protection in America, by giving an unnatural expansion to a manufacturing proletarianism, adds tenfold intensity to the evils of universal suffrage, her great political difficulty. The natural expansion of the American people as small but independent farmers, scattered over the face of the country, would be a sure guarantee for the safe working of Democratic institutions; but the unnatural and forced aggregation of masses of mere labourers in cities and manufacturing districts is here pregnant with serious evils. In England, our proletarian mobs have no political franchise; they are counterbalanced by a powerful middle class, and their excesses are checked by a strong police organization. Here the mob is master; and no wise statesman would wish to increase the power of such a master. Protection in America is at once a danger and a loss.

Now, the question naturally occurs, how is it then, that with so many reasons in favour of Free Trade and with so many inducements to eschew Protection, the enlightened people of the United States has lapsed into the slough of a semi-barbarous policy? The reasons, I think, are threefold. First, the nation has been too prosperous to look closely into the sources of national prosperity. They are too busy making money to care about philosophizing on the art of money making. Should adversity fall upon them, they will be more willing to take counsel with the economists. It was our 'commercial crises' and 'stagnations of trade' that repealed the British Corn-Laws. So long as the poor have a sufficiency of bacon and beans, and the rich see their town-lots, their land, and their niggers daily rising in value, they will not trouble their heads about theories of taxation and production. But let a pinch come, and they will be glad to inquire into the causes of national prosperity and ruin. Secondly, the low state of economical knowledge in America may, in part, be attributed to that superficiality of thought to which I have alluded above as characteristic of Western civilization. Economical knowledge is not a thing to be learned at common schools. It requires a mind of some independent strength to resist the influence of a host of popular prejudices and time-honoured fallacies. Thirdly, the progress of sound economical views in the State has been retarded by the peculiar position of parties. Interest makes the North Protective; and thus the weight, not only of numbers, but of intelligence, is thrown into the scale of barbarism, while the advocacy of more advanced notions is left to the Democracy of the South. Political economy has fallen on evil times in America, where the ablest statesmen and most vigorous thinkers are busy preaching Protection, and Free Trade has but the languid advocacy of Irish demagogues and Southern filibusters. Truth and error have changed places: commercial reform is supported by the vulgar; the wisest of the land are laboriously building up a superannuated absurdity.

I cannot think, however, that this anomaly will long continue. A people so intelligent cannot always remain the dupe of gross fallacies. Material circumstances will force on discussion, and so soon as the vigorous mind of the nation grapples with the question, the result cannot long be doubtful. The whole system of Protection will topple down, and the States will take, as becomes them, their place in the van of human progress. Already the straw is moving; coffee-drinkers are calling out for cheap sugar, woollen-manufacturers demand untaxed wool, and the South refuses to pay tribute to the manufacturers of the North. Everywhere the consumer has an uneasy sense of oppression. Let this feeling once grow into a clear and articulate conviction of the folly and iniquity of Protection, and the beginning of the end will be at hand. This vigorous people will make short work of a system at once so ruinous and so wrong.

Meanwhile I cannot but be proud, as an Englishman, that the 'Old Country' has herein taken the lead of younger nations. There are those even among ourselves who think that England's race is run; but no nation can be effete which takes the lead in wise and just legislation. England was the first to burst the withes of commercial restriction, and has thereby vindicated her claim to be a leader among the nations. The end of commerce is to bind together in one common brotherhood all the peoples of the earth; and

England, by inaugurating a wiser and more generous commercial policy, has given a fresh impulse to human progress. Of this peaceful triumph of common sense and sound science an Englishman may well be proud.

LETTER XVI.

SAVANNAH, 13th February, 1857.

In the railway from Montgomery to Macon I experienced another instance of that espionage, which I have already alluded to as so disagreeable in the South. A Scotch lady, who had married a South Carolinian, and lived sixteen years in the South, was giving me rather an animated and not very flattering account of slave life, especially in a religious point of view, when I noticed an elderly man, who had been seated at some distance behind us, move quietly up and take possession of the seat behind us. I at once broke off the conversation, having no doubt that he had caught stray words, and wished to play the eavesdropper. On mentioning my suspicions to the lady and her daughter, they agreed one could not be too cautious, as some persons who had expressed themselves too freely lately at Macon had been escorted to the station by a party of the inhabitants, and forced to take their departure. In politics there is

A SLAVE'S VIEW OF SLAVERY.

no toleration in the South. The slave-owner regards a wandering Abolitionist with about the same goodwill, that a manufacturer of gunpowder would a stranger who should visit his establishment with a lighted cigar in his mouth.

Since I came to Georgia I have had some conversation with a very intelligent slave. He was born in Virginia, and sold on account of the bankruptcy of his owner. He came first to Charleston: here he was parted from a sister, and has never heard of her since. I said, to try him, that I supposed the slaves were pretty well treated. Their treatment depends entirely, he replied, on the person they belong to. Indeed, how can it be otherwise? 'But,' said I, 'we are told that you prefer slavery, and would not be free if you could.' His only answer was a short, contemptuous laugh; but if he had spoken for an hour he could not have been more convincing. I almost felt ashamed of having made so silly an observation. He told me he had conversed with a free negro from the North, and that he understood a free man could 'get along' very well there if he behaved well. He did not add it in words, but I thought I could read it in his eye, that he would take the first feasible opportunity of trying for himself. Of course I gave him not the slightest encouragement, for I consider that that is not a matter for a stranger to interfere in; but that such feelings are fermenting in many an African heart, and those the best of the race, is to me a matter of perfect certainty; and if I wanted corroboration of the fact, I should find it in the suspicions and fears of the slave-owners.

On the way from Montgomery we had a glimpse of Georgian ploughing; the wretched plough drawn by one horse or mule, and held by a negro woman. On this point, however, I prefer giving you the authority of Olmsted, who is himself a practical farmer, and, being an American, will not be suspected of exaggeration. Travelling towards Charleston, he met in the train an elderly countryman, of whom he says— 'he described to me as a novelty a plough with 'a sort of wing, like, on one side,' that pushed off, and turned over a slice of the ground; from which it appeared that he had, until recently, never seen a mould-board; the common ploughs of this country being constructed on the same principles as those of the Chinese, and only rooting the ground like a hog or a mole, not cleaving and turning. He had never heard of working a plough with more than one horse. At another place he says—'the fact is, in certain parts of South Carolina a plough is yet an unknown instrument of tillage.' Such a state of things is almost incredible in a land that gave birth to Whitney's Gin (a Northern invention), and is only to be explained by the depressing influence of slavery. The agricultural system of the South is as far behind that of the North-West, as the latter is behind that of the Lothians.

Illinois and Georgia are about the same size, are both central States, and have nearly equal populations. I have been comparing them in different points of view, as fair representatives of the North and South; and the result is strikingly favourable to the former. Georgia has 58,000 square miles of area, Illinois has 55,405. The population of the former is 1,009,680; of the latter, 1,074,271. But here all similitude stops. Though Georgia is an old State and Illinois a young one, the progress of the latter is much greater. Her population advances at the rate of 7.6 per cent. per annum; that of Georgia, at 3.1 per cent. The ratio to the total population of the States has fallen, in Georgia, in twenty years, from 4.02 to 3.91; while in Illinois it has risen from 1.22 to 3.67. The unimproved lands in Georgia, in 1850, were over 16,000,000 acres; in Illinois, under 7,000,000. There were, in 1854, in Georgia, 884 miles of railway in operation; in Illinois, 1262. And then, as to political influence, the representatives of Georgia had fallen in twenty years from nine to eight; in Illinois, they had risen from three to nine.

Finally, Georgia contains 22.67 per cent. of immigrant Americans, and 1.24 per cent. of foreign immigrants. Illinois has 47.25 of the former, and 13.22 of the latter, making together, 60.47 per cent. of the whole population! Perhaps this last statement may help to explain all the rest. The great immigration is the secret of the progress of Illinois; but what is the secret of the immigration? Both States are fertile; in both nature holds out many inducements; the climate in Georgia is finer, the country is more salubrious. Why, then, is she left behind in the race of development and prosperity? I can see no reason, except that ever-recurring one—slavery. The hardy pioneer, himself a labourer, will not put himself in competition with brute labour, nor seek his fortune where labour is dishonourable. When Southern statesmen count up the gains of slavery, let them not forget also to count its cost. They may depend upon it, there is a heavy 'per contra' to the profits of niggerdom.

Even without these statistics, I could have guessed the different condition of these two States from my observation of their external appearance. Indeed, it was the striking contrast in the outward character of men and things in the two States that sent me to the census to hunt up their statistics. In Illinois all was life, and hope, and eagerness;

here a dull stagnation prevails. In Illinois the cars were crowded with emigrants, or speculators, or men looking anxiously for new homes. The value and worth of land was the universal topic. At every station a new city, at lowest a new town or village, was springing up; and on every hand the click of the hammer and the rasping of the saw betokened that new inhabitants had pitched their tents in the land of promise. In Georgia, how different! Some growth there is in one or two towns; some increase of cotton, too, there may be; but there lacks the animation and spirit of Illinois. There is none of that bustle or hopeful eagerness. You travel for a hundred miles, too, and see no village; and not unfrequently you pass lands where the young, green pines tell you that abandoned fields are returning to their primæval wildness. Look on this picture and on that, and tell me if you can account otherwise than I have done for the different positions of these two families of the same vigorous people. With all this, recollect that Georgia is the most go-ahead State of the South. It is the Southern Yankeeland. The Georgia Central railway was, I believe, the first central railway made, and has now been opened nearly twenty years. It is a most creditable concern, well made and well managed, and keeps better time than any line I know in the States.

The streets of Savannah, with one exception, are unpaved. This is not creditable to so ancient a city. In Iowa city, or St. Paul's, it might be pardoned; but here to drive or wade through sand a foot deep is too bad. When I remonstrated with an inhabitant, and suggested plank causeways, as stone is scarce, he objected, that they were already 'heavily taxed;' that the money was unprofitably squandered; and that they preferred their sandy streets to more ruinous taxation and corrupt expenditure. So these unpaved streets point to a yet deeper moral want.

Some twelve months ago there occurred in Savannah one of these events which shock our old-country ideas of law and order. A well-known gambler, Nat. Lewis, was playing billiards and drinking in a bar-room opposite this hotel. Late at night he demanded more drink from the barkeeper. The lad refused, alleging it was contrary to orders; on which Lewis drew a pistol and shot him through the head. For this he was tried, and, though three witnesses swore positively to his having committed the deed, and a fourth deposed that no one else could have done it, the jury not only acquitted him, but gave three cheers in honour of his acquittal. The jury, of course, was a packed one, the foreman being a brother-gambler of Nat. Lewis. And now this miscreant goes daily to the barber's shop adjoining the scene of crime, and sits down unblushingly to be shaved amongst decent men. In such a case as this, one is almost tempted to say that a touch of Lynch-law would not be out of place. Were an English community so unhappy as to have such an unhanged scoundrel amongst them, they would be very apt to take the halter into their own hands. That a jury can be packed, like that which acquitted Nathaniel Lewis, shows something wrong in the state of Georgian criminal law. This liability of juries to corruption is a serious objection to their use, and confirms my distrust of the institution when pushed to its extreme limit.

Lord Napier, I see, has been appointed Ambassador to the States. The appointment, I think, will prove a good one. He comes of a good stock, and is none the worse for being a Scotchman; for the Scotch are valued here, I really think, almost beyond their deserts. His station in society, too, is what it ought to be, and is a guarantee to the American nation that we have sent them one of our first people. What is wanted here is a first-rate gentleman, of good sense and manners, and of commanding influence; and none but one of the aristocracy can meet all those demands. A self-made man, at least a newly-made man, however respectable, has neither the weight nor the prestige, nor, finally, the social stamp which belong to an English nobleman. True, mere diplomacy is here out of place, and indeed is everywhere, I hope, out of date. What is wanted is plain truth and common sense, not finesse and Machiavellism, which, being interpreted, means simply —lying.

The more I consider of it, the more momentous does the American alliance seem to me. And by alliance I do not mean mere armed neutrality, a negative relation, but a true and hearty union and participation in the common end of the world's progress. The mind of the American people, I am persuaded, is ripe for such a friendly connexion between Old and Young England, if only we will take the necessary steps to gain their confidence and foster their affection. Before I came here, I had heard much of Anglo-phobia, and was prepared to meet in public and private with symptoms of jealousy and dislike of the English nation. But in this I have been most agreeably surprised. With few exceptions, such as a Hiberno-American Democratic tirade, or a Southern denunciation of British Abolitionism, I have met with nothing of the kind. There is, indeed, a certain jealousy of English interference; but this feeling is defensive, not offensive. All that the American asks of the Englishman is a fair and respectful recognition of his status as an equal in the ranks of civilization.

Conscious of his own growing power and intelligence, he resents as an insult the assumption of superiority: but meet him as an equal, and I am persuaded he would be our best and most faithful friend. The Americans are a warm-hearted, but a sensitive people. If we irritate their quick sensibilities, they will readily take offence : on the other hand, if we treat them cordially as relations, as friends, and, above all, as equals, we shall bind them to us as we can bind no other people. For at the bottom of their hearts, the Americans respect and love the English nation beyond all other nations. And well they may; for are they not bone of our bone and flesh of our flesh ?

Such being the case, it becomes a grave consideration with all who speak publicly to these two peoples how they speak. A heavy responsibility rests upon them; for, after all, the Press is the ruler of our day, and according to its wisdom or its foolishness will be the growth of international friendship or international hate. Words embitter even more than actions. The old revolutionary animosity has died out, and the feuds of last war have been forgotten; but Dickens' jibes still rankle in the American heart; and the sarcasms of the English press are bitterly resented. The Government has done its part towards a thorough alliance, an alliance in heart as well as in diplomatic form, by sending a worthy and accomplished gentleman to Washington. Now let the spiritual ruler, the Press, do its part, by speaking more generously and wisely; then we may look for the inauguration of the most powerful and beneficent alliance which has yet blessed the world— the alliance of the two great free nations of the world, with the common end of human progress— truly a Holy Alliance.

Apropos of American feeling towards Old England, I must tell you of an incident which I had from an eye-witness. This gentleman told me he was in the Boston Theatre when the news of the taking of Sebastopol arrived. Immediately the performance was stopped, the audience cheered, and demanded first, 'God save the Queen,' and then 'Yankee doodle.' There spoke out the real heartfelt feelings of our children. They like well enough to see our dictatorial arrogance snubbed, but at the bottom of their hearts they love John Bull—surly old rascal as he is.

Nothing is more remarkable than the contrast between North and South in point of newspapers. I do not, indeed, consider the amount of newspaper publishing as a correct or certain test of intelligence; but it is a very sure criterion of general activity, inasmuch as newspapers here are principally supported by advertisements. Instead of taking general statistics, let us compare Macon, in Georgia, and St. Paul's, in Minnesota. These two towns have each a population of about 10,000; but while Macon has only three weekly papers, St. Paul's boasts of four dailies and three weeklies.

The multiplicity of American newspapers has hardly, I think, received a sufficient explanation. Englishmen, for the most part, account for it by their cheapness; Americans, with pardonable self-complaisance, set it down to their superior intelligence. To me it seems the natural result of the social condition of the States. A new and sparse population must make known its presence, its needs, and its purposes; and this is best done through a public newspaper. In an old and thickly-peopled country, where everybody is everybody else's next-door neighbour, and knows precisely what he buys and sells, advertisements are rather a luxury than a necessary. But in a country with perhaps five or six inhabitants to the square mile, and where, probably, one-half of the population arrived by the last steamer, it is absolutely indispensable for the new-come Yankee to announce his advent and his benevolent intention of dispensing dry-goods, or giving 'cash for wheat,' or lecturing on spiritualism, or drawing teeth. Advertising is there a necessity of existence; and by advertisements the newspaper lives. Like circumstances have produced like results in Canada West and in Australia. Victoria has 350,000 inhabitants, and the *Melbourne Argus* has a circulation varying from 15,000 to 30,000 copies daily.

When the American paper really becomes a newspaper, the whole thing changes. It then becomes a political and literary institution, as well as a mere advertising sheet. The cost rises with the quality; and I believe the New York papers can hardly be afforded at the present price. They must charge higher if they are to give a better article. It will be curious if the price of the New York newspaper should be doubled, so soon after the vain attempt to bring down the London paper to the democratic penny.

LETTER XVII.

St. Augustine, Florida, 23rd February, 1857.

This is the oldest town in the States, having been founded in 1665 by the Spaniards. It retains few remains of its pristine state. An ancient fort, and a still more ancient gateway, are the only venerable mementoes of Spanish rule. The town itself is now a mere collection of wooden houses, very dull and uninteresting. The place is chiefly noted as a resort of invalids from the North, the climate of Florida having acquired some renown as a restorative for consumptive patients. In this respect its character is, I fear, better than it deserves. The climate is said to be very dry; but during the eight or ten days I have been in Florida, I have not seen one perfectly clear day. A fog, or at least a haze, generally prevails in the morning, and sometimes continues all day. There seem to be some exhalations which rise from earth or sea, and dim the atmosphere. Invalids used to go formerly to South

Carolina; then they advanced to Georgia; and now they flock to Florida. It is the same sad striving after health that sends people coughing over the South of Europe. There, too, they go further and further, as the faults of climate are, one after another, discovered—Montpelier, Nice, Rome, Naples; and now the poor consumptive must needs seek health or a grave at the Pyramids.

We came from Savannah to St. John's River by steam, coasting along the inland passages between the far-famed Sea Islands and the low, swampy coast. On the banks of the Savannah River we had an opportunity of seeing the rice plantations. Altogether, this is a miserable coast—low, sandy, desolate, and dangerous. There is not one good harbour between Chesapeake Bay and Mexico. Assuredly the Southern States of the Union, with their shoal coasts and bar harbours, were not intended by Nature for a maritime community. The division of labour between North and South was here clearly pointed out; and it says little for the political economy of the South if she fails to recognise the Divine intention.

Inland, for sixty miles, the eastern coast of the Southern States is an almost uninterrupted barren swamp. Nothing flourishes but the pine. It is beyond this desert margin that the rich soil commences, which has enriched the South with its luxuriant productions.

The St. John's is a beautiful and interesting river. It runs nearly North, so that, in ascending it, you are constantly going South, till at last you arrive at an almost tropical climate. It consists of a chain of lakes, connected by a river, which at last dwindles to a small stream. Near the entrance from the sea stands Jacksonville, the principal resort of invalids on the St John's; but there are also several hotels and boarding-houses on the banks of the river, the highest being Enterprise, about two hundred miles above Jacksonville. We ascended as high as Enterprise, and were amply rewarded for our trouble. The St. John's River differs from most other American rivers in having low banks, level with the water. The Lower Mississippi and Alabama have generally high banks of crumbling earth, whose constant 'caving in' gives the river a desolate and destructive look, and renders the water muddy and turbid. The St. John's, on the contrary, is more like an English river: its water is pure, and its banks are covered with beautiful overhanging trees, whose varied tints reflected in the bright water are extremely beautiful. There was the live oak, the palmetto, the cypress, and other fine trees, many of them evergreens. A characteristic feature is also a hanging moss, which grows here upon the trees, as also does the mistletoe. An occasional maple, with its red foliage, gives still greater richness and variety to the scene; and here and there groves of wild oranges, full of the glowing fruit, complete the picture. Then we had a variety of beautiful or curious birds to excite our interest: cranes, white and yellow, and herons, flapped lazily about the banks, or stalked among the reeds; wild turkeys were seen here and there, running through the woods, while paroquets flew overhead. Deer, too, were seen by those whose eyes were trained to wood-craft. I had to take these on credit.

But the inhabitant of the St. John's, *par excellence*, is the alligator; the number of these uncouth animals is astonishing. The hand of every man is against them, and they are slain by hundreds; but this havoc makes no perceptible inroad on their numbers. Our skipper killed seven or eight the day we ascended the river; and I was told that a party which went up the river beyond Enterprise, on a sporting excursion, some days before our arrival, killed with three guns seventy-five of these monsters. The river also swarms with fish, called here trout, but similar, I believe, to the black bass of the North; so that a sporting invalid might find both exercise and amusement at Enterprise in the pursuit of his craft. And if our sportsman wanted higher game than coons, or squirrels, or turkeys, he could at this moment take to stalking Red Indians. War with the Seminoles has again broken out, and is not likely soon to end. These Seminoles are originally Creeks; but, as the name is said to denote, they are runaways or outlaws from that once powerful tribe. The Seminoles are a very warlike race; they live in the almost impenetrable jungle of Florida, retreating, when hard pressed, to the 'Everglades,' inaccessible swamps, whither no white man can pursue them. Lying in the water, behind a log, they are invisible to a white man's eye, and, if need be, they can retreat to portions of the swamps to which they alone, of all living men, know the practicable access. Thus a handful of resolute men holds the southern portion of this peninsula against the whole military force of the Union. Pushed to extremity, the Red Man turns to bay; and a formidable enemy he then is. The warriors of the Seminoles are variously estimated at from 100 to 400 fighting men; the captain of the Volunteers at Enterprise thinks they are probably 250 strong; and this wretched fragment of a broken tribe defies an army. Billy Bow-legs, their old chief, says it will take three years to drive them out of Florida; and I think his estimate a modest one. Negotiations have, in the meantime, been opened; but the result is very doubtful. As to the spirit in which such 'negotiations' are conducted, I suspect that what De Tocqueville said twenty years ago may be said now with equal truth: 'It is impossible to destroy men with more respect for the laws of humanity.'

Meanwhile what is here called war is going on. An American family was murdered some weeks ago about thirty miles from Enterprise. The houses in the neighbourhood of Enterprise are now 'picketed,' *i.e.*, surrounded with palisades, and every settler is on the look-out. Companies of volunteers scour the country in what are called 'scouting parties;' but they can do little more than ensure the safety of the more settled parts of the country. They cannot bring the wary Indian to an open fight; neither can they hope to circumvent his vigilance. They harass and confine him, but that is all. Meanwhile they themselves are not a little harassed. Their captain confessed to me it was an irksome, thankless duty.

The only species of soldiers fit to cope with Indian warriors are Volunteers such as those I saw; and a rough lot they are. They are all inhabitants of these desolate, swampy forest lands; men who live chiefly by shooting and fishing; eked out, perhaps, with a little stealing. They are all good riflemen, and hold an Indian's life at about the value of a 'possum's. In all Indian wars, I am told (and by Americans), these white scamps are the aggressors. These Volunteers are all mounted; they will not serve on foot. They are paid twenty-eight dollars a month, and are found. They have no uniform, elect their own officers, and, as far as I could see, have little or no discipline among them. Saluting their officers is of course out of the question; and I was told one of them had the other day a regular shindy with his lieutenant. It must be a sorry business commanding such a ragamuffin crew.

Enterprise is the furthermost outpost of Southern civilization. It is not, as I supposed, a town, nor even a village; it is simply an hotel or boarding-house, with one or two adjoining workshops, and a wharf on the lake shore, at which the steamer lands her freight of dry goods and invalids. So it is with Picolata, Palatka, and other names doing duty as towns on the map of Florida. 'Enterprise' is really entitled to its name, and is interesting as a work of Yankee energy and decision. It is a well-built, well-furnished, comfortable hotel; a slip of high civilization planted on the very verge of savagism. The proprietor of hotel and steamer, Captain B——, is one of the most 'geniwine' specimens of Yankeedom I have come across. Judging by his name, I have no doubt he is a canny Scotch Lowlander by descent; but he could give me no information on this subject.

The Captain is far too busy with the present and future to bestow much thought on the past. B—— is quite a 'representative man' in this land of energy. He was born in Connecticut, but of course was too good a Yankee to remain at home. Some fifteen years ago he was an engineer on a steamer plying on the Charleston waters. Scraping together a few dollars, he purchased a small, worn-out steamer, and a crew of niggers; for you may be sure the Captain has no qualms on the subject of 'involuntary servitude'— always providing that it pays. So he went on his way rejoicing and money-making, till one day steamer, niggers, and captain were all blown into the air. The steamer went to shivers, no doubt being rotten to the core; the niggers, most of them, were blown to eternal smash; the Captain himself, who was up high in the wheel-house (on the upper deck), fell to the bottom of the vessel, broke his knee-pan, smashed his head, fractured sundry ribs, and scalded his whole side. But nothing could damp the energy of this untiring man. In a short time he was afloat again, in a better boat, and with a fresh crew; and soon after he was enabled to build the new hotel at 'Enterprise,' himself being landlord, skipper, pilot, and engineer, besides being the great alligator-killer of the St. John's. He is now reputed to be worth some 50,000 or 60,000 dollars. So it is that men here go ahead. But mark, it is your 'Northern men' who succeed, while the inhabitants of the place starve on precarious venison and scant potatoes, and curse Yankee luck and impudence.

The white inhabitants of Florida, as of all the Slave States more or less, constitute but two classes—the planters or rich class, and the poor class, variously denominated 'crackers,' 'white trash,' 'poor whites,' 'mean whites.' (N.B.—'Mean' is an Americanism for 'poor,' 'shabby.' They speak here of a 'mean' hotel, a 'mean' dinner, &c.) This social characteristic I consider the most remarkable and important feature of Southern civilization. It is only by keeping this clearly and constantly in mind, that we can at all understand the social and political organization of the South; and only thus can we duly appreciate the amazing difference between Northern and Southern development. The essence of Northern, as of English civilization, is the *progressiveness* of the labouring class, and the consequent rapid rise of an easy, affluent, well-educated, and law-abiding class, recruited from day to day, and from hour to hour, from the ranks of the lower class; the individuals raised being, from the nature of things, those most remarkable for energy, foresight, and self-reliance. Where men of industry, integrity, and intelligence can easily rise to a condition of independence, a nation is in a good condition, even though the improvident and sinful find their deserved portion of misery. On the contrary, where the labouring class forms a stereotyped, unprogressive caste, stagnation is the necessary characteristic of the community. The richer class may accumulate wealth, but there can be no dissemination of comfortable existence, no healthy growth of an independent, self-made, self-reliant class. Society is divided into a wealthy dominant class, and a wretched, ignorant class, at once insubordinate and servile. Such is essentially the social condition of the Slave States of this Union; and the cause obviously is the discouragement thrown over free labour by the institution of slavery. The white poor man disdains to 'work like a nigger;' he tries, instead, to live by his rifle or his fishing-rod. If these fail, he plants a few sweet potatoes, or loafs about the towns, doing odd jobs which have not the restraint of regular labour. He hates a trade; he will not be a smith or a carpenter, to compete with his rich neighbour's slaves, and probably be beaten by them. How, then, can such a man rise? How can he ever escape from his dependent and degraded position? How shall a man become a capitalist who will not first be a labourer? This is the secret of the 'white trash' of the Southern States. Hence the political rowdyism of slave communities, where an ignorant and idle mob, accustomed to the

PROGRESSIVENESS OF FREE SOCIETY. 223

use of deadly weapons, is constantly prowling about the country, and congregating in the cities. Hence, too, the want of material progress : there is neither efficient labour nor abundant capital. The very elements of civilization are wanting.

And yet this very charge of harsh and immovable social contrasts the defenders of the faith in slavery have the hardihood to bring against free society. The very contrary is the fact. It is the essence and the glory of free society that it gives power to the citizen to raise himself. There are no stereotyped classes, no castes, in free society. On the contrary, its most characteristic feature is that blending of conditions, that gradual shading of one class into another, that makes it easy for any citizen of ordinary energy and virtue to elevate himself both socially and morally. Who are our middle classes? Who inhabit the streets and squares of Liverpool and New York, and the villas and cottages that line our shores and ornament our river-banks, alike in 'Old' and 'New' England? Who own our stores, and ships, and factories? Almost without exception they are self-made men, or the sons of such; labourers turned capitalists; employers who but yesterday were employed. The whole mass of society is rising; only the dregs fall down into our wynds and alleys. And these 'dregs' the wiseacres of the pulpit and the press pick out as legitimate specimens of our industrial system! And slave-owners and slave-editors and slave-preachers shout—' Behold, free society is a failure!'

'Florida is the Paradise of an idle man.' So said a Georgian gentleman to me, and I believe it is pretty near the truth. The climate is mild and equable, so a man need not be particular as to house or clothing. Shooting and fishing will easily supply him with food; and, if he wishes to be very luxurious, by scratching the ground he may have a few sweet potatoes, or a little Indian corn. Land has been bought in Florida at a cent per acre; but for that matter our 'cracker' need not buy land at all—he may squat and take his chance of being turned out. It is not every one who would wish to dispossess a 'cracker,' so long as the cracker had his rifle and an ounce of lead. Having thus established himself on land of his own, or a patch of Uncle Sam's, he may also, if he pleases, become a grazier at small expense of labour or money. Having bought, borrowed, or stolen a few head of cattle, he simply marks them and turns them out into the woods. In the spring he collects the calves and puts his brand upon them; and this, absolutely, is all the care or trouble he takes, except catching them when a purchaser appears. In this way some of these Florida squatters accumulate vast herds of cattle, without any exertion on their part. Nay, so lazy and careless of comfort are they, that I am assured there are men in these forests owning 5000 or 6000 head of cattle who have not even milk to their coffee; 'and that,' said Captain B——, 'I call pretty damned shiftless.'

This easy, lazy, good-for-nothing kind of life is very common among all the 'poor whites' of the seaboard Slave States, but it seems to have reached its climax in Florida. Here the plentiness of game and cheapness of land attract many idlers from the neighbouring States; and many a man squats in Florida who has made other States too hot to hold him. Florida is the Alsatia of the Union. Some parts of the interior, indeed, are occupied by respectable planters, but this superior kind of settlement goes on slowly. Titles to the land are somewhat doubtful; the climate in the swamps is sickly; and then the vicinity of the Indians is a nuisance to the planter, not only on account of danger from attacks, but from the facilities it affords to the escape of slaves. A railway is now making across the isthmus, but with negro navvies railroad-making is slow work.

Florida has been a State since 1845. Its area is 59,268 square miles; its population (in 1850) 87,445, being only 1.48 inhabitants to the square mile. It possesses 349,049 acres of improved land, against 1,246,240 unimproved. Its principal production is cotton, but it stands last in the rank of cotton culture, its proportion of the whole cotton crop in 1850 being only 1.85 per cent. Altogether, Florida is a poor place, with little to attract either the capitalist or the labourer. The soil in general is sterile; indeed, Florida may be said to be one-half swamp and the other half sand. Tangled 'hammocks,' or jungles, alternate with 'pine-barrens;' much is mere morass. The coasts, surrounded with sandy shoals or coral reefs, and with dangerous bar harbours, afford no advantages for external commerce; while the interior, where fertile, is swampy and unhealthy. Barring a few districts, suited to the production of cotton and sugar, Florida is no land of promise for the Anglo-Saxon pioneer. For generations to come it must be a wilderness, the hunting-ground of the Seminole, and the haunt of 'crackers' and alligators.

When reviewing the state and prospects of Florida, one is naturally led to compare it with Minnesota, the one the Northern, the other the Southern Pole of American civilization. The contrast is striking; they do not differ more in their geographical situation than in their social condition. In the Free State all is bustle and animation, everywhere there is the din of industry and the buzz of hopeful expectation, while week by week a stream of some thousand emigrants, the very flower of the Union, is pouring into the State, bringing with them arts, and energy, and hope, and dollars. Here, in this poor Slave State, all is silence and stagnation; no cities are rising on the river-banks, no wharves are piled with goodly merchandise, no labouring man seeks here a home; those only come who will not labour, sluggards who are satisfied to share with the Red Man the beasts of the forest and the fowls of the air.

LETTER XVIII.

CHARLESTON, 28th February, 1857.

DURING the whole of my stay at Charleston, the pavement opposite the hotel has been lumbered with boxes of dry-goods, sometimes a hundred at a time. This disregard of police regulations is universal in America. You cannot walk out in any city of the Union without having the fact painfully impressed on your shins. Everywhere the public pavement is regarded as a convenience for the adjoining stores, rather than as a thoroughfare for passengers. Even in the most crowded parts of Broadway it is nothing strange to see a dozen hogsheads, or a score of packing-boxes, encumbering the pavement. In St. Louis, I noticed a newly-painted carriage standing on the pavement of a principal street, and attached to it a ticket, with a peremptory 'Hands off.' A nuisance so universal must be deeply grounded in the national character. The root of the evil I take to be that confusion so prevalent in the American mind between true liberty and individual licence. The Englishman intuitively recognises the subordination of every individual will to an overruling higher will. That authority he embodies in a mystical personage which he calls the 'Public.' Were such an outrage on public rights as I have described above to occur in London, the whole community would be up in arms. Half the street would be 'writing to the *Times*'—Civis, Nemo, Aliquis, and a whole alphabet of indignant capitals, would proclaim the wrongs of injured Cockneydom. Here, on the contrary, nobody cares twopence for the 'Public.' Everybody looks upon himself as an infinitesimal sovereign, and tolerates the despotism of his next-door tyrant, on condition of carrying out unmolested his own little despotisms in his turn.

From all the inquiries I can make, the money-cost of free and slave labour at the South, at this moment, seems to be very nearly on a par, and the preference for the one over the other arises either from local circumstances, or the inclination of the employer. On the Georgian railway Irish labourers were lately employed; now they have slaves. The American railway officials prefer the latter, but only, I suspect, because Irishmen refuse to be driven. On the Mississippi and Alabama rivers Irish and negroes are employed indiscriminately. On the St. John's only slaves are employed; few or no Irish go so far South. The captain of the Charleston steamer told me he paid eighteen dollars per month for slaves, and sixteen and seventeen for Irish; but he prefers the former, 'for,' said he, naively, 'if an Irishman misbehaves, I can only send him ashore.' The alternative in the case of the nigger was 'understood.' Then, as to waiters,—at the St. Charles Hotel, New Orleans, they are all Irish; at the Pulaski House, Savannah, they are all slaves; at the Charleston Hotel, Charleston, they are partly Irish and partly slaves. The experience of these three leading towns and principal rivers of the South proves that, in mere money-cost, there can be little to choose between free and slave labour in the South; and that the preference of the former to the latter is generally dictated by the habit of the employer, to expect unconditional submission from the labourers he employs.

But this, we must remember, is not a fair comparison of the cost of free and slave labour. Few Irish, comparatively, come to the South. There is a natural aversion in the free labourer to put himself on a footing with a slave. Free labour, therefore, is scarce and dear in the Slave States, and to form a fair comparison of the cost of free and slave labour, we must take the former as it exists in the Northern States, and contrast it with the slave labour of the

FREE AND SLAVE LABOUR. 231

South. Here the testimony of Olmsted is very valuable' as he is not only an accurate observer, but was himself an employer of agricultural labourers in the State of New York. In Eastern Virginia the average hire of slaves, at the time of his visit, was 120 dollars, with board, lodging, and clothing. The average hire of free labourers in New York, at the same period, he puts down at 120 dollars for Americans, and 108 for Irish or Germans, in both cases with board and lodging, but without clothing. The comparison of free and slave labour, therefore, would stand thus, board being included in both cases:—

	Dols.	Dols.
1 Irish Labourer	—	108
1 Slave	120	
Clothing, say	20	
	—	140
Difference in favour of Free Labour		32

less what may be saved off the board of the slave.

Such is the mere money view of the matter, and it is striking enough. But in estimating the cost of labour, an important element of calculation is the efficiency of the labourer. Now here there can be but one opinion, that voluntary labour is infinitely more efficient than compulsory labour. The most trustworthy opinions I can procure, agree in estimating one free labourer as at least equal to two slaves. Whatever may be the exact proportion of efficiency between free and slave labour, there are certain facts which prove that it must be great. One of these is the enforced use of mules instead of horses, wherever their management is intrusted to slaves, it being confessed by slave-owners that horses cannot stand the neglect and ill-treatment they necessarily undergo from slaves. Another material proof of the inferiority of slave-labour is the clumsiness and heaviness of the implements used in slave husbandry. Tools such as are used by the intelligent free labourers of the North, and which enable them to do a larger quantity of work, are quite unfit for slave use: 'They would not,' says Olmsted, 'last a day in a Virginian corn-field.'

One of the most important drawbacks to slave-labour is the loss by sickness, real or pretended. If a free labourer falls sick, the loss falls on himself, except so far as his employer may be actuated by purely charitable motives. Pretended illness is out of the question, as it would be at his own cost. With the slave it is very different. If he is really sick, you lose his labour; and if you suspect him of feigning illness and force him to work, you may lose him altogether, not to mention the inhumanity of the proceeding. If he feigns illness, you are equally at a loss how to act, not knowing whether he is really ill, or merely 'playing 'possum.' If it is bad with male slaves, it is still worse with females. Their ailments are more numerous, and, under certain interesting circumstances, their health may be made the pretext of any amount of evasion. In such cases, a poor distracted planter is absolutely at the mercy of the old negro nurse.

The nature of agricultural operations in the South has hitherto been compatible with the coarse labour of slaves. So long as only the fertile lands were cultivated, comparatively little labour was needed, and that of the rudest kind. Then slave-labour was available; and, although dear, it did not entirely absorb the high profits of fruitful virgin soils. But the case alters when, with the progress of society, inferior soils are called into cultivation. Then labour enters more and more largely into the cost of agricultural production, and not only more labour, but better labour, is required. From being the coarsest of human industries, agriculture rises to the dignity of an art, and finally, of a science. Every operation is directed by thought, and must be executed with intelligence and care. Here the rude muscular power of the poor negro is quite misplaced. Slave-labour may do while the hoe is the noblest implement of industry, but it is quite out of place among the refined processes, complicated machinery, and expensive stock of a high-farming establishment.

Now, in the Frontier corn-growing Slave States

this change is already taking place. The necessity for a better mode of culture is already felt, and tracts are written and agricultural associations formed to stimulate farmers to adopt more scientific methods. But neither pamphlets nor premiums can give the one thing needful, cheap and efficient labour. The need for 'improvement' is visible to all men. With exhausted fields, and an increasing population calling aloud for food, the husbandman would gladly use better methods; but all his efforts are paralysed by a system which affords him only dear and inefficient negro labour, and at the same time shuts out the cheaper and better labour, which his competitors in the neighbouring Free States have at their disposal. Let us have patience. The beginning of the end is at hand. The need is too pressing, and the interest too evident, that men's eyes should long be closed to so simple a truth.

Even the present cost of slave-labour, then, is preparing a revolution; but there is no reason to suppose that the gradual increase in the value of slaves, which has been going on for many years, has reached its maximum. This rise in the price of negroes is evidently caused by the demand for slave-labour outstripping the annual increase of the slave population, and this movement is likely to continue. And it is well it should be so: every dollar added to the price of the slave is a nail in the coffin of slavery.

Were the South an isolated community, she might be slow to recognise her true interest in the matter of slave-labour; but with the progressive North in her immediate neighbourhood, competing with her in industry, and striving with her for power, it is inconceivable that she should not soon awaken to the true cause of her laggard development. With a larger territory, she has not a third of the population nor (barring her slaves) of the property of the Union; every day she is falling further and further behind her more vigorous rival. If she would not soon become a mere appendage to the powerful and brilliant Republic of the North, she must cast off the incubus that now oppresses her energies. Southern writers and speakers admit and deplore the want of enterprise and progress in their country; but as yet they fail to attribute this deficiency to its true cause. They blame their so-called dependence on Northern manufactures; they blame the public for not patronizing Southern literature, the capitalist for not making Southern railways, and Government for not subsidizing Southern steam-ships; in short, they blame everybody and everything except the right thing,—their darling 'domestic institution.' Yes, slavery makes the South weak and poor; and if she would not be economically and politically obliterated, she must get rid of it one way or another. The South must extinguish slavery, or slavery will extinguish the South.

LETTER XIX.

CHARLESTON, 3rd March, 1857.

THE South, I feel sure, if she would maintain her place in the race of nations, must modify her social system: she cannot advance with the clog of slavery at her foot. And this I say in no unkindly spirit, but rather with the most heartfelt wishes for her prosperity, and a perfect appreciation of the difficulties of her position. Still the fact is there, stern and immovable—admitted, too, by the South in her secret heart, that slavery is a curse to the land. What, then, shall be done?

That is a question which the South herself must answer. She must work out her own deliverance. She only has the minute and local knowledge necessary for success; and she only has an overpowering interest to spur her on. Any external meddling can only do harm; it would only irritate and perplex. Nevertheless, there are some general considerations connected with this question which not only may be recognised by strangers, but which may present themselves most clearly to those who look on the matter calmly, and from a distance. They may see, on the one hand, that some schemes are essentially futile or objectionable, and, on the other, that there are certain general principles, which must be steadily kept in view in any mode of action that promises success.

One thing seems clear to me: the time for a wholesale deportation of the negro population has gone by. You cannot transport a people four million strong. The futility of such an idea is clearly proved by the ludicrously inadequate efforts of the 'American Colonization Society.' Between 1820 and 1856, inclusive, that society sent to Liberia 9502 persons. In the same period the increase of the slave population of the Union (supposing the average rate to have continued during the last six years) has been 1,999,527; so that Liberia has only absorbed the odd thousands, leaving an increase of nearly two millions to be disposed of. Even if practicable, colonization would only be justifiable with the full consent of the negroes. They were brought hither against their will, and should not be sent hence but of their own good pleasure. Undoubtedly they have a right to be heard in the matter. Now, with rare exceptions, I believe negroes dislike going to Liberia. Slaves themselves have told me so. They have been brought up among whites; they are accustomed to lean on the superior race, and in many cases have a strong attachment to them. They love the country, too, where they were born and bred, and which contains all their associations and old memories. For the negro, therefore, colonization is but a name for banishment.

Neither, on the other hand, can the whites spare the blacks. A negro exodus would ruin the South. The black race constitutes the sole available labouring class. By the last census there were in the Southern States 6,222,418 whites, 3,204,313 slaves, and 228,128 free coloured people. Leaving the latter out of view, we have 34 per cent. of the population consisting of negro slaves, by whom all the coarse labour and much of the mechanical work of the community are performed. How could the want of this great working-class be supplied? Who would till the fields when the 'nigger' was gone? Who would grind in the Philistine mill if the Ethiopian Samson were away? The country would starve. It would be a question, not of prosperity, but of existence. It is vain now to talk of the removal of the negro population. The white and the black races are united for better or worse. They must work and strive together, or they must go down to ruin together.

DIFFICULTIES OF EMANCIPATION.

The time, too, for any general scheme of emancipation and remuneration of the slave-owner is past and gone. The interests at stake are too vast and various, opinions are too conflicting, and feelings are too hostile, to afford the slightest chance of combined national action for slave-emancipation. The present money-cost of slaves is, of itself, an insurmountable difficulty. Major Beard, the great slave-auctioneer of New Orleans, (a most competent authority,) estimates the present average value of the slaves of the United States at 700 dollars each. Now, 4,000,000 slaves at 700 dollars, or 150*l.*, amounts to 600,000,000*l.*; equal to three-fourths of the national debt of Great Britain: a sum which assuredly will not be forthcoming for any scheme of negro emancipation. It is not by legislative or political, still less by philanthropic action, that this plague can be stayed. If slavery is to cease, it must be through economical influences. The interests of the slave-owner must free the slave, if he is to be freed at all.

Further, any regeneration of the social state of the South, to be satisfactory in its results, must be a work of time. The lessons of St. Domingo and Jamaica must not be forgotten. The safety of the whites and the elevation of the blacks must be alike provided for. Any sudden and wholesale manumission would be at once dangerous for the master and disastrous for the slave. The deliverance of the South must be a growth—a gradual progress towards enlightened and efficient industry. No philanthropic juggle, no legislative sleight-of-hand, can transform a horde of helots into a nation of noble workers. The social organization of the South can only be effectually bettered by a system, which will elevate the character and unfold the capacity of the slave, at the same time that it provides for his political enfranchisement. The elevation and the emancipation of the negro must go hand in hand.

Now, the ennoblement of the slave can only be effected by reversing those influences which have degraded him. High motives of action must be substituted for base ones. Free-will must rule instead of force, and voluntary contract take the place of the cowhide. By giving the slave an interest in his labour, we shall stimulate his energies, and raise him in his own esteem. His labour will cease to be a degrading and irksome drudgery. The idea of property, with all its civilizing influences, will be awakened within him, and the consciousness of voluntary exertion will gradually lead to that development of the power of will which lies at the root of all human ennoblement. So long as the negro is ruled by force, no forty-parson power of preaching can elevate his character. It is a savage mockery to prate of duty to one in whom we have emasculated all power of will. We cannot make a moral intelligence of a being we use as a mere muscular power. But let us treat the negro as a man, and we restore to him the consciousness of a human will. When we respect his rights, he will feel his duties. And so, gradually, the negro slave will rise from his abasement: he will work harder, more intelligently, and more cheerfully; he will become a better worker, and a nobler man; his self-reliance, self-control, and self-respect will grow apace, and at length he will approve himself fit for freedom and worthy of citizenship.

But how shall this regeneration be worked out? How are these general principles to be carried into practical effect? That is a problem for the South to solve; strangers may point to the end, but it is for the men of the South to devise the means. Nevertheless, there are facts already to be noted in the economy of the Slave States which indicate a dim consciousness of the course to be pursued, and which need only to be systematized in a bold and intelligent spirit to bring about the desired end. The instinct of self-interest has already taught the slave-owner, that he can accomplish more by a judicious admixture of the stimulus of hope applied to slave-labour than by a sole reliance on the principle of fear. Intelligent masters have found that with negroes, as with other men, interest is a more powerful instrument than force, and that slaves may be induced to do more and better work than they can be 'driven' to do. In the tobacco-factories of Richmond the slaves work hard for extra pay. So the lumber-men of the dismal swamp, cutting shingles by the piece, and the slave fishermen of North Carolina, working for wages, labour cheerfully and well. So it is, too, where piece-work has been adopted on plantations, allowing the negro to labour in over-hours for his own benefit; as also where slaves are allowed to hire out their own labour, paying a fixed sum to their owners, and putting to their own uses whatever they earn over and above. Wherever such rational methods are adopted, the old complaint of negro 'rascality' dies away. Nay, we are told that where slaves are allowed to profit in exact proportion to their exertions, 'the harder the work you give them to do, the better they like it.'

Even with free labour the amount of work done is greatly increased, and the efficiency of the labourer heightened, by accurately proportioning reward to exertion, by means of 'piece-work.' Now, there seems no good reason why the principle of piece-work should not be applied to that condition of *quasi* freedom, which is here proposed as the precursor of emancipation, and the best preparation for entire freedom. In all the higher occupations of slavery, such as mechanical trades, it would seem a simple arrangement that a certain portion, however small, of the slave's production should be allotted to himself, so that his exertions should have the constant stimulus of interest.

Whatever property the slave acquires by any of the means indicated, he should be permitted, nay encouraged, to use in purchasing his own freedom, and, still more so, that of his children. In this way the young would be trained up to a rational use of liberty; and only those adults would be enfranchised who had proved their fitness for freedom by the very act of self-emancipation. Such a scheme, you may remember, was long ago sketched by Michael Scott in *Tom Cringle's Log*.

There is, indeed, one weighty objection to self-emancipation, as to all emancipation, which must not be overlooked, namely, the repugnance of the white population to live on terms of equality with a community of freed-men. They feel affection for the negro as a dependent and protected race, but they cannot brook the idea of equality with those whom they have so long regarded as inferiors. A drunken Kentuckian expressed this feeling coarsely but pithily, in my hearing: 'I like a nigger,' said he, 'but I hate a damned free nigger.' So deep-seated is this feeling, that De Tocqueville considered it an insurmountable bar to emancipation; and even Jefferson thought the difficulty could only be got over by removing the emancipated slaves *en masse* from the country, and importing free labourers in their stead. His plan was, that, after being emancipated and 'brought up, at the public expense, to tillage, arts, or sciences, according to their geniuses, &c.,' the negroes should be 'colonized to such places as the circumstances of the time should render most proper,' and that, ' at the same time, an equal number of white people, from other parts of the world, should be sent for, and induced, by proper encouragements, to migrate into Virginia.' When Jefferson proposed his plan of emancipation, there were probably some half-million slaves in the States (the number by the census of 1790 was 697,397). Even such a number would be difficult enough to deal with; but with four millions of human beings the idea of colonization is simply absurd. Such an exodus would require a new Moses and new miracles.

The truth is, the presence of the negro population in the Southern States is now a matter of necessity. And this necessity is the best antidote to negro antipathy. When the Southerner finds that he must emancipate his negroes to avoid ruin, and that his freed-men can neither be removed nor replaced, he will be reconciled to an inevitable fate; he will put his prejudice in his pocket, and learn to respect the labourer whose destiny is inseparably bound up with his own. Time will soften asperities of feeling, and just men will gradually rise to a fair appreciation of their liberated bondsmen. In the North the feelings of the whites towards free negroes have been greatly softened of late years, and there cannot be a doubt that, with time, a similar change would take place in the generous-hearted South.

The gradual nature of self-emancipation, too, would give time for prejudice to subside. The increase of freedom would be too imperceptible to be offensive. Emancipation would be graduated, not only according to the character of the slaves, but according to the geographical position of the States. Henceforth, as hitherto, freedom must proceed from North to South. If emancipation is to be at all, it must begin in the frontier, or corn-growing Slave States. There the proportion of slaves is smallest, and there slave-labour is least profitable. Then, the superior intelligence of the slaves in the frontier States, and the close vicinity of the Free States, makes slave-holding troublesome, precarious, and costly. With so many reasons in favour of social reform in the frontier Slave States, and with so few difficulties in the way, it is inconceivable that an intelligent and spirited people will long hesitate to undertake the work. And when they do, a marvellous success will reward their efforts. The direct effect of a judicious and practical system of negro emancipation would be to double the efficient power of the slave population, and greatly increase the value of the land. The five frontier States contained, in 1850, 863,589 slaves; so that, supposing an increased efficiency of only fifty per cent., the measure in question would be equal to an accession of nearly half a million of labouring inhabitants to these States. Another immediate and certain effect would be a large increase in the value of land. The average value of an acre of land in the Free States (exclusive of California) is 20.84 dollars; in the five frontier Slave States, containing much of the most fertile land in the Union, with easy access to the best markets, the average value is only 12.49 dollars. It cannot certainly be thought extravagant to presume that a successful substitution of free for slave labour would add at least 5 dollars to the value of the acre. Now, these five States contain 58,425,223 acres, which, at 5 dollars, would amount to 292,226,115 dollars. The direct results, then, of a judicious system of self-emancipation to those five States may be set down as equal to an increase of half a million of labourers, and an addition of nearly 300 millions of dollars to the value of land.

But this gain, enormous as it is, sinks into insignificance when compared with the indirect benefits which must inevitably accrue from the rush of capital and labour that would take place from without. At present the natural flow of immigration is dammed back from these States by slavery; but remove that obstruction, and they would be overflowed with the wealth and population, not only of the North, but of Europe. Then the rich soil, great mineral resources, and glorious climate of these favoured lands would have their due effect. Marvellous as has been the progress of the Northern States of the Union, it is, I am persuaded, nothing compared with that which is in store for the South, so soon as she shall have the virtue and wisdom to remodel her institutions in the spirit of freedom.

South Carolina is the centre of Southern aristocracy. The average number of slaves held by South Carolinian slave-owners is 15.04; in Virginia it is only 8.58. The average size of her farms is 541 acres; while the general average of the Slave States, not including Texas, is 344. Her wealth and power, however, are not in proportion to the aristocratic pretensions of her society. The average value of land in the Slave States is 7.81 dollars per acre; in South Carolina it appears to be only 5.08 dollars, according to the census tables; and even this is suspected to be founded on grossly exaggerated returns. In point of population, South Carolina, in 1820, held the eighth rank among the States of the Union; thirty years after, during which time the cotton culture made so vast a spring, she had sunk to the fourteenth place. In 1820, the ratio of the population of South Carolina to the total population of the United States was 5.22; in 1850 it had fallen to 2.88. The immigration to South Carolina has been less than to any other State, with the single exception of North Carolina, the whole population born out of the State being, in the case of the former, 7.69, and of the latter, 4.22. On the other hand, the slave population of the State is large, and rapidly increasing. From 1840 to 1850, while the white population only increased 5.97 per cent., the slave population increased 17.71 per cent. The proportion of the slaves to the white population, which in 1830 was 54.2 per cent., in 1850 had risen to 57.5 per cent., being 18.1 per cent. higher than the average of the ten cotton-growing States, and 40.4 per cent. higher than the average of the five frontier Slave States. It is difficult to understand, how men can shut their eyes to the evident connexion between slavery and stagnation which these facts indicate, and how they should persist, to their own ruin, in hugging so fatal a delusion as the belief in the profitableness of enforced labour.

The political importance of South Carolina is dwindling with the declining prosperity of her people. The number of her representatives has fallen, in thirty years, from nine to six, notwithstanding the increase of her negro population. Were only the white population represented in the same proportion as are the Free States, South Carolina would have only three representatives. The proud old Palmetto State would send to Congress the same number of representatives as the upstart Wisconsin, a State not nine years old! If the South is serious in her desire to uphold her political influence, she must take the necessary means for increasing her wealth and population. It is vain for her to seek to accomplish this object by any combinations of political jugglery. No party manœuvres can uphold the power of a community, whose industry is paralysed by a social gangrene. Hitherto the aristocratic prestige of the South has given her a political influence, not warranted by her material power. Descent and hereditary station have a power over men's minds which is founded, more or less, on reality. But, at best, this influence is shadowy and passing; it cannot long survive the material superiority that gave it birth.

Here, as elsewhere, the aristocratic element must give way to the industrial. Old family names are dying out; new men and new interests are rising into prominence and power. Henceforth the South can only retain her political influence by the wise and vigorous development of her resources.

Charleston is finely situated on an angle formed by two magnificent rivers. I was disappointed, however, by the general appearance of this capital of the South. On the whole, it has somewhat of a poverty-struck look. There are one or two good streets, but even in them shabby wooden houses alternate with the finer buildings. Even in the back streets the shops, with a few exceptions, are singularly mean, and many of them such as would be thought shabby in an ordinary Scotch village. The want of capital is painfully apparent in the busy portions of the town; the principal streets are paved—the first paved streets we have seen since leaving New Orleans—but in the suburbs the sand turns up again. There are many large imposing houses, with pillars and verandahs, no doubt the residences of the aristocratic Southerners; the rest of the habitations are small and poor-looking. There seems no middle class; only rich and poor. In the streets are to be seen more equipages than usual in the States, but they are far from handsome, and, in some cases, very paltry; many of them have only one horse. The only appearance of style about these equipages is the almost universal presence of two negro servants, many of them dressed in livery. Charleston boasts one palmetto-tree, standing enclosed with an iron railing, near the post-office. This, I believe, is now the sole palmetto in the 'Palmetto State.' With the rejuvenescence which, I trust, awaits her, perhaps her palmettos may again flourish and abound. This, and better growths, I sincerely wish her.

LETTER XX.

CHARLESTON, 8th March, 1857.

BY far the most imposing edifice in Charleston is the Orphan Hospital. The massive grandeur of its sandstone architecture towers conspicuous among the wooden shanties with which it is surrounded, and the stranger is at a loss to guess to what purpose this palatial anomaly can be devoted. The Charleston citizen hastens, with no small complacence, to inform him that it is an institution for orphan children. As in duty bound, I visited this imposing charity, and found it physically unimpeachable, clean, airy, elegant. As to its purpose and moral bearing, that, I confess, remained very questionable to me. By the original act of incorporation, which dates back so far as 1783, the obligation was imposed on the Orphan-house of 'providing for the poor, and maintaining and educating poor orphan children;' but an additional ordinance, passed in 1790, provided that it should also support and educate the children of 'poor, distressed, and disabled parents, who are unable to support and maintain them.' This ordinance has been interpreted to include 'foundlings.' The last report (1855) of the Institution says:—'Its ear has been attentive to the tale of sorrow and woe, and its portals open for the admission of the orphan, the foundling, and the offspring of poverty.' On the next page the Report rises into the sublime of sentimental bathos, thus:—' Who can describe the agony with which another mother pinned to the frock of her deserted daughter, a few days old, this inscription, and caused the infant, in a basket, to be laid at midnight at the door of the porter's lodge:—' It is desired that this child should be placed in the Orphan-house, upon the fund in the hands of the City Council for the benefit of foundlings.''

Thus an institution mistakenly founded for the relief of orphans (a class naturally limited) is first extended to the children of the improvident, and then to those of the sinful. It was absurd to take children from log-huts, rear them in a palace, and return them as apprentices to wooden shanties; but to treat thus magnificently the progeny of the reckless and sinful, is to encourage improvidence, and hold out a premium on prostitution. Thus, with the natural proclivity of error, unreasoning charity degenerates into worse and worse forms of evil; and an institution which begins simply as an absurdity, ends by becoming a social nuisance. America should take warning by England, where perverted charity has probably done more to debase the poor than all other causes combined. Our poor-laws and our 'charitable trusts' are a standing lesson to all nations. It is especially needful that Americans should guard themselves against this specious folly at this moment, when they are so rapidly accumulating wealth, and the temptation is great to earn vulgar applause by public donations. The 'golden opinions' thus cheaply bought will prove to be a base counterfeit, and a wiser generation will curse the vanity of the charitable blockheads, who sought to ennoble their memories by a costly degradation of the poor. On this score our clergy and other teachers of the people have much to learn. It behoves the Christian minister, in our day, to study scientifically the nature of charity, and to beware how he inculcates the Mahommedan virtue of indiscriminate almsgiving.

In the lower part of Charleston there is a magnificent structure rising near the river, of beautiful Massachusetts granite. This beautiful and substantial edifice is to be—the Custom-house; that is, if it can be built before the tariff falls. It seems a curious retribution, that the Americans have been prompted to build up such striking and lasting monuments of their own blunders. When Protection shall long be numbered with the follies that have been, these granite evidences of economical ignorance will remain to reprove the nation that built them.

Another imposing edifice in Charleston is the 'Military Academy,' with which is connected a subsidiary 'Academy' in Columbia. These military and other 'colleges' are pregnant symptoms of the aristocratic, semi-feudal character of South Carolinian society. The only point in which South Carolina takes the lead among the other States is in the provision made for the education of the higher classes. The disproportion of the funds devoted to the education of the rich and the poor, in South Carolina, will appear best by comparing the educational appropriations of that State with those of Massachusetts. The comparison stands thus:—

	Massachusetts.	S. Carolina.
	Dollars.	Dollars.
Colleges, (Annual Income)	107,901	104,790
Public Schools ,,	1,006,795	200,600

In Massachusetts, therefore, one-tenth of the whole expense is devoted to 'Colleges;' in South Carolina, one-half. If the South Carolina aristocrats neglect education on the whole, at least they do not neglect the interest of their 'order.' It is true that in the Military Academy the 'State supplies to the beneficiary cadet all his expenses,' — *i. e.*, there is a class of eleemosynary cadets admitted to the academy; but who pays their 'expenses?' The State; and who is the State? Why, the taxpayers. The South Carolinian lords give a dole out of the people's taxes to a certain number of the people's sons, under the name of a military education, and then take credit for the liberality of their institutions. Well might a late governor of South Carolina say in his message to the Legislature :—'Education has been provided by the Legislature but for one class of the citizens of the State, which is the wealthy class.'

One evening in Charleston we heard an interesting lecture from Mr. Hayne, a young gentleman of an aristocratic South Carolina family, who has devoted himself to literature, and takes this method of impressing his views on his countrymen. Mr. Hayne is a favourable specimen of that refined class in the South, to which hereditary ease and affluence have given birth. There can be no doubt that, with the progress of industrial development, both in the North and South, this class will be rapidly reinforced, and that through their influence a corresponding increase will take place in refinement and substantial knowledge. Mr. Hayne himself is evidently a man of fine abilities and good scholarship. He has sat at the feet of Coleridge, and, in common with most persons trained in that school, attributes more power to the fancy than to the sterner faculties of the soul. Like all men of this idiosyncrasy, he is at war with the material tendencies of the age, which he thinks can only be counteracted by a stronger infusion of the æsthetical element into national education. This dread of an overwhelming materialism, which perturbs so many minds, lay and clerical, on both sides of the Atlantic, seems to me altogether unfounded. The material results of modern civilization cover the land, and are evident to the bodily eye, while its spiritual creations escape our notice. Secretaries of State sum up, by bale and barrel, the annual products of material industry, and trumpet them forth to the world in congratulatory statistics; but who shall measure the forces or estimate the creations of the invisible spirit? Nevertheless, to me it seems manifest that there is a strong under-current of spiritual life in the society of our day, and that the most marked characteristic of this society is a reaction from the blank materialism of the last century. What are the writings of our best authors but vehement protests against an unspiritual existence? What was it but this spiritual movement that shook the dry bones of our churches? Coleridge, Carlyle, and Emerson were but organs, thrown out by the fermentation of their respective churches, to give articulate utterance to this impulsion, and to minister to the spiritual needs of the people. Mr. Hayne, and those who think with him, may take comfort. Spirituality is not dead; the steam-engine has not supplanted the soul.

The most interesting portion of Mr. Hayne's lecture, for me, was that in which he applied his ideas to the political circumstances of the South. I was never more impressed with the agitated state of the Southern mind, than when I saw this refined young man carried away at once by his feelings, and the calm scholar transformed in a moment into the violent politician. A nation must be strangely perturbed when even its calmest spirits are thus agitated; when neither study, nor retirement, nor refinement can ward off the contagion of the epidemic violence. The lamest part of Mr. Hayne's address was his conclusion. While denouncing *Uncle Tom's Cabin* as a gross libel, he yet admitted its great power, and poured scorn on all attempted retorts in the same vein. A higher literary power, he said, must be evoked to repel this fierce attack; and the means of doing so was a more generous and enlightened patronage of literary talent. But such expedients cannot answer. The talent that can cope with hostile genius needs no patronage; and a talent that would stoop to be patronized will hardly cope successfully with genius. In literary as in industrial development, the South has but one effectual means of forwarding her progress, and that is to knock off the shackles that impede her.

In the course of his lecture, Mr. Hayne alluded to a curiosity of literature in the history of *Uncle Tom*, which was new to me. *Uncle Tom*, it seems, was published originally in a Washington newspaper, and excited no attention. It was only when it issued as a coarse and cheap reprint from a Boston book-store, that it flashed like a meteor over Europe and America. There is luck, it would seem, even in genius.

In Charleston, as you know, the public sales of negroes are conducted in the open street, in front of the Court House. We attended one sale, which greatly interested us. The negroes announced to be sold, 'under decree in Equity,' were a mother and five children. On arriving at the Court House, we found the family to be sold standing in a row by the Court House steps. A dozen or two of men were gathered in groups hard by, and one man was, apparently, examining the 'lot.' The children were all of different shades of colour, the eldest being nearly pure white. It was some time after the appointed hour before the sale commenced; and as we paced up and down on the opposite pavement, many furtive glances were thrown across at us, as if to ask what was our business there. Several negro women, too, stopped as they passed on the opposite side of the street, looking anxiously across, and whispering to each other. At length the auctioneer arrived, and we crossed over to the scene of action. The family was put up in one lot, at so much a head. The bidding was spirited, but it soon was manifest that the contest lay between two men, one of whom seemed determined to have the negroes at any cost. The competition grew keener and keener; the crowd grew excited, and laughed outright at each bid; it was clear that the price bid was more than the negroes were worth, but neither party would give in. At last the lot was knocked down at 640 dollars a head to one of the bidders, who, turning to his competitor, said, in an excited tone—'You have made me pay a hundred dollars a head for charity;' on which a bystander remarked to his neighbour, that no doubt he had been commissioned by one of the family to whom the negroes had belonged to buy them in, to prevent them falling into the hands of strangers. This is one of the thousand modes by which, I doubt not, individual virtue strives to modify a general wrong. It is inexpressibly consoling to find human nature vindicating her nobility under such adverse circum-

A CONVERTED ABOLITIONIST.

stances. This softening down of slavery is no less honourable to the dominant race than beneficial to the subjected.

I have been reading Dr. Nehemiah Adams's *South-Side View of Slavery*—a book which was recommended to me, as a good exponent of the views of Northern favourers of slavery. Dr. Adams is a Boston minister, who went to the South a rabid Abolitionist, and returned, after a stay of three months, a rank pro-slavery man. The history of his book tells the character of the man. He is one of those soft-hearted, soft-headed men with whom Abolitionism is a sentimentalism; whose maudlin philanthropy has no sure basis of intellectual and moral conviction. They do not regard slavery as a moral wrong—as a lese-majesty of the human will, interfering with the duties and destinies of man as a moral intelligence. It is the 'unhappiness' of the slave, the so-called 'horrors of slavery,' over which they snivel and snuffle. Such men easily pass from one extreme to another. Apostacy is the natural revulsion of a weak mind. A diseased sensibility, uncontrolled by stable principle, yields to every varying influence; and the fanatic of the North becomes the apostle of slavery in the South. By his own account, Dr. Adams went to the South with his brain seething with 'Uncle Tom.' He expected to meet nothing but 'Topsys' and 'Legrees;'

and when, on the contrary, he saw pleasant little black faces, and met with refined Southern slave-owners, the revulsion of feeling changed him, at once, from an opponent to an apologist of slavery.

Far be it from me to doubt the Doctor's testimony as to the humanity of the slave-owners of the South, and the general average comfort of the slaves. This information, however, he could have got nearer home, and in a more undeniable form, from the census tables. The rate of increase in population, among masses of men, is, *cæteris paribus*, in proportion to the comfort of their existence; and the rate of negro increase in the Slave States, especially when compared with the slave decrease in Cuba, is proof positive of general good treatment. But no comfort and contentment of the slave, however great, can justify slavery. Nay, the contentment of the slave is to me the completest condemnation of slavery; for it proves that he has fallen low enough to barter his birthright for a mess of 'mush.'

LETTER XXI.

Columbia, 13th March, 1857.

The whole country from Charleston to Columbia is very desolate; there is not a town or village of any consequence on the whole route of 130 miles. The face of the country, with its almost interminable forest, is more that of a newly-settled country than of one which has been in the possession of a civilized race for generations. Yet the civilization of North and South Carolina counts by centuries, while that of Minnesota or Iowa counts by years.

The negroes one sees at the stations of the railways have a very different look from the smart servants of Charleston. Yesterday was Sunday, and yet some of these poor creatures whom we saw hanging about the stations were absolutely in rags: some, too, had marvellously foul linen. I cannot conceive how Southerners have the face to compare these poor creatures with our working people. Such figures as we saw yesterday might perhaps be found in our wynds and closes; but to compare them with our respectable working people is a perfect mockery, and could not be persisted in, if English people were in the daily habit of visiting this country, and observing for themselves.

The dwellings of the slaves which we have seen from the railway seem in fit keeping with their clothing. As far as such a passing glance can inform one, they consist of a log hut of one apartment, with a brick chimney outside, a door, and an aperture with a wooden shutter for a window. They resemble considerably the poor *châlets* on the Swiss table-lands, where they drive their cattle to in summer. Altogether, taking into consideration the difference of climate, they seem to me much on a par, as to comfort, with the hovels of our Highland cottiers. Most undoubtedly they are very, very far beneath the comfortable cottages, or 'flats,' which contain the decent labourers of Scotland. The clothing of the slaves is generally of a uniform make and colour; a uniformity which gives them, to an English eye, more the appearance of convicts than of labourers.

On the Southern railways one has generally abundance of room, a luxury much wanted in the North; and one which I presume is much more agreeable to the traveller than to the railway proprietor. A traveller told me, he was the sole passenger in a night train between Charlotte and Columbia. The truth is, there never can be a sufficiently large middle-class (the chief travelling class) in a slave community to pay a railway by its passenger-traffic; it must pay by freight or not at all. The sparseness of population, too, destroys all local traffic, confessedly the most profitable part of railway traffic in England. Here the passenger-trade is almost solely the through traffic from one considerable town to another, and these are often at great distances from each other. The earnings of the Georgian Central Railway, in 1855, amounted to 1,428,682 dollars, of which only 278,103 dollars were derived from 'passage and mails.' A director of the line informed me that the mails amounted to about 40,000 dollars, leaving 238,103 dollars, or about 17 per cent., as the contribution of the passenger-traffic.

I hear much abuse of the 'poor whites,' or, as they are called here, 'Sandhillers.' A slave said to me, the other day, he thought them the laziest people on the face of the earth. For my part I cannot but believe, that there is a possibility of improving the condition of the 'mean whites' of the seaboard Slave States. Indeed, these poor 'sandhillers' seem to me to have been somewhat hardly dealt with. Every one has his fling at them; nobody has a good word for the poor devils. Even Irishmen and niggers jeer at the 'lazy' white rascals. Now, there must be a cause for this 'laziness.' Why should the 'sandhiller' and 'cracker' alone, of all Americans, be 'lazy?' Laziness is not an American sin—over-activity rather. Whenever we find whole bodies of men affected by an anomalous failing, instead of railing at them we should set about discovering the cause of the anomaly. It will generally be found lurking in some ancient legislative injustice or abuse. The chronic apathy of Irish and Highland cottiers, and English chawbacons, may be traced to old feudal abuses of land-owning; and the vagrancy of the 'poor whites' of the Slave States is owing to that institution, which shuts out capital and prevents the copious employment of free labour. The poor sandhillers are the unconscious victims of a vicious social organization, which excludes the civilizing principle from their country. The same cure must be applied to Southern as to Irish vagrancy and listless beggary: the obstruction must be removed which dams-out capital.

No one can study the social condition of the Slave States of the South, without being struck with the prevalence of bloody duels. I have not seen any accurate statistics on this subject, but the following cases have fallen under my notice, in my desultory perusal of the public papers since my arrival in the

States. Soon after I landed, Mr. Tabor, editor of the *Charleston Mercury*, was killed in a duel. About the same time, two cotton-brokers of New Orleans, whose names I have forgot, fought a duel, in which one of them was shot. I was introduced to the survivor when I visited New Orleans, and an ugly dog he was. I heard there the remark made that he had killed 'a better man than himself.' I also was informed that the victim of this duel had been almost forced into it, and had declared when he went out that he did not know what he was fighting for. The cause of quarrel was ostensibly some dispute about cotton; but I heard it whispered that the old '*teterrima causa*' was at the bottom of the 'difficulty.' During my stay at New Orleans, another fatal duel took place, of which I have not the exact date. It took place at Napoleon, in Arkansas, the Boulogne of the State of Mississippi. The parties were Dr M'Collough and a Mr. Mason, a merchant of Napoleon. 'The former was wounded slightly, and the latter, it is supposed, fatally.'—*Vicksburg Times*, January 22. The day before my arrival at New Orleans from Havana, another fatal duel had taken place there. On this occasion the combatants were Mr. G. W. White, a book-keeper in a hardware store, and Mr. Packenham Le Blanc, a deputy-sheriff. They fought 'with double-bar-

relled guns, at fifteen paces,' and at the first fire
Mr. Le Blanc was shot through the heart.—*New
Orleans Picayune*, Jan. 22. The scene now changes
to Georgia; and here we have two fatal duels, on the
same spot, within a week. 'Screven's Ferry,' it
seems, is the 'Chalk Farm' of Savannah. At this
inauspicious spot, on the 16th of February, 1857,
there met 'Daniel S. Elliot and Thomas S. Daniel,
Esqrs., both citizens of Savannah. The weapons used
were rifles, distance twenty-five paces. Mr. Daniel
fell at the first fire, and expired immediately, the ball
having penetrated his heart.'—*Savannah Republican*,
February 16, 1857. On the 23rd of the same
month, and on the same bloody ground, another duel
took place, 'in which the parties were D. S. Kimbrough and James P. Hendrick, both citizens of
Columbus, in this State. The weapons used were
rifles, and they fought at forty paces distance. Upon
the second fire Mr. Hendrick fell mortally wounded.'
—*Savannah Republican*, February 24. And now we
have to return once more to New Orleans. The
South Carolinian, published in Columbia, South Carolina, under date 11th of March, has the following:—'*A Duel between Two Editors.*—New Orleans,
March 7.—A duel was fought to-day in Mobile between Mr. Nixon, Editor of the *New Orleans Crescent*,
and Mr. Breckenridge, Editor of the *New Orleans*

Courier. At the second fire Breckenridge was shot through both thighs; the left was broken.'

Thus in seven months we have seven bloody encounters, six of them occurring in the three principal towns of the South—an amount of barbarous bloodshed which certainly cannot be paralleled in any civilized community of Christendom. When Herr von Hinckeldey, the Prussian Minister of Police, was shot last year by a reckless young aristocrat, the whole of Europe rang with indignant denunciation; while here, citizens murder each other with 'double-barrelled guns,' at the rate of some twelve per annum, and the fact is recorded as coolly as the arrival of a Cunard steam-ship, or the variation of a cent a pound in the price of cotton. The people of the South were very wroth at the credence given in Europe to the 'Arrowsmith hoax;' but the fault lies with the character she has too justly earned for sanguinary manners. A community which, by its own showing, kills off its man a month, cannot wonder if rawbone stories are told of it, nor complain if they are believed.

The people of the South are apt to account for their duelling propensity by the aristocratic character of their society. They attribute it to a punctilious sense of honour, and a spirit peculiarly impatient of injury. This plea, I fear, is somewhat too flattering. The aristocratic element of Southern society is now-a-days too much weakened, to give a tone to the manners of the whole community. Neither does it appear that those who engage in these sanguinary encounters are, by any means, exclusively the *créme de la créme* of Southern society. And again, if aristocratic influence were the producing cause of the duels, why is it that the custom has fallen into disuse and disrepute in England, where the same influence exists in an incomparably stronger degree? To me it seems the prevalence of duelling in the South is to be attributed partly to her peculiar social institutions, and partly to the imperfect state of her political organization. The existence of a dominant class necessarily leads to violence. Trained up from youth to the unrestrained exercise of will, the superior race or class naturally becomes despotic, overbearing, and impatient. In their intercourse with their inferiors this leads to unresisted oppression; but with their equals, armed with similar power and fired by the same passions, it breaks out into fierce strife. Hence the broils of the feudal aristocracy, which gradually softened down with their decreasing power into milder and milder forms of single combat, and at last disappeared when the predominance of their class was all but extinguished by the growth of a great industrial community. In this country the

AFFRAYS.

relation of master and slave produces the same effect on the character of the dominant class, as was formerly produced in Europe by that of lord and serf. There is the same imperious will, the same impatience of restraint, the same proneness to anger and ferocious strife. The passions which are developed in the intercourse with inferiors show themselves, though in a different form, in the intercourse with equals. Thus, by an inevitable retribution, wrong is made self-chastising, and the hand of the violent man is turned against himself.

Duelling is not the only form of this national proneness to acts of violence; rather, it is the modified form which it assumes among fair and honourable men, who even in their anger disdain to take advantage of an adversary, and who have at least sufficient self-command to give a semblance of reason to their passion. There are others, whose hasty impulses disdain even this slight self-restraint, who carry with them habitually the means of deadly injury, and use them on the slightest provocation. In reading Southern newspapers one frequently encounters such paragraphs as this: '*Affray at Madison, C. H., Fa.*— An affray took place at Madison, C.H., Florida, on Monday, the 1st instant, between Messrs. Dickson, Morris, and Bishop, the *two latter* of whom were fatally shot.'—*New Orleans Picayune*, Dec. 18th,

1856. Or take this from the *Lincoln* (Tenn.) *Journal* of Nov. 24th, 1856, referring to a Mr. Thompson and a Dr. Pugh who had quarrelled about politics:—
'The parties then closed for a fight. Thompson threw Pugh—friends interfered to separate them, and while in the act of raising Thompson, Pugh inflicted a terrible wound with a knife in the abdomen of Thompson, letting out his intestines. Thompson drew a pistol and fired; the shot missed Pugh, but took effect in the side of another man, passing through into the hip of another.' The *Journal* adds: ' Pugh and Thompson — one a physician and the other a merchant—resided near each other, and though differing in politics, were personally *very warm friends !*'

The custom of carrying arms is at once a proof of proneness to violence, and a provocative to it. This habit, I am informed, prevails very extensively in the South. When coming down the Mississippi, a Colonel B——, to whom I had been introduced, pointing to a crowd of men of all ranks clustered round the cabin stove, said: 'Now, there is probably not a man in all that crowd who is not armed; I myself have a pistol in my state-room.' On the St. John's River, when the alligator-hunt was at its height, I was surprised by the sudden appearance of several revolvers which some young men in the boat drew from their pockets, and with which they kept up a continuous fire on the poor alligators. But apart from all information, it is quite evident from the history of these rencontres, and the ready recourse to deadly weapons, that the practice of carrying arms, if not universal, is very general. Another proof is the negative one, that in the advertisements of masked balls and similar public entertainments, it is frequently announced that carrying arms will not be permitted.

The tendency to personal violence which is thus engendered by the social institutions of the South, is no doubt aggravated by the want of a thorough political organization. When justice is so lamely administered as in New Orleans, men naturally take the law into their own hands. The instinct of self-preservation makes a man arm himself when the law cannot protect him. But this wild justice easily degenerates into lawless violence, and a bloodthirsty ferocity is developed among the ruder members of the community; the higher classes defend themselves with 'rifles at fifteen paces,' the lower make a shift with brass knuckles and bowie-knives.

LETTER XXII.

COLUMBIA, March 18th, 1857.

COLUMBIA is a pretty little town, and the capital of this State. I wonder how many Englishmen are aware that the capitals of South Carolina, Georgia, and Louisiana, are, respectively, Columbia with 6000 inhabitants, Milledgeville with 2216, and Baton Rouge with 3905. It certainly is strange it should be so, when these States possess such cities as Charleston, Savannah, and New Orleans, situated on important navigable rivers, and with respectable populations. This mania of the Americans for placing the capitals of their States according to a trigonometrical measurement, without reference to any other consideration, is a curious specimen of the predominance of the synthetic over the analytic faculty in the American mind, which makes them easily sacrifice important details to a fancied symmetry. To make a capital of a paltry town, merely because it happens to be the geographical centre of the State, seems to me contrary to common sense. A capital should be the centre of affairs, the centre of intelligence, the centre of society. An American capital is simply the centre of a map. There are no conveniences for public business in such a place; there are neither the men nor the things required. No lawyers, editors, eminent merchants, to aid with their knowledge and advice, or to do the work required. There are no public buildings, no banks, no libraries, no centres of traffic and information, such as abound in a city that is a capital by nature. There are not even the accommodations necessary for the crowds who are drawn thither at the periods of legislation. All is scramble, discomfort, and confusion. I am persuaded that the annoyance of being banished to a third-rate country town, such as most American capitals are, is one of the reasons that makes the State legislatures distasteful to all but those who are indifferent to the refinements of society, or who are willing to forego them to favour their own ends. Neither can it be doubted that, by placing the Government in small towns, a great encouragement is given to corruption. The seductive influences which would be powerless on the population of a great city, are irresistible when exercised on the few thousands of an American State capital. And, in fact, if I am well informed, they have a strong tendency to become nests of jobbery and corruption.

Now, more than ever, the impolicy of this banishment of the State Governments to provincial villages will become apparent. The more the means of communication are perfected, the more necessary it is to be near the centres of communication. The natural site of a metropolis is at the convergence of a system of steamers, railways, and telegraphs. Columbia has no more right to be the capital of South Carolina than has Warwick to be the metropolis of England.

The evil is not political only. The great want of American civilization is concentration. The true policy of America, therefore, should be to draw together the available elements of intellectual power into the truly metropolitan centres of the several States, instead of dissipating them needlessly, and even prejudicially, over the small towns of the interior. The want of metropolitan concentration is a serious drawback to the higher progress of America.

From all I can see or hear of the American Post Office, it seems to me to be on an unsatisfactory footing, both in a financial and political point of view. The expense is great and rapidly increasing. According to the American almanac for 1857, the excess of expenditure over income, in 1855, was

2,626,206 dollars; whereas the average excess for the four previous years was only 1,610,316 dollars.

Great part of the increasing deficit arises from the greater cost of carrying the mails. This has more than doubled between 1850 and 1855, having risen from 2,965,786 dollars in the former year to 6,076,335 dollars in the latter. The transportation of the mails leaves a profit on the whole; but the profit is altogether due to the Northern States, while the Southern mails of themselves would leave a heavy loss, as thus :—

Transportation of Mails, 1855.

	Dollars.
Profit by Free States	1,962,428
Loss by Slave States	896,759
Net Profit	1,065,669

Of this gain almost the whole is due to the North-Eastern States, the North-Western States, including Ohio, doing little more than clear the expenses. The gain of the Eastern States alone amounts to 1,930,631 dollars. In the Slave States, on the other hand, the loss is principally incurred in the ten cotton-growing States, which show a deficit of 818,631 dollars; while the five frontier Slave States are only accountable for a loss of 78,127 dols. The cause of the difference here exhibited is very evident. In the North-Eastern States the business is greatest, and the distances are smallest; in the South-West, it is exactly the reverse. The cost increases and the returns diminish according to the sparseness of population, and *vice versâ*.

One cause of the great expense of transporting mails in the United States is the very extensive and, I believe, much-abused privilege of franking. Not only 'the President, ex-Presidents, the Vice-Presidents, ex-Vice-Presidents, Mrs. Harrison, and Mrs. Polk;' not only members of Congress, delegates from Territories, and governors of States, but countless secretaries and assistant-secretaries, comptrollers, auditors, registrars, solicitors, chiefs, chief clerks, and superintendents have, more or less, the ' privilege of franking.' Moreover, ' exchange newspapers,' magazines, &c., between editors, pass free. With such a host of privileged defrauders of the Post Office, all besieged, no doubt, by troops of friends, male and female, for the use of their name, it is no wonder that the cost is heavy on those who do pay. That the privilege may be greatly abused cannot be doubted. I myself know of one case where a noted statesman's name was used to circulate, gratis, a printed letter relating to a projected railway; and as the principal on this occasion had no time for such work, he merely gave his assent, and his signature was affixed by two or three gentlemen who happened to be present. The circumstance was related by two of them, in my presence, as a good joke. The privilege is the more unnecessary in the States, as the members of Congress are paid already; and if their remuneration is not thought enough to cover the expense of postage, it would be better to increase it than to create a privilege so liable to abuse.

With all its costliness, the transportation of the mails seems badly done. There is an irregularity in American mails which would drive Englishmen mad. When I was at Montgomery, at the beginning of February last, there were nineteen mails due from the North; and during the whole of this winter and spring there have been continued complaints on this subject in Congress, in the newspapers, and among all manner of men. For a time the snow served as a valuable apology, but long after this excuse had melted away the irregularity continued.

One angry editor, no doubt fuming at the detention of his own 'articles,' thus vents his displeasure at the 'franking system,' as the efficient cause of the delay:—' The United States mails carry gratis to all parts of the country every conceivable paper and document that the wisdom of lawgivers and the wit and ingenuity of lawyers can contrive. Patent-office reports by the million, scientific reports, reports of surveys, legislative reports, bank statistics, reports upon commerce and navigation, land-office reports, speeches, financial reports, law cases, census reports, messages, and political speeches, &c. &c., make up a grand total to be computed in bushels, cart-loads, and tons, and all carried for nothing and to no purpose, —often, too, to the exclusion of readable newspapers and valuable correspondence. Is it a wonder that with such an abominable and senseless clog our mails are frequently days and weeks behind time?' One cannot help sympathizing with the angry editor, whose own lucubrations were doubtless among the 'readable newspapers' kept back by the weighty literature he deprecates. There is much truth, too, in what he says; but it is not all the truth. A deeper cause of this postal mismanagement is, no doubt, the inefficiency which characterizes all Governments when they undertake ordinary business affairs. It is, doubtless, difficult to draw the line which should separate private and public undertakings. There is much debatable ground in that region of politics. But the transmission of letters, parcels, books, newspapers, magazines, and money,—in short, the business of a modern post-office,—seems to me peculiarly adapted to individual enterprise, and in every view unfit for Government interference. In despotic countries the Post-office, like the railways and the telegraph, is kept in the hands of the Government for police purposes; but that consideration, thank God, does not weigh in England or America. There we have to look merely to the commercial side of the question—how can our letters be carried best and cheapest? Now, it seems clear to me, that a principle of industry that can traverse the ocean with regular lines of steamships, and cover the land with an intricate system of railways and telegraphs, might surely be trusted with organizing a mode of transmitting daily a few tons of letters and newspapers. 'Nay, have we not already the requisite organization in such establishments as Pickford's admirable carrying company, and the excellent 'Express' companies of Adams and others in America? I have not a doubt that Pickford would take over our whole Post-office business at six weeks' notice, and manage it better than ever it has been managed by all our lordly Postmasters. As it is, every improvement of our postal system has been forced with much ado on our officials from without; the public being regarded as a surly brute to be kept at bay, rather than as an excellent customer, whose every wish is to be gratified.

Besides this commercial consideration, there are in America strong political reasons, why the postal business should not be in the hands of Government.

The patronage of the Post-office is the source of great and corrupt political influence. There were on November 30, 1855, 24,770 post-offices, the officers to which, besides all other officials connected with the department, are appointed either by the President himself, or by his nominee, the Postmaster-General. Such an army of sycophants scattered over the whole face of the country, each dependent for bread on the favour of the administration, is a power that cannot be viewed with complacency by any thinking American. Now, the only way to get rid of this evil would be to hand over the whole concern to a private company. Wall-street would find the funds and the brains necessary for the undertaking in a fortnight.

I have just seen in the newspapers a curious case of Lynch-law in Iowa. It is interesting from the queer jumble of law and lawlessness it presents. Indeed, what strikes a European most in the States is the melodramatic contrast of high civilization and semi-barbarism which he now and then encounters. Even the wildest excesses of Lynch-law violence are perpetrated with a tragi-comic gravity that is sublimely ludicrous. On the occasion referred to, the whole proceedings were conducted with the most exemplary decorum, and a punctilious observance of Newgate etiquette. The culprit was allowed time for ghostly preparation : a clergyman offered up a prayer, and at the fatal moment a numerous body of citizens laid hands upon the halter, to mark the common will of the community. The whole ceremony could not have been more imposingly performed under the joint ministrations of Calcraft and Dr. Cotton. The very culprit seemed impressed with the respectability of his exit, confessing his guilt, and warning sinners in the most orthodox strain of Tyburn piety. Altogether a most edifying piece of business. And, after all, there is a rude natural fitness in Lynch-law : loose laws and loose clothes are needed for frontier life. The stiff decorum of London police were as misplaced in Texas or Nebraska, as the knee-breeches and top-boots of the English farmer would be irksome to the free-and-easy pioneer of the West.

LETTER XXIII.

AIKEN, SOUTH CAROLINA, 23rd March, 1857.

I HAVE already said, that the natural increase of the slave population is the best proof of the absence of any general and extensive misery. The annual increase of the slave population in the slave-holding States, from 1820 to 1850, was 3.6 per cent. During the same period the increase of the whites in those States was 4.0 per cent. The difference is too small to lead to any important conclusion one way or another. The difference between the whites in the Free and Slave States during the same time is much greater than between the white and slave population of the Slave States; the annual rate of the former being 5.5 per cent. against 4.0 per cent. in the latter. On the whole, then, we may conclude that the average treatment of the North American slave is such as not to interfere materially with his natural rate of increase.

There is every reason for believing, also, that for

many years previous to the breaking out of the present strife between North and South, there had been a gradual amelioration in the condition of the slave. Slaves themselves have informed me that, on the whole, their condition had decidedly improved of late years; and that especially in the towns, where the check of public opinion operates, they are considerately treated. The slave-owning community have participated in the growing humanity of the age; and the greater consideration for people of inferior station, which is the noblest characteristic of our times, has doubtless had its due weight in softening the bondage of the slave of the South. Neither can it be doubted, that the force of public opinion has had great effect in improving the condition of the slave. The slave-owner is aware that the eyes of Christendom are on him and his institution, and that any marked abuse of his power will, if known, bring down on him the execration of the civilized world. This consideration may not act directly on the more coarse and ignorant slave-holder, but it does act powerfully on the better class, and through them on the inferior. For there are few men so brutified, as to be insensible to the moral indignation of their neighbours and fellow-citizens. When a brutish slave-owner exerts his power with ferocity, he is put under the ban of public execration; and there cannot be a doubt that this moral police is one of the strongest engines for the amelioration of slavery. American slavery is comparatively humane, because it is in the hands of a highly civilized people. This is at once its best defence and its deepest reproach.

It is certain, however, that there still occur exceptional cases of great barbarity. No doubt public opinion in general controls the violence of slave-owners; but there are men whose fierce and brutal passions are amenable to no control, and whose savage nature finds vent in deeds of great brutality. Here is such a case from the *Savannah Republican* of the 6th of February, 1857 :—
'*Brutal Murder of a Slave by his Owner.*— Michael Boylan, a German, residing on Lover's Lane, near this city, was arrested yesterday by Sergeant Wilson and Privates Richardson and Walter, of the mounted police, on a charge of whipping his own slave, a man named Stepney, to death. The circumstances of this outrage, as we have learned them, are as follow : — It appears that the negro had been absent for some time, and was taken on Tuesday last, and was carried to gaol by Constable Jones. He was then whipped, and turned over to his master. Yesterday Boylan, while under the influence of liquor, renewed the punishment, and continued it until the negro sank under the inflic-

tion, and died. Sergeant Wilson is of opinion that but for his prompt arrival on the spot, the negro would have been buried, and the crime concealed, as the coffin was already prepared, and a hole dug to receive it.' An exceptional case, we shall be told. True; but why have we never an ' exceptional case' of a slave-owner hanged for such a bloody outrage?

In judging of the welfare of the slaves, it is necessary to distinguish the different conditions of slavery. The most important distinction, both as regards numbers and its influence on the well-being of the slave, is that between house-servants and farm or field-hands. The house-servant is comparatively well off. He is frequently born and bred in the family he belongs to; and even when this is not the case, the constant association of the slave and his master, and master's family, naturally leads to such an attachment as ensures good treatment. There are not wanting instances of devoted attachment on both sides in such cases. There is even a danger that the affection on the part of the owner may degenerate into over-indulgence. It is no uncommon thing to make pets of slaves, as we do of other inferior animals; and when this is the case, the real welfare of the slave is sacrificed to an indiscriminating attachment. I was struck with the appearance of the slaves in the streets of Charleston on a Sunday afternoon. A large proportion of them were well dressed, and of decent bearing, and had all the appearance of enjoying a holiday. I was informed they were principally house-servants belonging to the town; and there could be no doubt the control of public opinion, natural to a large city, had exercised a favourable influence on the condition of these poor people.

The position of the field-hands is very different; of those, especially, who labour on large plantations. Here there are none of those humanizing influences at work which temper the rigour of the system, nor is there the same check of public opinion to control abuse. The 'force' is worked *en masse*, as a great human mechanism; or, if you will, as a drove of human cattle. The proprietor is seldom present to direct and control. Even if he were, on large estates the numbers are too great for his personal attention to details of treatment. On all large plantations the comfort of the slave is practically at the disposal of the white overseer, and his subordinate, the negro-driver. There are many estates which the proprietor does not visit at all, or visits perhaps once a year; and where, during his absence, the slaves are left to the uncontrolled caprice of the overseer and his assistants, not another white man, perhaps, being within miles of the plantation. Who can say what passes in those voiceless solitudes? Happen what may, there is none to tell. Whatever the slave may suffer there is none to bear witness to his wrong. It needs a large amount of charity to believe that power so despotic, so utterly uncontrolled even by opinion, will never degenerate into violence. It could only be so if overseers were saints, and drivers angels.

It is often said that the interest of the slave-owner is sufficient guarantee for the good treatment of the slave; that no man will voluntarily injure the value of his property. This reasoning assumes, first, that slave-owners will take an intelligent view of their own interests; and, secondly, that they will be guided by the passion of gain rather than by other passions. But we find the Cuba slave-owner working his slaves to death, at the rate of 3 per cent. per annum. And again, slavery is a system which evokes passions more powerful even than the love of gain. Against the action of these angry passions, the distant calculation of mere profit can avail but little with men of violent dispositions.

But even if we grant the restraint placed on the passions of the master by considerations of pecuniary interest, we cannot allow the same effect to be produced on the overseer. On the contrary, the interest of the overseer is to exhibit a large production as the result of his exertions; and the more remote consideration of being a prudent husbandman of his forces will only affect a superior mind. On this point I prefer giving the opinions of slave-owners themselves. In an article in *De Bow's Review*, on the management of slaves, I find some interesting remarks on this subject, in a report to a committee of slave-holders. After pointing out the interest of the owners in the good treatment of their slaves, it continues :—' There is one class of our community to whom all the motives referred to, to induce us to kindness to our slaves, do not apply. Your committee refer to our overseers. As they have no property in our slaves, of course they lack the check of self-interest. As their only aim, in general, is to get the largest possible crop for the year, we can readily conceive the strong inducement they have to overwork our slaves, and masters are often much to blame for inadvertently encouraging this feeling in their overseers.'

It appears, then, that nothing but high principle on the part of the overseer could ensure the good treatment of the slave on large plantations. But all testimony concurs in representing the overseers as a very inferior class in point of character. A Virginian slave-owner used this language to Olmsted :—' They (the overseers) are the curse of this country, sir; the worst men in the community.'

Yet these are the men on whom devolves, practically, the management of the great bulk of the agricultural slave population, in the cotton, rice, and sugar districts.

Midway between house-servants and plantation-hands stand the farm-servants of small proprietors. Of all slaves these are, probably, the best off. They are neither spoiled like pet domestics, nor abused like plantation cattle. They live much in the farmer's family, work with himself and his children, take an interest in his affairs, and, in return, become objects of his regard. Such is the condition of many slaves among the small farmers in the upland districts of Virginia, Kentucky, Tennessee, Georgia, and the Carolinas. The same applies also to many proprietors in Texas, and, I believe, Arkansas. In general it may be affirmed, that the welfare of the slaves is in an inverse ratio to their numbers.

While it is right to acknowledge the growing humanity of the slave-owner, it should not be forgotten that there are certain evils inherent in the system which no humanity can compensate. Of all the evils to which the slave is exposed, the most universal in its application, and the most pestilent in its effects, is the practical outlawry to which he is subjected by the refusal of his evidence in the courts of justice. He is thus exposed defence-

less to oppression. For him the court of law is no sanctuary. The dominant white man is on the bench, in the jury-box, and—unanswered—in the witness-box. No wonder that a conscientious Governor of South Carolina should say to his people:—
'The administration of our laws, in relation to our coloured population, by our courts of magistrates and freeholders, as these courts are at present constituted, calls loudly for reform. Their decisions are rarely in conformity with justice or humanity.'

The slave trade, though not universal in its application, is another hideous evil; and though many escape its grievous calamities, there are few who do not suffer from the dread of its application to themselves or those whom they love. So long as the slave trade continues there can be no sense of security for the slave, and without security it is a mockery to talk of happiness. This trade is a sore subject with the defenders of slavery. It is difficult to weave it handsomely in among the amenities of the patriarchal institution. They fain would make a scape-goat of the 'Trader,' and load all the iniquities of the system on his unlucky back. Men who own hundreds of slaves would scorn to meet on equal terms with a slave-trader. Now there seems little justice here. If slavery and the slave trade which it necessitates be in themselves right and proper, it is a wrong to visit with ignominy the instruments of the system. But conscience will not be put down; our intuitions are stronger than our logic, and the slave-owner has the 'noble inconsistency' to condemn his institution in the person of the agent who is essential to its existence.

The shame felt at the slave trade prompts the South to cry 'exaggeration.' But the extent to which it is carried is conclusively proved by the statistics of the slave population, from which it appears that, during the last thirty years, the number of slaves has rapidly increased in the Southern or slave-buying States, while in the Northern or slave-breeding States, the slave population has been almost stationary. The following is the exact statement:—

Increase of Slave-Population, 1820—1850.

Average increase per cent. per annum.
Northern or slave-breeding States 93
Southern or slave-buying States 5.93

Now it will hardly be asserted that the amenities of negro life on cotton, rice, and sugar plantations are so overwhelming as to account for a natural yearly increase of 5.93 per cent., while their brethren in the frontier States show only an increase of .93 per cent. The increased proportion, therefore, in the Southern Slave States, must be due to the importations of the

'Trader.' On the whole, it is time this odious traffic were getting itself abolished. The slave-trader in these days is too gross a solecism. He and his living freight are quite out of place in steamboats and railway cars, the special organs of modern civilization.

It is true, I believe, that till of late the condition of the slave had for a long time been gradually improving; but it is no less true that the present strife between North and South has been very prejudicial to the position of the slave, and has materially added to the rigour of his treatment. Indeed the South admits this, and makes it a charge against the abolitionist North, that she thus injures the cause of the slave. The knowledge that the slaves participate deeply in the interest of the struggle, and the fear that they may break out into overt acts of insubordination, have led to measures of severity that would not have been dreamed of a few years ago. In some States emancipation has been prohibited; the presence of free negroes is generally discouraged, and everywhere the slaves are subjected to more strict and annoying police regulations. The slave-owner fears his slave more and more, and surrounds himself on every hand with legal safeguards.

Nor are his fears without sufficient cause. The position of the African in America at the present day is very different from that of slave countries where the slave trade is permitted, and the ranks of slavery are recruited by fresh imports of semi-savage captives. Here there is no fresh infusion of the barbaric element, and the whole population grows up more or less under the influences of American civilization. Such a community must needs improve from generation to generation. No barrier, legal or social, can effectually shut out from them the subtle influences of intelligence and virtue. Already the negroes in the Northern Slave States have achieved a notable enlightenment. So in the towns throughout the Slave States they have made great progress. Many slaves have learned to read in spite of all prohibitions. The very prohibition has stimulated exertion. They desire the more ardently what is so peremptorily forbidden them. With the unerring instinct of self-preservation, the slave perceives that the secret of his deliverance lies in that intellectual power which is so strenuously withheld from him.

In Richmond, I am informed, almost every slave-child is learning to read. Even in Columbia, the capital of South Carolina, hundreds of slaves can read, and twenty or thirty negroes regularly teach reading in the evenings to their fellow-slaves, receiving a fee of a dollar a month Other slaves are taught by friendly whites. I have myself seen this going on in the corridors of an hotel. On plantations the slaves teach one another. If an intelligent negro comes from the North to a plantation his fellows help with his task, and in return he teaches them to read.

But the surest and most powerful means of education for the negro is his constant association with a superior race. The African has not yet been many generations in this land. Some native-born Africans are, I believe, yet alive. Yet even in this short time the association with a civilized race has wonderfully improved them. Nothing strikes me more than the intelligence of some of the negroes whom I encounter. This is especially the case in the towns, and wherever they are brought into contact with white men. This mental progress must rapidly go on, as the labour of the slave is turned to more varied and higher uses, and as he is more and more associated with the superior race. In factories, on railways, and other public works, slaves are now extensively employed. Such employments are the most efficient schools for labourers in their stage of cultivation, and must assuredly have a strong influence in developing their intellectual powers. The numerous servants in private houses, hotels, steamboats, &c., will also supply a large body, educated by contact with a superior class. Even the means of material development which are raising the condition of the community at large, the means of rapid intercommunication and universal dissemination of intelligence will have their due effect on the education of the negro race. They cannot live in the atmosphere of American progress without participating, more or less, in its effects.

The very struggle to perpetuate and extend the institution of slavery must tend to undermine it; for it excites the curiosity and interest of the slaves, and stimulates them to acquire information, and to cultivate their understandings, that they may understand their position, and take advantage of their opportunities. The late Presidential contest did more to awaken the negro race to a sense of their rights and wrongs, than could have been effected by the propagandism of a thousand Abolition societies. Thus the slave-owner is himself the prime agent in arousing the slave to insubordination. He it is who, above all other men, stimulates the zeal of his slaves. The fanatic of the North, the Yankee pedlar, the underground agent himself, can do little in wakening the slumbering passion for freedom in the negro breast, compared with the pro-slavery champion who stirs up strife, and causes discussion, and excites passion throughout the land.

There is no plantation so remote but what the echoes of this national warfare reach it, awakening to new thoughts and impulses all but the utterly degraded. Then there is another and no less powerful Abolitionist agent constantly at work—the slave-dealer. Through his means a constant stream of Northern intelligence is spread over every plantation of the South. The most intelligent slaves are, as a rule, the most insubordinate, and these it is whom the trader purchases in the North and sells in the South. Every such slave thus bought and sold is an emissary of Abolitionism, more powerful, more subtle, and more sure of opportunities, than any whom the most rabid Abolition Society could employ. If, as is frequently the case, he can read, then he is the organ of information for the whole plantation. It needs but little of such leaven to leaven the whole mass with insubordinate and violent thoughts. Thus, by a striking retribution, the passions of men are made to recoil upon themselves: the slave-owner is made the chief of Abolitionists, and the slave-trader becomes the arch incendiary.

The danger from the insubordination of the slave population seems to me a serious and growing evil. Slave-owners, in general, affect to make light of it; but the intense eagerness with which they deny all evidences of insubordination, and the severity with which they punish supposed incendiaries, prove that a vast amount of distrust and fear lurks under their bravado. The insurrectionary movement in the Slave States during the autumn of 1856, though not formidable in itself, was alarming from the extent to which it spread, from the power of organization it evinced, and above all from the amount of disaffection it implied. The alarm in Tennessee during my visit in the beginning of December was great. At Clarkesville eight or ten negroes were hanged by a Vigilance Committee, aided by impromptu Lynching by an infuriated mob. That matters were not much better in the neighbouring State of Kentucky will appear by the following:—'*The Negro Insurrection.*—The ringleaders of the attempted negro insurrection at Hopkinsville, Kentucky, have been hung. A white man was discovered painted black, who had been in the neighbourhood several months, and had passed off as a negro. He was sentenced to receive nine hundred lashes; he died before the whole number was inflicted.'

The movement was not confined to the Northern Slave States, but extended also to the South. I had positive information of its existence at Jacksonville, in Florida, though the papers there denied the fact. Under the head of 'Precautionary Measures at Jackson, Mississippi,' I possess a notice prohibiting the usual resort of negroes to Jackson at the Christmas holidays, 1857. Similar measures were adopted elsewhere. To my knowledge a Committee of Vigilance was formed at Memphis at the time of my visit in December. About the same time I read the following :—'*Louisiana Intelligence.*—The Board of Select men of Baton Rouge (capital of Louisiana) has passed an ordinance creating a night police for that city.' On the 27th Jan., 1857, in the same city, 'Mr. Hyam's Bill preventing the emancipation of slaves was passed (in the Senate), with an amendment by Mr. Munday, to the effect that masters might free slaves in any case where the said slaves had given information of an insurrection among the servile population.' That the insurrectionary movement had spread to Texas appears from the following paragraph in the *Galveston News* of the 11th Sept., 1856: 'We learn from the *Columbian Planter* of the 9th, that two of the negroes engaged in the insurrection at Columbus were whipped to death; three more were hung last Friday.' Another Texan paper, *True Issue*, of Sept. 5th, says: 'Some two hundred, we learn, have been severely punished under the lash, and several are now in gaol awaiting the more serious punishment of death, which is to be inflicted to-day.' I likewise saw notices of disturbances in

Virginia. From one end of the country to the other the alarm was universal, though great pains were taken to keep the matter quiet, both to prevent it reaching the ears of the negroes, and to prevent undue panic among the whites. On such a volcano is based the institution of slavery.

The remedy proposed for this state of things is repression, severity; ever more severity. This will not do. Statesmen have yet to learn the law of social dynamics, that compression only increases the explosive force of disaffection. Terrorism does not pacify a people. It only changes complaint into conspiracy. Can the South exist with its whole labouring population in a state of chronic insurrection? Can a community of six millions afford to have four millions of conspirators in its bosom? Curfew laws, passes, increased police, 'mounted patrols'—all will not avail so long as the generating cause of discontent exists. The only way to extinguish slave disaffection is to extinguish slavery.

LETTER XXIV

Knoxville, East Tennessee, 28th March, 1857.

When I first entered the Slave States I could see no prospect of improvement. Indeed, things seemed going from bad to worse, and I had to fall back for comfort on the intuitive trust of the human heart on the ultimate prevalence of the right. But a nearer acquaintance with the state of the country has led me to believe, that even now influences are at work which may bring about a revolution in the internal economy of the Slave States.

I put no faith in political or philanthropic nostrums. If the South is to be regenerated, it must be by economical influences. Slavery will be abolished now, as heretofore, simply because slavery is unprofitable. An unworthy motive, some may say. True; but it is the way of God to bring good out of evil, turning even our unworthy motives to His own good ends.

The course of emancipation has always been from

North to South, and so it will continue. In 1780 there were emancipated Massachusetts and Pennsylvania; in 1784, Connecticut and Rhode Island; in 1792, New Hampshire; in 1799, New York; and in 1804, New Jersey. Now, what has determined this stream of freedom to flow, almost by compass, in one direction? The course was neither moral nor political, but geographical, or rather industrial, founded on topographical peculiarities. The people of the North-East were not more virtuous, nor were their politicians wiser than those to the south and south-west of them; but they had a more rugged climate and more barren soil, which together made husbandry impracticable with slave-labour. All emancipation, in the United States, has proceeded from the recognised unprofitableness of slave-labour. So it has been in Europe, where serf-labour has given place to hired labour, because the latter was found, on the whole, a better bargain. And these emancipations have universally and signally proved beneficial to all parties concerned—blessing those who gave, and those who received freedom. On the other hand, the emancipations which philanthropy dictated, in the British and French colonies, have not as yet borne the happy fruits which were expected of them: so difficult is it for man to bless his neighbour by direct efforts: to succeed he must watch the laws of the divine economy, and follow them modestly, yet trustingly.

To me it seems clear that the course of social reformation which, for half a century, has seemed suspended, is now about to be renewed. Many circumstances are combining to bring about this result. Foremost among these is the strong demand for cheaper and better labour in the South. This applies both to the corn and cotton-growing Slave States. Notwithstanding the rapidly-extending area of agricultnre in America, population still presses on subsistence. The consequent demand for food tells especially on the frontier Slave States, where much good land would be available, if only the needful labour were at hand to till it. But the negro labour is deficient both in quantity and quality, and yet it prevents the influx of cheaper and better free labour. The need is made more pressing by the emigration of many farmers' sons from the South to California and the North-west, attracted by more brilliant prospects than their native States afford.

The same demand for labour exists in the Southern Slave States, arising from the high price of all the staple productions of the South, but especially of cotton. The increase of cotton culture is regulated by the increase of the slave population. This is somewhat more than three per cent. per annum for the whole

Slave States; but in the cotton States it is nearly six per cent., almost the whole natural increase of the frontier States being drained towards the South. By this increase of slave population, and improved methods of production, the total annual increase of the cotton production has been latterly about nine per cent. per annum: but as the demand has increased at the same time about sixteen per cent., the pressure of demand on supply still continues. The average price of cotton, which had been falling regularly for thirty years, up to 1850, has risen since that time as under:—

Average Price of Cotton.

		Cents.
Ten Years, ending 1830	. . . .	13.3
,, ,, 1840	. . . .	12.4
,, ,, 1850	. . . .	8.2
Five Years, ,, 1855	. . . .	9.6

Since 1855 the price of cotton has risen still higher.

Now, slave-labour being a limited commodity, any increase in the demand for it immediately raises its price. It is estimated that every additional cent per lb. of cotton adds a hundred dollars to the average value of negroes. This rise in the price of slaves is an important consideration, not only in the economy of cotton culture, but in the whole social system of the South. There is no doubt that cotton culture, in its earlier stages, by giving increased value to negro property, arrested the progress of emancipation; but the exorbitant value now attained bids fair to reverse this influence, and to force on a renewal of emancipation, in order to enable negro labour to compete with free labour. Inefficient labour may pay when the labourer costs only 500 dollars; but when he costs 1000 or 1500 dollars, his inefficiency becomes ruinous.

With an abundant supply of good labour, a rise in the price of cotton would be a clear gain to the planter: as it is, it hurts him in two ways; first, by raising the price of negroes, it enhances the expense of his own production; and secondly, it affords a strong stimulus to the cotton culture of other countries. Thus it increases the cost of production at home, and stimulates competition abroad. Now, the only way to rid himself of both inconveniences would be to adopt free labour. The command he then would have of cheap and efficient labour would enable him to produce cotton, in such abundance and at such a cost as would set all competition at defiance. At present the cotton culture of the South is limited by the slow increase of a single horde; but with an unlimited immigration of free white labourers, in addition to free negro labour, there are no bounds to the development of cotton culture, on the millions of acres of fine cotton lands yet unoccupied in the sunny South.

Neither could any country pretend to compete with the South in point of cost of production. Her soil, climate, and nearness to the best markets, aided by her rivers, railways, and, above all, an energetic population, would ensure her triumph over every rival. Her one sole want is good and cheap labour. Will the South continue this evil, or will she remove it? Will she perpetuate this self-inflicted paralysis of her powers, inviting the competition of the East, and lowering herself to the level of Asiatic barbarism? Or will she do as conscience and interest alike command her, and remove the only bar to her progress? It is for the South herself to say.

The imperious necessity which exists in the cotton States for an increased supply of labour is clearly recognised by the South, and has given rise in South Carolina, among extreme politicians, to the proposal to re-open the slave-trade. Our cotton monopoly, says Governor Adams, Governor of that State, can only be maintained by a sufficient supply of cheap labour: a sufficient supply of slave-labour can only be got by importation; *ergo*, the slave-trade must be re-opened. The Governor's logic is undeniable, but his statesmanship is very questionable. A policy which is opposed not only by the combined convictions of Christendom, but even by the common sense of the Slave States of the South, can have little wisdom in it. If Governor Adams wishes more, and better, and cheaper labour, let him free his negroes, or rather let him allow them to free themselves. Again, South Carolina has already about sixty per cent. of slaves; how many more would she have? Would Governor Adams guarantee her existence with seventy or eighty per cent. of slaves in her bosom?

It is said white men cannot labour in a tropical climate. But the Southern States are not a tropical region, neither is cotton a tropical product. It flourishes only in the belt between the tropical and the temperate zones. In that delightful climate white men work well and pleasantly. White men labour all day long in Louisiana at the heaviest work. Nay, in Texas, the most southernly of the Slave States, cotton is even now produced by free (German) labour; and better cotton, too, than any grown by slave-labour. This cuckoo-cry of climate is a mere pretence, and is become a weariness to all men. The white race can labour anywhere. Free white men do labour in all climates; in Asia, South America, and in burning Africa itself; why not in North America? The rice swamps? some one says. And what then? The whole rice production of the United States is only worth some 4,000,000 dollars per annum. *That* is not a consideration on which to hang a national policy. As to sugar, its days are already numbered. No nursing can prolong its sickly existence. The next 'amended tariff' will remove that stumbling-block from the path of American statesmanship.

Now, what power of resistance can the South oppose to the immense economic force, which this demand for labour is bringing to bear upon the institution of slavery? Is the South an unanimous whole, animated in defence of slavery by one spirit, one interest, one fanaticism? At first sight it appears so. If we listen only to her orators, editors, governors, and other organs of public opinion, we should say the South is unanimously in favour of slavery. But if we look closer into the social state of the South, and weigh the meaning of silent, yet expressive facts, we shall see that, under this seeming unanimity, there is much diversity of sentiment; that among the States themselves there is division; and that within the States there is still further variety of interest and opinion.

The most marked and the most important difference existing in the Slaves States is that between the frontier and the cotton States; the former bordering on the free States, and partaking, more or less, of their characteristics; the latter removed further, both geographically and industrially, from the influences of freedom. The former include Delaware, Maryland, Kentucky, Missouri, and Virginia; though no doubt East Virginia partakes much of the character of a cotton State. To the latter belong Tennessee, (though West Tennessee is essentially frontier in its nature), North and South Carolina, Georgia, Alabama, Mississippi, Louisiana, Florida, Arkansas, and Texas. To make the difference in their social and industrial condition more apparent, I append a table, compiled from De Bow's *Compendium of the Census*, showing the density of population, the value of land, the per centage of slave population, and the holdings of slaves in each State :—

FRONTIER AND COTTON STATES.

	Density per sq. mile.	Slave Population.		Value of Land per acre.
		Per Cent.	Average Holdings.	
Frontier States.				Dollars.
Delaware	43.18	2.5	2.84	19.74
Maryland	52.41	15.5	5.63	18.81
Kentucky	26.07	21.4	5.47	9.15
Missouri	10.12	12.8	4.55	6.50
Virginia	23.17	33.2	8.58	8.28
Average . . .	30.99	17.1	5.41	12.49
Cotton States.				
Tennessee	21.99	23.8	7.07	5.16
North Carolina . .	17.14	33.2	10.19	3.22
South Carolina . .	22.75	57.5	15.04	5.08
Georgia	15.62	42.1	9.92	4.20
Alabama	15.21	44.4	11.70	5.30
Mississippi	12.86	51.0	13.41	5.17
Louisiana	12.55	47.2	11.81	15.20*
Florida	1.48	44.9	11.17	4.06
Arkansas	4.02	22.4	7.85	5.88
Texas	0.89	27.3	7.51	1.42
Average . . .	12.45	39.4	10.56	5.46

By this table it appears that the material progress of the frontier States, as seen in the density of their population and the value of their land, has been more than twice as great as that of the cotton States; the average density of the former being 30.99 against

* No doubt erroneous.

12.45 in the latter, and the value of land 12.49 against 5.46. In regard to slavery, again, these relations are reversed. The cotton States have more than double the per centage of slaves, or 39.4 against 17.1, and their slave-holdings are nearly twice as large, viz., 10.56 against 5.41.

The difference between the frontier and cotton States, in regard to their servile population, is not only great, but it is progressive, the per centage of slaves diminishing in the former and increasing in the latter, as under:—

Per Centage of Slave Population.

	1820.	1850.
5 Frontier States	22.0	17.1
10 Cotton States	35.4	39.4

So that while the proportion of slave to free inhabitants fell in the frontier States, during thirty years, from 22.0 to 17.1, in the cotton States it rose from 35.4 to 39.4. The greater number of slaves held by each owner in the cotton States is a fact of much significance, as bearing both on the political and industrial condition of these States. Slaves are the principal species of property in the Slave States. According to his property in slaves is a man's wealth and influence estimated, as in England by his possession of land. The comparatively large holdings of slave property in the cotton States indicate a more aristocratic society; and this element culminates, as might be expected, in South Carolina, where the average holding is 15.04, or nearly three times the average of the frontier States. The average holdings in the frontier States is materially increased by the addition of the aristocratic Old Dominion. Without her the average would only amount to 4.62.

There is yet another marked distinction between the frontier and cotton States. The former, from their proximity to the Free States, are more open to the influence of free ideas, and more subject to the evasion of their slaves. I have been struck with the different look of the Northern and Southern slaves. In the frontier States the slave has a freer, bolder, though perhaps a gloomier, presence. It is clear that he better knows his rights, and more keenly feels his wrongs. The frontier slave is a nobler man, and therefore a more unwilling slave.

Again, the neighbourhood of a Free State gives the slave facilities for escape. The slave of the frontier State not only is a more unwilling slave, but he has an easier road to freedom; he has only to pass the frontier line, and though his master's legal claim continues good, he finds friends who set the law at nought. For there is no denying the fact; the Fugitive Slave Law is a dead letter. Conscience has triumphed over all the quirks of lawyers and compromises of politicians. The free men of the North will not be legislated into slave bloodhounds.

The statistical returns of manumitted and fugitive slaves correspond with these observations. Of the total slaves manumitted in 1850, seventy-nine per cent. belonged to the five frontier States, with only twenty-seven per cent. of the slave population; and of the fugitives, Maryland alone has twenty-seven per cent., with less than three per cent. of the slave population. This element of insecurity must daily increase, as improved means of information and communication are multiplied, and as the growing intelligence of the slave enables him to turn these facilities to account. Already a secret and powerful organization exists, which, under the name of 'The Underground Railway,' facilitates the escape of slaves; and it is not to be doubted that the power of this and similar organizations will increase with the growing discontent of the slaves, and the increasing zeal of their friends across the border. Thus the slave-owner's property is becoming more insecure at the same time that its value is rising. The risks and inconveniences of slave-holding are increasing; the agricultural value of the slave is diminishing; the slave-owner is burning his candle at both ends.

At first sight it might appear that the high price of slaves makes it the interest of the frontier States, in their character of 'breeding' States, to continue the system. But the gain is quite illusory. With every rise in the value of slave progeny, there is an increase in the amount of parent capital invested. The stock rises, *pari passu*, with the produce. A negro stud, at present prices, is a dear investment, and the capital, if realized, might be re-invested in stocks as profitable, and more secure. The slave-breeder runs the risk of his capital running off. No doubt a negro paterfamilias, whose every woolly-headed pledge of love is worth 300 or 400 dollars so soon as born, is a very paying investment; but as any fine morning he may disappear by the Underground Railway, a prudential patriarch would be sorely tempted to hand him over to the 'trader,' and invest the proceeds in a 'section' in Iowa or a 'town-lot' at Chicago.

To me it seems clear, that the views and interests of the frontier States are very different from those of the cotton States, and that in them the slave power will look in vain for hearty and unanimous support, if, indeed, it does not meet with open opposition. Symptoms are not wanting of anti-slavery feeling in the frontier Slave States; and even without the gift of political second-sight. one cannot but see the shadows of coming changes. Delaware is already, to all intents and purposes, a free State. A slave population of two and a half per cent., every year decreasing, is surely too trivial a remnant of the curse to make it worth her while to bear much longer the plague and shame of slavery. Maryland, by her late Presidential vote, showed how completely she is separated in spirit from the fanatical portion of the South. In Missouri and Kentucky, Abolitionist movements have already taken place; and perhaps, ere long, the grand 'Old Dominion' herself will re-assert the noble abhorrence of slavery that yet breathes and burns in the words of her wise men of olden time. The progress of emancipation will be in an accelerating ratio; for the resisting force will be getting less as the invading force gains in strength. Every Slave State emancipated will count as a double gain to the cause of freedom.

I am not here indulging in mere hallucination; there are economical facts to bear me out. The demand for lands in the frontier States for increased corn culture, and the recognised impossibility, in the opinion of unprejudiced practical men, of high farming by slave-labour, are the basis of my anticipations. How soon or how late they may be verified, is of course beyond my knowledge; that depends on an unforeseen combination of favourable or unfavourable circumstances.

Among the cotton States themselves are two, peculiar in position and character. Arkansas and Texas, situated on the west bank of the Mississippi, are also essentially frontier States; and there also the slave power may encounter hostile feelings and interests. Arkansas and Texas have been chiefly settled by the smaller farmers of the principal cotton States, who have been crushed out of their original homes by the aggrandizement of their more aristocratic neighbours. In the older cotton States the constant tendency is towards extension of land-holding and slave-holding. Whatever a planter gains, and that is saved from the ravening maw of Newport and Saratoga, is invested in more cotton-land, and more niggers to till it. The small fry bought out in this process betake themselves across the Mississippi, and settle in the cheap yet fertile lands of Arkansas or Texas. The latter also contains a considerable population of foreigners, chiefly Germans, with an admixture of Northerners—a population which, small as it is, may yet exercise a mighty influence on the destinies of the nation. You will observe that the more democratic character of Texas and Arkansas is marked strongly in that most essential point, the number of slaves held by each proprietor. The average of the two is 7.68, against 11.29 in the eight aristocratic States. The proportion of slave population, also, is much less than in the eight larger States, being 24.8 in the former to 43.0 in the latter. In respect, therefore, to the all-important element of slavery, Texas and Arkansas hold a middle place between the frontier and the eight other cotton States; and, indeed, approach more nearly to the former than to the latter.

It is from Texas, especially, that opposition to slavery may be expected. Bordering on free Mexico, it affords, in its Western portion, great facilities for the escape of slaves, and will, on that account, be less affected by slave-owners. There is, besides, in that region, a considerable population of Germans and Northern men, strongly opposed to slavery, and proving by their example the possibility of successful cotton culture without the aid of slavery. These men will strenuously oppose the introduction of slavery into Western Texas, should a New State be there erected, as most likely will soon be the case. Thus, the slave power may find itself vigorously assailed in the rear, and that by its own fancied allies, at the moment it is directing all its energies to oppose the enemy in front. Placed thus between two fires, slavery could not long sustain the unequal combat.

Besides these great divisions between the States,

there are minor divisions in the interior of the several States, which will prevent united action in defence of slavery. Thus the planters of the lowland districts are socially and politically opposed to the small farmers of the upland districts. The former are the aristocracy of the South—the slave power *par excellence;* the latter are essentially a democracy, and have but a slight interest in the institution of slavery. In the upland districts of Virginia and Tennessee, the per centage of slave population is, respectively, 11.3 and 8.6; while in the aristocratic lowlands it is 47.5 and 31.7, or nearly four times as great. In Beaufort, Colleton, and Georgetown—three important planting counties on the seaboard of South Carolina—the slaves constitute eighty-four per cent. of the total population, while in the three upland counties of Pickens, Spartanburg, and Greenville they only amount to thirty per cent.

In the mountainous regions of the Slave States—even of the Carolinas—there is an industrious yeomanry, who till their farms, themselves and their sons, with little negro help. This is a stalwart, laborious, independent population; the pith of the Slave States. The Alleganies are the backbone of the United States, and their inhabitants are the strength of the American people.

This yeoman class is also—as in the North—

decidedly democratic in its political leanings. The slave-aristocracy has hitherto managed—mainly by working on their pro-slavery prejudices—to enlist this fierce democracy in the cause of the oligarchical supremacy of the South; but this political manœuvre cannot succeed much longer. The democratic farmers of the upland districts will not always consent to sacrifice themselves for the benefit of the lordly planters. Already there are symptoms of defection. The more intelligent of the yeomen are tiring of this catspaw system. Their direct interest in slavery is too slight to make it an object of pre-eminent importance in their eyes, and they feel even more keenly than the North the undue political influence which the planter-aristocracy wields, by virtue of its slave representation.

Further; among the commercial class of the South there is much concealed hostility to slavery. This is particularly the case in the large trading towns of the frontier States; in Wheeling, Virginia; in Louisville, Kentucky; and, above all, in St. Louis, Missouri. In St. Louis there are about 30,000 Germans, all to a man opposed to slavery. Indeed, slavery in St. Louis exists only in name. When the time comes, the party of freedom in the Slave States will find itself suddenly endowed with unlooked-for strength. Two-thirds or three-fourths of the commercial business of the South are carried on by Northern men or foreigners. At present these men hold their peace; they bide their time. But many of them hate the system they are forced to endure. They see clearly the evils for themselves and others of a system that is forced upon the community by a privileged class, and will lose no opportunity of putting an end to it.

The late Presidential election gave pregnant proofs of this latent hostility to slavery among Southern men. The Fillmore vote consisted of two elements —first, a conservative pro-slavery element; and secondly, a concealed anti-slavery element. Only in Maryland was the combined force of those two parties sufficient to influence the electoral vote; but the large popular vote throughout all but the most aristocratic States shows the latent strength of the opinions. The electoral vote of the South for Mr. Fillmore was only three per cent., but the popular vote was upwards of twenty-nine per cent.; and of this undoubtedly a large proportion was a silent protest against slavery. It is impossible, for instance, to interpret otherwise the significant vote of the German Democrats of St. Louis in favour of a Know-nothing candidate for the Presidency.

Lastly, in the matter of slavery, the young of the South are opposed to the old. Age naturally cleaves to old fanaticisms, while the open mind of youth embraces gladly new truths. Among the aristocracy of the South, pride of intellect and pride of station may help to perpetuate hereditary error; but the young farmers of the hills, and the young traders of the towns, have opened their eyes to the curse that is upon them, and assuredly they will not rest until it is annulled. As yet there is no form, nor even consciousness, in their movement; but, if I mistake not, the anti-slavery feeling of the Young South will yet prove the most irresistible element of Abolition power.

With such elements of disunion within itself, how can the South withstand successfully the various influences that threaten her institutions? Hitherto the political influence of the slave power has been great; but that influence was based mainly on old associations and a *prestige* fast fading away. If the slave power is to stand, it must be on rational and practical grounds, not on old romantic memories. On the whole, it seems to me that the slave aristocracy holds its power by a very frail tenure: and hence, perhaps, its violence. It is the spasm of conscious weakness; the convulsive clutching at a departing sceptre.

LETTER XXV.

RICHMOND, 8th April, 1857.

I WAS struck with the thriving looks of East Tennessee, as compared with Middle and West Tennessee; the more especially as the eastern portion of the State is mountainous and rugged in its formation, while the middle and west are the favoured seats of the tobacco and cotton production, those pets of the South, though, like many other pets, very ungrateful in the long run. Here, again, statistics support, in a most remarkable manner, the evidence of one's senses. In America, the census is as good as a guide-book to the traveller. Look at the relative proportions of slavery in the three districts, in 1850:—

Slave Population, 1850.

	Slaves.	Per cent.
West Tennessee	84,126	31.7
Middle Tennessee	132,846	27.9
East Tennessee	22,487	8.6

The proportion of the slave population in the cotton-growing West is almost four times as great as in the agricultural and pastoral East; and the relative prosperity and smiling look is somewhat in the same ratio. This distinction in the internal condition of this Slave State shows the difficulty of making very accurate classifications of these communities. Eastern Tennessee should be ranked with the frontier, and Western with the cotton States. An approximation to accuracy is all that can be attempted.

We entered Virginia at last. Western Virginia pleased me even more than East Tennessee. The face of the country is mountainous and woody, yet diversified with well-cultivated fields, and the habitations of a population sufficiently dense to give life to the scene. The agriculture seemed good. In one field we noticed five ploughs with three horses each. The 'spirit of improvement,' however, is not quite universal; a little further on we saw once more the wretched Southern plough with the single mule in front and the negro woman behind. In general, however, the fields in Western Virginia, as in all the mountainous regions of the South, are mostly tilled by white labour. There are comparatively few slaves, and these are in the hands of the wealthier proprietors. In many cases lands are leased for periods varying from one to five years, either at a fixed rent, or for a stipulated proportion of the produce. The farmers' sons either work with their parents, or, after reaching their majority, hire themselves out as labourers. In these industrious regions there is a poor labouring class. The non-labouring whites, here called 'loafers,' are few in number; they abound chiefly in East Virginia, where they can prey on the negro hordes, corrupting them, and robbing them.

The rich proprietors raise here tobacco, and at present prices large profits are realized. I heard of 130 dollars per acre, and even more, being cleared by tobacco-growing in 1856. The consequence of all this industrial movement has been a great rise in the value of the good land. Land has been bought in this district lately for eighty dollars per acre. In the East it may be had for fifty cents to one dollar per acre. This rise in the value of land, and the improved cultivation of it, are the natural results of that pressure of the American population on the production of food which is now working a silent revolution in the affairs of this great nation. Whoever looks merely to the social and political events of American history, without weighing carefully the industrial elements of her progress, as modified by the laws of population and capital, will fail alike to interpret the past and to foretel the future.

There was thus much to please and interest me in

my progress from East Tennessee to West Virginia; but what pleased and interested me beyond everything else, was the positive information I received regarding the progress of Abolition sentiments in this region. The truth is, I believe, that Western Virginia, and more or less all the Frontier States, have become abolitionized without knowing it. The spell of slavery is still so strong in these lands, the old ideas have still so strong a hold on the imagination, if not on the understanding, and the terrorism exercised by the fanatical believers in slavery is so powerful, that the strength of the heretical element is unknown alike to those who have discarded the old faith and to those who hold by it. This heresy, the faith in freedom, at once fatal to the slave power and big with promise for the Slave States, is principally confined to the young. It is the fresh and unbiassed intellect of the country that, as might be expected, has first thrown off the incubus of an oppressive hallucination. The open and candid mind of youth could not but be struck with the momentous lesson, which the glaring contrasts of North and South impressed upon their minds. Their interests, too, backed the conclusions of their understandings. Why was it, they asked themselves, that they were left to mope and moulder in ignominious obscurity, while the youth of the North were rising into affluence and power? Why had they to leave their homes to prosper, and seek in California or Illinois the fortune they could not find in Virginia? It was hard for youths, glowing with American hope and energy, to sit idly, day by day, before their dull stores, discussing the philosophy of free and slave society, while their rivals in New York or Chicago were rising to fortune and eminence. They have inquired, and have found the cause of their depression; and having found it, we need not doubt that they will remove it. All that is wanted is a little time for self-recognition and self-organization. As yet they do not know their power. When the movement does begin, it will be astonishing; it will astonish these youthful revolutionists whom it will bear along to victory, no less than the old-fogie fanatics whom it will overwhelm. It will be the movement of a social avalanche.

I have already alluded to the Know-nothing Presidential vote in St. Louis as a silent protest against slavery. Within these few days the Abolitionists of Missouri have taken stronger ground; they have essayed overt action in the Legislature, and, when beaten there, have boldly thrown themselves on the popular vote. Their success has been triumphant. In the municipal elections of St. Louis, the Abolitionist candidate has been elected by a large majority.

The blow will embolden the North and discourage the South. It is the beginning of the end.

The anti-slavery feeling in Western Virginia among the young is very strong. One young man from Russell County, in the extreme West, told me it was a decidedly Abolitionist county. The inhabitants resent especially the terrorism which represses the free expression of opinion. As Americans, they feel it degrading to be gagged, and they are prepared to demand, in a voice that cannot be resisted, the free thought and free speech guaranteed to them by the Constitution. Whoso attempts to put down free speech on slavery matters in Western Virginia will have a tough job of it. As my friend expressed it, should any one be imprisoned for Abolitionist sentiments, 'there is not a jail in West Virginia would hold him.' These intelligent young men feel, moreover, that their interests are sacrificed to the supposed interests of the slave-owning oligarchy. They understand well enough that the slave-power is cozening them of their votes on false pretences. They see through the Democratic dodge, and, Democrats though they be, they voted stoutly for Fillmore, not daring, as yet, to support an Abolitionist. They neutralized their influence by voting against the candidate of the South. Attempts were even made to get up a Fremont party, and in Botetourt County, as I learned on good authority, a strong vote would have been given for Fremont but for the threatened violence of the pro-slavery party. So hollow and rotten is the slave power, even in her most boasted strongholds.

I spent some days at Buchanan, in the valley of Virginia, at the foot of the peaks of Otter. I could have fancied myself in Scotland. The hills, the river (James), the people, the kirk—everything had a mountain look, and a pleasant, homely flavour. This valley of Virginia, between the Blue Ridge and the Alleghanies, which I hold to be, naturally, the paradise of America, was principally settled by Scotch Lowlanders, the lower part of the valley being occupied by Germans. These sturdy Caledonians have proved excellent citizens, and yet maintain much of their peculiar modes of thought and action. They have done good service to the land of their adoption, and the land that sent them forth to dare and to do may well be proud of her noble children. The respect, too, is reciprocal; for Auld Scotland is still a venerated name in the Valley of Virginia.

The old Scotch names still flourish luxuriantly here. You find Crawfords, Cummings, Paxtons, Prestons, Carruthers, Wallaces, Wilsons, Campbells, McDowalls, Monroes, Alexanders, with many more.

The old Scotch devotional spirit, also, with a tinge of the old Whig asceticism, still animates these sturdy mountaineers. 'Promiscuous dancing' is still a sin abhorred in the Valley of Virginia, as it ought to be, wherever our Confession of Faith is held in pretended reverence. But we believe only what we like in our creeds, and slur over unacceptable texts. Not so the good honest Presbyterians of Virginia: they stick by the letter of the law, and hold in orthodox abhorrence the iniquity of the reel, and the more modern abomination of the polka. Instead of these carnal vanities, the youth of these exemplary regions seek delectation in the ministrations of a Presbytery meeting, or the more stirring excitements of a revival. During our stay of near a week at Buchanan, a Presbytery meeting was in progress, and from morn to noon, from noon to dewy eve, there was continual preaching, a never-ending drone.

Revivals, too, are common; but these are not confined to the Presbyterians; they flourish even more luxuriantly among the Methodists and Baptists. One often sees such notices as the following:—

'*Revival.*—A considerable religious revival is in progress at the Third-street M. E. Church in this place, under the ministrations of the Rev. Messrs. Rasser and Hall. There are twenty or twenty-five penitents at the altar.'—*Lynchburg Virginian*, 9th of April, 1857.

Or this :—

'*Revivals at Richmond.*—The revival at the Leigh-street Baptist Church is progressing, as also that at the Wesley Chapel, in the Valley, and scores of mourners are flocking to the altars every night.'—*Virginia Paper*, April, 1857.

Similar devotional outbreaks have taken place of late at Tincastle, Virginia; Raleigh, North Carolina; and probably elsewhere: but with what permanent benefits to the community or the 'penitents' themselves I have no means of knowing.

But the Presbyterians of Virginia, like their 'dour' Whig forefathers, love fighting quite as well as psalm-singing. Presbyterianism is essentially a church militant, and the spirit of Drumclog yet lives on the spurs of the Alleghanies. Here, also, this tough Scotch yeomanry has striven faithfully and honourably for civil and religious freedom. Hear what a Virginian historian says in their honour:—' As Presbyterians, neither they nor their forefathers would submit to an ecclesiastical hierarchy; and their detestation of civil tyranny descended to them from the Covenanters of Scotland. Hence, in the dispute between the colonists and the Mother country, the Presbyterians of the Valley—indeed of the whole country — were almost unanimously Whigs of the firmest and most unconquerable spirit. They were among the bravest and most effective militia when called into the field. General Washington signified his opinion of them when, in the darkest day of the revolutionary struggle, he expressed his confidence that, if all other resources should fail, he might yet repair with a single standard to West Augusta, and there rally a band of patriots, who would meet the enemy at the Blue Ridge, and there establish the boundary of a free empire in the West.'* The brave old Whigs!

It is strange to find in Virginia united, and yet distinct, the two races that in old times strove together in our own island; east of the Blue Ridge the descendants of the Episcopalian Cavaliers; to the West, the sons of the Scottish Covenanters. The former are the tobacco lords of the seaboard, owning many slaves and working little themselves; courteous, chivalrous, and reckless as of old. The latter plough the steep hillsides of their new mountain home, living laborious days like their fathers before them. And between these two races, inhabiting one State, yet divided by descent, creed, character, and history, a new struggle is about to take place, not

* Howe's *Historical Collections of Virginia*, p. 454.

less momentous than that which established the religious freedom of our country. The sons of the men who crushed the priest-power of England will be foremost in extinguishing the slave-power of America. The issue of the contest cannot be doubtful. The right and the true must prevail against all the powers that earth or hell can bring against them.

The climate in the Valley of Virginia seems eminently healthy. I have noticed more blooming complexions, especially among the children, during my short stay in that district, than in all my wanderings in the Northern States. One can well understand how a race, originally strong and large, and living the vigorous life of warriors, hunters, and husbandmen in these mountain solitudes, should expand into the gigantic proportions that astonished me on my first entrance into Kentucky. Of course the strongest and boldest would play the pioneer; but even those left in Virginia are of great size, and I have no doubt the Six-foot Club could find more *bonâ fide* recruits among the inhabitants of the Valley of Virginia, than in any community of equal extent on the face of the globe.

The moment we crossed the Blue Ridge, we entered a district as different in its social aspect as in its geographical position. Let us look for a moment at the statistical characteristics of the two regions :—

Slave Population, 1850.

	Slaves.	Per cent.
East Virginia	409,295	47.5
West Virginia	63,233	11.3

You will observe by this statement, that the per centage of slaves is more than four times greater in the East than in the West ; and that the absolute number of slaves in the East is more than six times greater than in the West. The practical fruits of this state of matters were visible the moment we entered the Eastern district. From Lynchburg to Richmond, a distance of one hundred and twenty miles, the country presented the same desolate, half-cultivated appearance that had distressed us in the cotton States. The habitations of men were few and rude, and instead of the well-ploughed fields, or promising wheat lands of West Virginia, we had whole tracts of 'old fields,' the exhausted lands again becoming a wilderness, easily recognisable by the never-failing characteristic pines.

Besides the difference of opinion on the matter of slavery, East and West Virginia are opposed to each other politically. The West complains that the East, by means of her slave representation, has more than her due political weight.

The slave population of the East being 409,295, is equivalent to a white population of 245,577, while three-fifths of the slave population of the West is only 37,941. Thus it comes to pass that the West, with 488,453 whites, has only a population of 526,147 to be represented, while the East, with only 406,347 whites, has a representation based on a population of 651,924. I put it thus into a tabular shape:—

	White Population.	Political Population.
East Virginia	406,347	651,924
West Virginia	488,206	526,147

That such a state of things should irritate the West need not surprise us, and accordingly we find that political dissension on this point has, at times, threatened to split Virginia into two separate States, divided by the Blue Ridge. Thus, it appears that not only on the question of slavery, but also on the momentous one of slave representation, the North has powerful allies in the South herself.

Richmond pleases me more than any city of the South. From its situation on several hills, with a plain stretching away below, it has been likened to Richmond on the Thames (whence the name), and also to our own Edinburgh. Cockneys will probably deny the former likeness, and as a patriotic Scotchman I protest against the latter. Still, Richmond is a fine town. There is more life and bustle, too, in Richmond than in most Southern cities; and yet there is not all the appearance of wealth and business that one would expect in the capital of Virginia. When Eli Thayer and his Yankees, with the help of the Covenanting freemen of the valley, shall have regenerated the Old Dominion, Richmond will have grander buildings, more gorgeous stores, and a busier, blither population. That this blessed revolution may arrive, and that speedily, is the most earnest prayer of my heart. That it will arrive, is the settled conviction of my understanding. It is impossible to misinterpret the handwriting on the wall.

LETTER XXVI.

RICHMOND, VIRGINIA, 15th April, 1857.

BEFORE leaving the South, I will now, at the risk of some repetition, bring together the main facts, which seem to me to indicate the issue of the present struggle between North and South. We shall here be best guided by the statistics of the progress of the two sections. The history of the Past will be the surest prognostic of the Future.

By the annexed table you will see that, in every point of comparison, the progress of the Free States has been from 50 to 100 per cent. greater than that of the Slave States. The density of population in the former is nearly double, the annual increase a half more than in the latter. The Free States have improved one-half more of their lands; their lands have three times the average value, and there is double the amount of agricultural implements upon their farms. With an inferior climate, and, for the most part, inferior soil,

FREE AND SLAVE STATES.*
1850.

	POPULATION.		INDUSTRY.						PUBLIC WORKS.		EDUCATION.		REPRESENTATION.	
			Agriculture.					Agricultural and manufacturing products per head of population.			Illiterate Whites.			
						Produce per acre.			Canals per million of population.	Railways per million of population.			1790.	1850.
	Density per square mile.	Annual increase, 1790 to 1850.	Improved Lands.	Average value of Lands.	Average value of Agricultural Implements.	Wheat.	Maize.				Natives.	Foreign.		
	Percent	Percent.	Percent.	Dollars.	Dollars.	Bushels.	Bushels.	Dollars.	Miles.	Miles.	Percent.	Percent.	Percent.	Percent.
FREE STATES	21.91	9.71	14.72	19.00	.77	12.4	31.1	105.85	274	1000	2.40	6.37	53.8	61.5
SLAVE STATES	11.35	6.59	10.00	6.00	.36	9.8	19.6	65.67	116	500	8.37	9.09	46.2	38.5

* Compiled from De Bow's *Compendium of the Census* and the *Treasury Report of 1853.*

the Northern man produces fifty per cent. more wheat and Indian corn than his Southern neighbour. The total industrial production of the North, per head of its population, is sixty per cent. greater than that of the South. In public works the Free States have double the amount of that possessed by the Slave States, in proportion to their relative population. The Slave States, on the other hand, have nearly four times the amount of ignorance among their native white population, and considerably more even in their foreign immigrants, showing that only the inferior class of foreign labourers emigrate to the South. Finally, the political influence of the Free States, as indicated by its representation, is rising, while that of the Slave States is falling.

Perhaps of all tests of progress, the movement of population is, under ordinary circumstances, the surest. In this respect the superiority of the Free over the Slave States is very marked. Take, for example, the increase of population from 1790 to 1850:—

Increase of Population, 1790—1850.

	1790.	1850.	Increase.	Per Cent.
Free States	1,968,455	13,434,922	11,466,467	9.71
Slave States	1,961,372	9,612,969	7,651,597	6.59

Thus, in 1790, the population of the present slave-holding and non-slave-holding States was as nearly as possible equal. In 1850 the population of the Free States was nearly fifty per cent. greater than that of the Slave States; the average annual increase having during this period been likewise about fifty per cent. more in the former than in the latter. And yet, during this time, the South had the benefit of a monopoly in the production of a staple, the increasing use of which is one of the marvels of modern civilization.

From this sketch of the relative progress of the North and the South, it is easy to cast the horoscope of their fortunes. The supremacy of the North is assured. Already she excels her sister in every element of power, and the rate of her progress is infinitely greater. Nothing but her oligarchical organization and the prestige of old associations—now almost extinct—saves the South from political subjection. Nor is this all. Independent of her internal preponderance of strength, the North is daily gaining accessions of power from the formation of new States. Minnesota and Oregon already swell her ranks; and in no long time Kansas and Nebraska will probably be added to her forces. The numbers of the States will then stand twenty to fifteen; so that even in the Senate the power of the Free States will be represented by forty members, against thirty for the South. Thus the supremacy of the Free States is not a mere political speculation, it is a mathematical certainty. The predominance exists already, and every day is adding to it.

What, after all, is this 'South' of which we hear so much? Let us look a little into this matter. The population of the slave-holding States, in 1850, consisted of 9,612,969 souls, if we allow souls to negroes. Of this number of inhabitants, 6,222,418 were white, and the remainder free coloured, or slaves. But of all this six and a quarter millions of white people only 347,525 persons possessed slaves; so that even of the white population of the South, 5,874,893 had no direct interest in the institution of slavery.

But further, when we analyse a little more closely the holdings of these 347,525 slave-proprietors, we find that the oligarchical element of the slave-power is confined to a very limited number of slave-holders. One-fifth of all the slave-holdings consist of a single slave, and nearly one-half of less than five slaves. It must be further borne in mind that all the slaves belonging to a proprietor are not available labourers: his holding includes women, children, and those incapable of work from age, infirmity, or other causes. The usual calculation is, that, of a well-assorted, fresh-bought 'force,' one-half are efficient hands. In hereditary or older gangs not more than one-third can be counted on. Assuming, however, that on the average one-half of every holding consists of available labourers, we must cut down still further the number of wealthy planters. Certainly the term planter, as opposed to farmer, cannot apply to any slave-holder with a less available force than ten working hands. Let us, then, deduct all those properties of less than twenty slaves (equal to ten working hands), and the remainder will represent those planters who may be truly said to constitute the slave-power of the South. The figures would stand thus:—

Total Slaveholders		347,525
Owners of 1 Slave . . .	68,820	
,, under 5 ditto . .	105,683	
,, under 10 ,, . .	80,765	
,, under 20 ,, . .	54,595	309,863
		37,662

According to this statement the whole number of agriculturists, deserving the name of planters in the Southern States, cannot be put down at more than 40,000; and that this is rather an over-estimate than otherwise, appears from an examination of the statement of 'occupations' in the census, where only 27,055 persons are put down as 'planters.' Such, then, is the paltry handful of proprietors to whose supposed interests, and real ruin, is sacrificed the prosperity of millions of their fellow-countrymen.

Looking to the white population alone, there are more than 6,000,000 of people whose interests are absolutely opposed to those of the slave-power; and if we think it worth while considering the rights and feelings of black men, the total number sacrificed is nine millions and a half.

The old prestige of a once powerful aristocracy, and yet more, the spell of an ancient and fanatical faith, still give a show of stability to the slave-power of the South. But in reality it is hollow: heresy has undermined it. A dominion built on opinion is destroyed by doubt. But here there is not only doubt, there is utter unbelief in the old fanaticism, and a new faith has arisen in the evangile of freedom. And the disciples of this new faith are young, strong, and enthusiastic, among the first and ablest of the land. Slavery in the South is doomed; for her own best hearts have vowed its downfall.

The truth is, slavery cannot continue in the South. The governing class of the South is too highly-civilized to co-exist with slavery. The incongruity is too great between a barbarous institution and a refined people. Slavery and high civilization are a contradiction, a monstrosity, an absurdity. The South has not had justice done her by the world; nor has she done justice to herself. Strangers have concluded that the South was barbarous, because she holds by a barbarous institution, while the South herself exalts slavery as a powerful element of her high civilization. Both are wrong: the South is a refined community, but it is in spite of slavery; and the contradiction between her social system and her state of culture is so gross that it cannot long continue. Slavery may subsist in Brazil or Cuba, among degenerate, sensual races, but it cannot exist side by side with Anglo-Saxon civilization. Whether viewed geographically or historically, slavery and civilization are manifestly incompatible. The course of all modern civilization has been from serfdom to freedom. Are the Southern States of the American Union to exhibit the sole anomaly ? Are they alone, of all nations, to reverse the course of history and civilization? Or is it not more probable that they, too, ere long, will follow the usual course of human progress, and rid themselves of this fatal anachronism. I respect the people of the South too highly to doubt it.

Let us be just to the South. Let us not wrong the slave-owner in denouncing slavery. The system is a vicious one; but there are conscientious men who regard it as a good institution, and yet more who look on it as a necessary evil. We must not forget that the slave-owners of these States have been born and bred in a land of slavery, and that they inherited the prejudices with the property of their fathers.

If we take a generous view of the position of the South, she will appear entitled to our kindliest sympathies. Herself a high-spirited and refined community, she is brought into antagonism with all civilized society. The convictions of the world condemn her. She is the pariah of civilization. The consciousness of this moral outlawry galls a people at once sensitive and proud, and hence those outbursts which seem to us to partake almost of the character of frenzy, are but the exacerbations of that chronic irritation which is gnawing continually at its heart. The South, too, knows full well the evils connected with her social system. Who should know them better? In her secret heart she feels and deplores the plague that is upon her, but she is too proud to confess her pains. With Spartan fortitude she smiles in the world's face, while her inward vitals are consumed.

The South feels, further, that the constant agitation to which she is subjected is fatal to her progress. She yearns for quiet, that she may follow peaceably her industrial concerns. But this desire of her heart is in vain. Unrest is the necessary condition of her existence. It is not the work of external agitators, as she vainly thinks; it is the necessary consequence of a social system, antagonistic to civilized opinion and incompatible with her own high culture.

The state of feeling in the South points out the tone which other communities should adopt towards her. She must be treated with the consideration and respect due to her position among cultivated nations. All exasperating language must be studiously avoided, and the honest condemnation of slavery tempered by a generous appreciation of the peculiar difficulties of the South. It is not a sycophantic truckling to her prejudices that will please the South, but that open yet courteous expression of dissent which well-bred disputants owe to each other. There has been too much denunciation, too much vituperation. Surely it is possible to condemn slavery, and lament its evils, without pouring vials of wrath on the heads of those who are its chiefest victims. Especially it behoves foreign nations to eschew all vain meddling with the internal polity of the Slave States. When the occasion demands, it is our duty to state our convictions simply and freely; but it is an insolent assumption of superiority for one nation to lecture another on its duties, and organize forces to modify its institutions. There is a Pharisaical party amongst us who look upon themselves as the conscience-keepers of the world, and who have done more to attach the character of domineering insolence to the English name than our haughtiest politicians.

It only remains to ask, Will the slave question of the Northern States be settled without a disunion of North and South? I think it will. The more I study American character and American opinion, the less I believe in the probability of disunion. No doubt the violence of politicians, and the impulsiveness of the people, may precipitate the country into disunion policy, contrary to their sober judgment and desire, but, barring such political accidents, the sense of the American people in both sections will preserve the Union. Nothing has struck me more in my intercourse with the American people than the strength of their nationality. In the early history of the United States, the attachment of the Americans to their native States was an absorbing passion; it was the great difficulty which the wise founders of the Union had to encounter. And this was natural at the time. The American nation was unknown, a poor rickety creation, hardly able to sustain its own existence. The chief States, on the contrary, were comparatively old and honoured communities. One can easily conceive the feeling that made John Randolph prouder of being a Virginian than an American.

But now all this is reversed. The American nation is everything: the States are nothing. Citizens of the original States may still look back with pride on their provincial history; but in the face of the world the American citizen values himself as being one of the great American people, not on 'hailing' from Wisconsin or Alabama. Whatever may be the sectional feelings of the States at home, the foreign policy of the country, and the pride attached to the importance of the nation in the affairs of the world, must always preserve, and even increase, the feelings of American nationality. It is the American flag, the American navy, American power, and the American people that occupy the first place in the modern American's affections. To him, therefore, disunion appears less the severance of a federation than the civil war of a compact nationality. In name the States'-right doctrine still exists; seemingly it is even triumphant: on the contrary, federalism is nominally dead. And yet, if we look more to inward fact than outward seeming, it is evident that the force of events has produced that very fusion of State interests into a national unity which the federalists desired, and which their successful opponents denounced as a centralizing despotism.

The whole course of modern American history has tended to develop this national feeling. The good and the bad in the American character have alike contributed to establish it. The ambition of the people of the Union makes nationality a necessity. It can carry out its 'manifest destiny' only as a powerful people. Its industry contributes no less to fuse provincial and sectional interests and feelings into a national whole. The division of labour which nature appointed to the different States, and which inter-provincial Free-trade has confirmed, tends irresistibly towards industrial unity of interest and sentiment. The emigration from State to State is another bond of union. It produces an interlacing of interests and affections which neutralizes the old insulating prejudices of State individuality. With ties of kindred and friendship binding him to a variety of States, the modern American unconsciously becomes more and more national, less and less provincial.

Then the increased means of material communication, whether of thought or person, tend naturally to union in idea as well as in fact. Disunion was possible when States were separated by weeks of travel, and intelligence was fitful and slow. But with a daily mail, and hourly telegraph, and express trains, a closer political union necessarily follows from the material nexus. Even the progress of democracy itself, by levelling the State institutions, has helped to rob them of dignity and authority. No man of mark cares to be relegated for months to the obscurity of a State provincial-capital, to be mixed up with boors, and rowdies, and third-rate attorneys-at-law. These legislative bodies, even in States like Virginia, have lost their weight in men's eyes, and the Central Government has been proportionally strengthened. The rise of great cities, too, as a necessary element of industrial progress, is adverse to the insulated provincialism of States'-right ideas. Such cities as New York, Boston, and Philadelphia have, morally and politically, more or less of a metropolitan influence, and tend, unconsciously but irresistibly, to impress the idea of nationality on the American mind.

But perhaps the strongest reason why disunion between North and South is, for the present, impossible, is the division of opinion in the South itself. The question of slavery could alone cause disunion; but on this question, as I have stated, a serious schism exists already in the Southern States. The aristocracy and democracy, the lowlands and the uplands, the planters and farmers, the old and the young, are of different minds on the momentous interests in question. As yet this schism is 'filmed o'er,' but the first note of civil war with the North would rend in twain the population of the South.

The democratic, slave-hating youth of the Slave States will not separate from the North for the sake of an institution they have learned to abhor. On the contrary, any serious attempt at disunion would only precipitate the crisis of abolition. But the cry of disunion, except with a few fanatics, is not a serious one. It is a bugbear set up to frighten the timid and timeserving in the North. It is a pretence of politicians, not seriously desired by any considerable section of the people. It is opposed to all their prepossessions, and even as a political 'cry,' cannot long serve the purpose of manœuvring statesmen. The very use of this 'cry' shows how strong the fear of disunion is.

So long as the American Union continues to grow naturally it will continue; for it will retain all the natural elements of cohesion: harmony of race, religion, language, laws, and history, cemented by industrial and material connexion. It is when she shall have forcibly added to her confederation elements of heterogeneous nature, and have extended her empire beyond reasonable limits, that the Union will break of its own weight and fall asunder. But though political disunion may be far distant, moral disunion already exists; and for this there is no remedy but the removal of the bone of contention. The abolition of slavery is the only radical cure of that sectionalism which now afflicts the otherwise United States. Peace never will exist while slavery continues. Destroy slavery and the distinction between North and South falls, and with it the angry passions that now exist. If the lovers of union, who, in the North, would sacrifice principle for 'peace,' could take a larger view of politics, they would reverse their timorous, spiritless policy, and strain every nerve to overthrow an institution, whose existence must ever keep alive a warfare of ideas between the Northern and Southern sections of the country.

LETTER XXVII.

NEW YORK, 24th April, 1857.

THANK Heaven! I am once more in the North Behind me is despotism and desolation; around me is freedom and prosperous industry. One breathes more freely. The little step from South to North is a stride from barbarism to civilization; a leap from the sixteenth to the nineteenth century.

I did not stay long in Washington. I hurried on from the sham to the real metropolis of the States. In truth, it is not the politicians but the people of this country that interest me. America has outgrown her politics. This is the case with all advanced civilizations: as society approaches its ideal, the material government loses its significance. Laws and lawgivers are but obsolete lumber, when the eternal law of justice lives and rules in the people's heart. But there is another and a less flattering reason, why the politics of America are a weariness to the world and an affliction to her best sons. America is not ruled by her noblest men. The American ballot-box riddles away the gold and retains the dirt. It was not always so : once the great and good of the land were its rulers; and things have come to a sorry pass when Soulé and Douglas sit in the seats of Washington and Hamilton. Nevertheless, it were a gross blunder to suppose that the American people has degenerated with its politicians. It was under our Sidmouths and Castlereaghs that the public opinion was matured in England, which in these latter days has swept away so much intolerance, privilege, and monopoly. So, in America, under a crass Democracy, there has grown up a cultivated conservative class—the sheet-anchor of the nation. The strength of this intellectual power is unknown even to itself. As yet it is chaotic, and only begins to find fit organs in the press. But to those who have faith in the just and the true, its ultimate supremacy cannot be doubtful.

The American puts his trust in his common schools. For my part, I have small faith in the power of spelling-books and catechisms to teach man his political duties. The life of the citizen, I take it, is the only school of citizenship. The American is educated by his freedom : he thinks and acts for himself, instead of having a prefect or a director of police to think and act for him. This is his true and ennobling 'self-government,' not his infinitesimal share in the election of policemen and presidents. Now the necessary tendency of a school directed and paid by Government is to weaken this autocratic spirit, and nothing it can teach can compensate this essential injury. I confess it seems strange to me that the American, with his horror of a State Church, should take so kindly to a State-school. In principle they are identical: the essence of both is an authoritative moulding of the human soul. Be this as it may, I should tremble for America if her common schools were her sole bulwark against mobocracy. But she has another and a better safeguard. Her true security is her prosperous industry. Let her only give free scope and natural expansion to this noble power, and it will raise up a body of wise and virtuous citizens, who will save her from the ruin threatened by a low Democracy.

Last night I listened to an admirable address from Lord Napier, at the St. George's Festival. Evidently our ambassador has got beyond the Talleyrand school; he sees a higher use of human speech than to hide human thought. There is much to hope from a man who can cast the slough of officialism. I know of no higher calling than to stand on the keystone of the bridge between two noble nations, and beckon good will to both. Lord Napier, I think, is worthy of his errand. He need set himself no higher aim than to prove himself a statesman who has the talent, without the temper, of the Napiers. But, after all, it is little that statesmen can do to make or mar alliances. In our days, a people is its own best ambassador. The press is our best representative abroad, as it is our chief ruler at home. Neither is it a parchment alliance that is wanted: the thing needed is an alliance of the heart. And this union already exists between the superior minds of both nations; nay, I was astonished to find so little hostility to England, even among the lower order of Americans. Except in the diatribes of some obscure Democratic paper, or the spoutings of some ex-rebel or ex-revolutionist, I scarcely saw a trace of it. In private I had everywhere assurances of the desire of all sensible Americans for a cordial, but an equal, friendship. Trust me, we have the love and respect of every American whose love and respect is worth having. And if so, what matter if the vulgar do not do us justice? Enough for us to have the esteem of her wisest and worthiest. The love of one Emerson outweighs the hate of a whole wilderness of Mitchels. For God's sake, then, let us not confound the noble people of America with her pothouse politicians and the *canaille* of her cities.

Never were two nations so eminently fitted to aid

and comfort each other in the joint work of civilization as the English and Americans of the present day. There is precisely that mixture of accord and discord that makes the finest harmony, and that adaptation of gifts and needs that gives to union its greatest efficacy. This power of mutual helpfulness rests on material and on moral grounds. First, England and America are serviceable to each other from the diversity of their productive powers. A grand division of labour separates their occupations, and so unites them by a common industry. Secondly, and chiefly, they are fitted for mutual aid by the peculiarities of their respective idiosyncrasies. By temperament and by intellect they are curiously suited to complement each other's powers and correct each other's failings. The one nation has the vigour and decision of youth, the other the endurance and wariness of age: the one loves enterprise, the other delights in thoroughness. American ardour stirs up English phlegm: English caution checks Yankee impetuosity. So with their intellectual faculties: the audacity of American genius is best tempered by English judgment; while the sound sense of the older nation is quickened by the fire of the younger. Dovetailed together, the English and American minds would give the best practical intellect the world has seen. To make it perfect, and fit it for the highest uses of human thought, we must add German depth and French lucidity.

The State of New York, I find, is busy tinkering at her Liquor Law. Truly it is weary work this clouting of unsound legislation. It is the old story; you patch up one hole and make a new one. Is it not strange that your legislative tinker never asks himself whether his law be worth the patching? To me it seems clear, that here and at home temperance legislation is on a wrong scent, and must try back for a better principle. The upper classes entirely mistake their calling when they attempt to force virtue on their inferiors. Even were it possible to shut out temptation, and so produce an outward decency, we should only emasculate the moral will of the people. Virtue is not flight from evil, but victory over it; and to step in between man and his trials, or between sin and its penalties, is a profane and pestiferous meddling with the Divine government. The business of the higher classes is to set a good example to their inferiors, and let their improved morals filtrate slowly down to the lower strata of society. The law has no business with sin; it has only to do with crime. The overt act, not the hidden motive, is the proper object of legislative repression.

I need not tell you that the tone of the better portion of the American press is rapidly improving. From the little I have seen of the conductors of the higher class of American newspapers, I am satisfied that the progress in this direction will be marked and continuous. The stereotyped ideal of a Yankee editor, in the vulgar English mind, is a literary ruffian, with a pen in one hand and a bowie-knife in the other, stabbing, indifferently with either weapon, whosoever dares to differ from him. You call on him, and find a scholar and a gentleman, who has probably travelled from one end of Europe to the other. This is an instance, among a thousand, of the extreme difficulty of estimating aright the civilization of a people so progressive. The change itself is of essential moment. The pen is the sceptre of the modern world; and it is a matter of national concern that it be wielded worthily and gracefully. No doubt there are still rowdy newspapers in New York; but their power is rapidly on the wane. Coarseness and violence are no longer the necessary attributes of the premiership of the press. On the contrary, the chief authority is passing more and more into the hands of those journals, which are conscientiously labouring to make themselves worthy organs of the moral and intelligent Conservatism of the nation.

The elevation of the American press is noticeable

in another aspect. It is a sample of that self-schooling power which is a chief excellence of the Saxon race. The Saxon dares to look fact in the face. Hence his love of publicity. He proclaims his shortcomings to himself and to the world, and so cures them. This gift of self-healing is the surest pledge of English and American progress. There is everything to hope for a nation that has the nerve to probe its own sores.

At this moment the New York pulpit is thundering against the 'Mammonism' of the city. If it speak true, Sodom and Gomorrah were virtuous, compared to Wall-street and Fifth Avenue. To me, I confess, the indiscriminating denunciations of money-making, so rife in our day, seem somewhat unphilosophical. After all, money-making is but industry; and, if work be the end of man, the ordinary motive to labour must be respectable. With the vile, money-making is the love of pelf; but with nobler workers it is the love of power. The same ambition now sets the Yankee to cure cod and build clippers, that sent forth his Norse forefathers to the poetic villanies of piracy. His love of gain may be excessive, but it is the excess of a noble desire. Indeed, I do not flatter the Americans when I give them this high praise; that, for the most part, their faults are but exaggerations, or distortions of their virtues. Their dollar-worship is overstrained ambition: their lawlessness is a perverted passion for liberty : their superficiality springs from that Titanic energy that grasps at the impossible. Nay, what is Lynch-law itself but a caricature of that need of justice which is the crowning glory of the Anglo-Saxon character?

LETTER XXVIII.

NEW YORK, 29th April, 1857.

THE price of beef may seem a topic somewhat out of my beat; but whoever feels strongly the connexion between material and moral progress must watch with interest the cost of national subsistence. Statistics teach us that morals stand in direct relation to the cost of food. Marriage is regulated by the price of grain; virtue rises and falls with wheat; and chastity might be quoted with corn in the *Mark-Lane Express*. Now, in New York, the cost of subsistence has been doubled within the last ten years; and, according to the Report of a 'Society for the Improvement of the Condition of the Poor,' the price of bread and beef, in November, 1856, was higher in New York than in London or Paris. This is ominous; it marks a strong pressure of population on subsistence; and a few cents on the pound of beef or bread may cause a social revolution—may repeal the tariff,

SCARCITY OF FOOD.

abolish slavery, shake the Union, and change the whole course of American history.

The cause of the enhanced price of provisions is apparent from a glance at the census. Between 1840 and 1850, the agricultural population of the Union fell from 78 per cent. to 45 per cent. of the whole; while the manufacturing population rose from 17 to 30 per cent. During the same period the increase of population was 36 per cent. With the single exception of Indian corn, the production, per head of population, of all grain, potatoes, cattle, sheep, and swine, was smaller in 1850 than in 1840; and this in the face of a vast increase in the area of production. During the same ten years the exports of 'breadstuffs' were doubled, having risen from 13,075,993 dollars to 27,809,933 dollars. The upshot of all this is a scarcity of food. Protection has evidently misdirected industry, and American statesmen cannot too soon reverse a policy which has already caused scarcity, and threatens to cause still graver evils.

Among the enlightened merchants of New York there is, I find, a strong feeling in favour of some stable system of national currency. The need is great. The rag-money of America seems almost as rotten now as when the financial earthquake of 1836 shook the country to its centre. But the time for this reform is not yet come; the sovereign multitude is still fanatical in its faith in paper, and its horror of a national bank. The dictum of an ignorant old soldier still outweighs all rational argument.

Civilization has her peculiar errors, as she has her peculiar diseases. A smattering of science breeds confusions unknown to simple ignorance. Thus only can we explain the muddle of modern ideas on capital and currency. It would seem a simple proposition, that nothing can increase the available capital of a community but the increase or economy of the commodities which constitute capital; and that no juggle of borrowing and lending, no hocus pocus of deposits and discounts, can add one peppercorn to the material elements of national production. And yet there are men, priding themselves, too, on their practical common sense, who believe in the creative energy of waste-paper, and who think the wealth of a country can be indefinitely multiplied by flooding it with worthless 'promises to pay.'

The best remedy for all this nonsense, and, at the same time, the best currency reform, both here and at home, would be the establishment of a strongly-founded National Issue Office—a paper Mint. It should have no banking business, neither deposits nor discounts. Banking is a trade, and therefore no concern of Government. On the contrary, when the law makes notes a legal tender, the State is bound to see that they have real value. In America the need of a substantial National Board of Issue (I would sink the word Bank), which should secure at once the universality and the soundness of the currency, is even more pressing than with us. The idea of thirty-two distinct currency systems in one nation is ludicrous, and the inconvenience is intolerable. On the other hand, the insecurity of the present system is ruinous. When I passed through East Tennessee, the whole community was paralysed by the failure of a bank, which had contrived to issue 1,400,000 dollars' worth of notes on a paid-up capital of 7000 dollars.

For myself, I have religiously avoided all contact with American paper money. The first note I received in the United States was refused immediately afterwards when I offered it in payment. This was more than either my finances or my temper could stand. From that time I preferred paying the fixed tax of a premium on gold to running the risks of a sliding scale of insolvency, varying from one per cent. discount to utter worthlessness. Besides, their notes are filthy. Until I came to America, I had always supposed a Scotch bank-note was the dirtiest and greasiest thing in nature; but I soon found that an American note presents an accumulation of more grease and dirt, with the additional disadvantage of not always being worth 100 cents in the dollar. For your Scotch abomination you have at least the satisfaction of getting 'One Pound on Demand.'

Touching emigration, a hard-headed Scotchman said to me just now: 'Tell the people at home, if they are doing well, to stay where they are.' This, I believe, is about the sum of all that can be said wisely on the subject. Let well alone. A high rate of profit and cheap land give greater scope to industry in America than in England. But the climate and the mode of life are trying both to mind and body. A man must work harder, and stand more, to keep up with this high-pressure people. If a young man of five-and-twenty, 'without encumbrance,' cannot 'get along' at home, he may come here, provided he be very active, very strong, and very sober. He will have a good chance of getting on; and, if he does not die of dyspepsia, may live to make a fortune. But under no circumstances let any one come to this country who hates work, or who loves whisky. Laziness, in America, is ruin; and to drink is to die of delirium tremens.

Caleb Cushing has been rating the men of Massachusetts, for not taking the lead in what he calls the 'manifest destiny' of the nation, but what plainer men call aggrandizement. Cushing has the fatal gift of clothing vulgar ideas in noble rhetoric—a rhetoric especially pestilent when addressed to a young and ambitious nation, whose imagination is already fired with the grandeur of its empire and the splendour of its history. It is Satanic work to lull the conscience and kindle the ambitions of this fiery people. Assuredly the American nation, like all high civilizations, has some noble mission; but it will not learn it from Caleb Cushing. Divine messages are not declared from stumps, nor to mass-meetings. The function of this Union is the ennoblement, not the subjugation, of America. To return to the ferocities and felonies of their buccaneering forefathers were to abdicate their high office as the leaders of Western civilization. America has many noble men who feel the sacredness of the national calling, and who, I trust, will have power to guide their countrymen aright. Let the American people take counsel with these high-minded men, in Massachusetts, or wherever else they may be found; and, as they value their salvation, let them be deaf as adders to the false teachings of their Caleb Cushings.

And England, too, must see to it, that she treat American progress in a right spirit. If we are to look on America as a rival power, which can only expand at our expense, we shall never get rid of old, mean jealousies, and our policy will be to hem her in with hostile settlements, seizing on every marshy river-mouth and rocky islet, as a vantage-ground from which to battle with her onward progress. If, on the contrary, we view American civilization in a more generous and cosmopolitan sense, as a part of that great work of human ennoblement in which all cultivated nations are fellow-labourers, we shall be careful not to cross her path, and will seek rather, as far as duty and honour permit, to withdraw from all vague possessions and dim 'protectorates,' which bring us into collision with her expanding power. In so doing, we shall also best study our real interests. The most generous policy is also the wisest.

Some say the Americans have no physiognomy— a great mistake, I think. To me their physiognomy seems most strongly marked, bearing deep impress of that intensity which is the essence of their being. The features even of the young are furrowed with lines of anxious thought and determined will. You read upon the nation's brow the extent of its enterprise and the intensity of its desires. Every American looks as if his eye were glaring into the far West and the far Future. Nay, his mental physiognomy is determined by the same earnestness of purpose. The American never plays, not even the American child. He cares nothing for those games and sports which are the delight of the Englishman. He is indifferent to the play either of mind or muscle. Labour is his element, and his only relaxation from hard work is fierce excitement. Neither does he laugh. The Americans, I imagine, are the most serious people in the world. There is no play even in their fancy. French wit is the sparkle of the diamond, that dazzles a *salon:* the American imagination flashes its sheet-lightning over half a world.

The same terrible earnestness is, I am persuaded, at the bottom of that ill health which is so serious a curse to American life. No doubt other things contribute—climate, stimulants, sedentary occupations, and so forth—but the deepest-rooted cause of American disease is that overworking of the brain and over-excitement of the nervous system, which are the necessary consequences of their intense activity. Hence nervous dyspepsia, with consumption, insanity and all its brood of fell disorders in its train. In a word, the American works himself to death.

LETTER XXIX.

NEW YORK, 4th May, 1857.

Is America a success, or is it not? That, after all, is the question that most nearly concerns Europe, and the world. That America, on the whole, is a success cannot now be denied. It has prospered; and prosperity is a rough, but trustworthy criterion of national excellence.

As to the causes of American success there may be more difference of opinion. The Democratic theory is simply that a community, long depressed by monarchy, sprang, at the touch of Democracy, into noble and prosperous activity. This solution does not meet the facts. The colonies prospered before their independence; nay, judging by the growth of population, their prosperity was greater before than after the Revolution. Between 1749 and 1775, the population of the colonies rose from 1,046,000 to 2,803,000, or 6.46 per cent. per annum. From 1790

THE SUCCESS OF AMERICA.

to 1820, a nearly similar period, the aggregate population of the United States increased from 3,929,827 to 9,638,131, or at the annual rate of only 4.92 per cent. On the other hand, we have communities both in North and South America living under Democratic institutions, and yet sunk in hopeless stagnancy.

To me American success seems the product of a noble race, acting with all the helps, and none of the hindrances of older civilizations, on circumstances in themselves singularly favourable. First as to race. The American is not a Saxon; he is an Englishman, one of that cross-breed which Emerson calls 'the best stock in the world.' And of this strong race the strongest came here—men scorning submission, and ready for that struggle with Savage Man and Savage Nature which was still more to brace their nerves. These men brought, too, noble faculties—the power of organization and of self-rule. And their self-rule was that real autocracy, the power of each individual man to think and act for himself. This autocratic faculty, the noblest a people can possess, was further unfolded by their colonial isolation, and by the equality of their condition. Again, this picked band of a picked people was set down in a land of peculiar promise. It had, in profusion, all the elements of industrial production, while seas, gulfs, lakes, and rivers gave those means of locomotion without which all other elements are null and void. Further, a vast variety of soil and climate created a natural division of labour most favourable to production, and which there was no temptation to annul by self-imposed restrictions. Then, America has been favoured by history no less than by nature. She has had the benefit of all those inventions which have revolutionized the productive powers of man. Canals, the steam-engine, the steamboat, and later, just as it was needed, the railway, with its familiar spirit, the telegraph; these are the obedient genii that have helped on the great work of American prosperity.

Such were her aids; but America was no less happy in the absence of those clogs which have hampered the progress of European nations. In England all our great reforms have been repeals—repeals of bigotry, of privilege, undue influence, and monopoly. Nay, what was the French Revolution, what the Reformation, but a repeal? All modern history is but the repeal of feudalism and ecclesiasticism. Now America was saved all these impediments. She had neither State Church nor feudal aristocracy; she had no privilege to put down, no monopoly to abolish, and no debt to pay. She started in the race of progress the youngest athlete, and the least encumbered. How different from old John Bull, toiling along with the Archbishop of Canterbury, the Lord Chancellor, the Chancellor of the Exchequer, and the National Debt upon his back! Must we not marvel at the 'gameness' of the sturdy veteran, that still keeps a foremost place in the race of nations?

The burdens which America bears are chiefly these: Protective laws, pseudo-democratic institutions, and slavery. The first of these she will soon throw off: a protective policy cannot long co-exist with education and publicity. The second will be a greater trial. Not the least evil of ultra-democracy is the difficulty of its reformation. Reform can only be effected by that power which itself is to be reformed. Nevertheless, here also, we may hope much from the strong sense and conservative spirit of a cultivated class, rising every day in power. Finally, there is Slavery. Peaceably or violently this incubus must now be got rid of, if America herself is to continue. American civilization and American slavery can no longer exist together. In the face of the world they have closed in deadly conflict; and the one or the other must be destroyed. For my part, I cannot believe it to be the Divine purpose, that a remnant of barbarism should overthrow the civilization of a new world. Slavery must succumb.

America, then, in my view, is a success, but a modified success. During the last half century her social condition has improved—her political condition has fallen off. There is more power in the nation, more worth and wisdom in the people, but there is more corruption and more oppression in the Government. Believing strongly in the supreme force of truth and justice, I feel assured that the spiritual power which has been unfolded in the good and wise of the community will prevail over the pest of bad institutions; but it will be a hard struggle, and America will need all her energy and all her virtue.

Meanwhile, what is more befitting for us Englishmen, than to watch with intensest study and deepest sympathy the momentous strivings of this noble people? It is the same fight ourselves are fighting—the true and absolute supremacy of right. Surely, nothing can more beseem two great and kindred nations, than to aid and comfort one another in that career of self-ennoblement, which is the end of all national as of all individual existence.

THE END.